PLUCKING THE EAGLE'S WINGS

PLUCKING THE EAGLE'S WINGS

America's Prophetic
Cycles, Patterns and Destiny

By Dr. Perry F. Stone, Jr.

All Scripture, unless otherwise indicated, is taken from the King James translation of the Bible.

ISBN 0-9708611-0-9

The International Office for the Voice of Evangelism
P. O. Box 3595
Cleveland, TN, 37320
(423) 478-3456
Editor: Kathleen R. Gordon

Printed in the United States of America at Pressworks, Cleveland, TN

TABLE OF CONTENTS

I would like to say a special thanks to my dear friend and colleague, Bill Cloud, for his excellent research concerning the Hebrew connection with America's early history, which has been a wonderful contribution to this project.

INTRODUCTION

America in Bible Prophecy

Is the United States of America mentioned in Biblical prophecy? Would the Almighty God weave thousands of end-time predictions into Scripture only to omit any reference to America, a nation that has become the lighthouse to the world by proclaiming the Gospel of Christ?

After many years of research, I have discovered that some of the greatest truths in Scripture are often hidden within the text. To discover these truths, we must compare verse with verse and word with word, and study the many patterns and cycles locked within the Bible. This type of research is new to many people, but as you are about to discover, once you clearly see the cycles and patterns, your eyes will be opened to experience a fresh level of knowledge and revelation.

In this book, you will see the remarkable connections between America and ancient Israel. The parallels begin with the discovery of this new land by the Vikings, and later by Christopher Columbus. They continue with Hebraic patterns relating to the founding of America and the American Revolution. The imprint of God's design will even be seen in the symbolism on the federal buildings in Washington, D.C.

We will take a journey into the prophetic destiny of several American presidents, including the 43rd president, George W. Bush. We will explore the nagging questions relating to the "zero cycle" and the strange deaths of America's presidents, and look at the unusual prophetic implications of election 2000.

I will share with you how the great division between traditional Christianity and the Jewish people is being healed. You will learn why America may be on a collision course with its final destiny, prior to Christ's return. The greatest Gentile nation on earth has an assignment to complete and we may be on the road to fulfilling this end-time mission over the next several years.

The spiritual link between America and Israel will be revealed in the pages of this book. Understanding this link will help you realize that current events may yield significant insight into God's blueprint for America in these last days.

Chapter 1

THE EAGLE IN BIBLE PROPHECY

Is America in Bible Prophecy?

Since America became a nation, Bible scholars and students have wondered if America is mentioned in Bible prophecy. Surely the most powerful Gentile nation on earth, a nation that has financed the preaching of the Gospel of Christ, would be mentioned prophetically in Scripture.

America's history has been one of faith and freedom. Just as the Hebrews crossed the Red Sea to enter the Promised Land where they would be free to worship Jehovah, the Pilgrims crossed the Atlantic to find a land of religious freedom. They believed that they were fulfilling a Divine assignment. Their faith in the God of the Bible was evidenced in the Mayflower Compact signed on November 11, 1620, which read in part:

> "In the name of God, Amen. We, whose names are underwritten, the Loyal Subjects of our dread Sovereign Lord King James, by the grace of God, of Great Britain, France, and Ireland, King, Defender of the Faith, etc. Having undertaken for the glory of God,

and the advancement of the Christian faith, and the honor of our king and country, a voyage to plant the first colony…"

Some 150 years later, the concept of inalienable rights and liberties becomes fundamental to the Declaration of Independence, the Constitution of the United States, and the Bill of Rights. The word inalienable means *unchangeable, immutable, undeniable* and *absolute*. The authors of the Declaration of Independence and the Constitution believed that life, liberty, and the pursuit of happiness were granted to all of mankind by the Almighty. These cherished American rights came from God first, and were proclaimed, not established by, the Declaration of Independence and the Constitution. No government can lawfully take away these absolute, undisputed rights that were first granted by God.

The fact that God and the Bible are pertinent to the way people live is fundamental to the theory of government expressed in the Declaration of Independence and the Constitution. God sanctions government in both the Old and the New Testaments. Harry Truman expressed his belief that America's founding documents were based upon the Torah, the book of Isaiah, and the four Gospels. The role of civil government is explained and sanctioned by God in the New Testament. It states:

"Let every soul be subject unto the higher powers. For there is no power but of God: the powers that be are ordained of God. (Note: Jesus told Pilot that his authority as Caesar was from His Father in heaven.) Whosoever therefore resisteth the power, resisteth the ordinance of God: and they that resist shall receive to themselves damnation. For rulers are not a terror to good works, but to the evil. Wilt thou then be afraid of the power? Do that which is good and thou shalt have praise of the same: For he is the minister of God to thee for good. But if thou do that which is evil, be afraid: for he beareth not the sword in vain: for he is the minister of God, a revenger to execute wrath upon him that doeth evil. Render therefore to all their dues: tribute (note: taxes) to whom tribute is due, custom to whom custom; fear to whom fear; honor to whom honor. Owe no man any thing, but to love one another: for he that loveth another hath fulfilled the law. Love worketh no ill to his neighbor: therefore love is the fulfilling of the law."

(Romans 13: 1-4; 7-8)

The Founders understood the Divine source of our liberties and the role of civil government as protector, not author, of those freedoms. Our Founding Fathers understood this to be the most appropriate and desirable way to pursue happiness!

It is not the purpose of this book to define the personal faith of our Founding Fathers. However, I take exception to the attempt of revisionists to write God out of American history, thus causing an erroneous interpretation of the Founders' intent. The impact of deism on the Founders has been distorted. Deists did not believe in organized religion, the divinity of Christ, or the relevancy of the Bible. However, even they asserted that nature itself demonstrates the existence of God (Source: *Webster's Encyclopedia*, 1941).

Thomas Jefferson, the primary author of the Declaration of Independence, believed in the existence of a Supreme Being who was the creator and sustainer of the universe. Jefferson supposedly rejected Christ's divinity. Interestingly, he wrote to William Short on October 31, 1819, that he was convinced that the fragmentary teaching of Jesus constituted the "outlines of a system of the most sublime morality which has ever fallen from the lips of man." Said to be a Unitarian, Jefferson wrote to Ezra Stiles on June 25, 1819, "I am of a sect by myself, as far as I know" (Source: Monticello Research Department, Rebecca Bowman, August 1997).

Although there is evidence that some of the Founders rejected organized religion and the relevancy of the Bible, they were not the majority. I encourage you to also read the original documents of the Founders to collect all of the facts. Don't be deprived of knowing America's complete heritage by believing only the revisionists' reports.

To interest you in the facts we never see in public school history books, let's read the actual words of some of our Founders concerning Christ. Special recognition here is due to author David Barton for his scholarly research and faithful service to American history. Then we will move on with our prophetic study.

Founders' Own Words from Their Last Will and Testaments

"First of all, I . . . rely upon the merits of Jesus Christ for a pardon of all my sins." Samuel Adams, signer of the Declaration

"To my Creator I resign myself, humbly confiding in His goodness and in His mercy through Jesus Christ for the events of eternity." John Dickinson, signer of the Constitution

"I resign my soul into the hands of the Almighty who gave it in humble hopes of his mercy through our Savior Jesus Christ." Gabriel Duvall, U.S. Supreme Court Justice; selected as delegate to the Constitutional Convention

"This is all the inheritance I can give to my dear family. The religion of Christ can give them one which will make them rich indeed." Patrick Henry

"I render sincere and humble thanks for His manifold and unmerited blessings, and especially for our redemption and salvation by his beloved Son. . . . Blessed be His holy name." John Jay, original Chief Justice, U.S. Supreme Court

"I am constrained to express my adoration of . . . the Author of my existence . . . [for] His forgiving mercy revealed to the world through Jesus Christ, through whom I hope for never ending happiness in a future state." Robert Treat Paine, signer of the Declaration

"I think it proper here not only to subscribe to . . . doctrines of the Christian religion . . . but also, in the bowels of a father's affection, to exhort and charge them [my children] that the fear of God is the beginning of wisdom, that the way of life held up in the Christian system is calculated for the most complete happiness." Richard Stockton, signer of the Declaration

Copies of these wills may be obtained from State archives, historical societies, or from David Barton c/o WallBuilders, P.O. Box 397, Aledo, TX 76008-0397.

Founders' Comments as They Lived and Worked

"My hopes of a future life are all founded upon the Gospel of Christ and I cannot cavil or quibble away [evade or object to] the whole tenor of His conduct by which He sometimes positively asserted and at others countenances [permits] His disciples in asserting that He was God" John Quincy Adams (Source: *The Select Writings of John and John Quincy Adams*, Alfred A. Knopf, 1946, page 292).

"Now to the triune God, The Father, the Son, and the Holy Ghost, be ascribed all honor and dominion, forevermore Amen." Gunning Bedford, signer of the Constitution (Source: Funeral Oration Upon the Death of General Washington, Gunning Bedford, Wilmington: James Wilson, 1800, p. 18).

"You have been instructed from your childhood in the knowledge of your lost state by nature; the absolute necessity of a change of heart, and an entire renovation of soul to the image of Jesus Christ; of salvation thro' His meritorious righteousness only; and the indispensable necessity of personal holiness without which no man shall see the Lord" Elias Boudinot, Revolutionary Officer and President of the Continental Congress, to his daughter (Source: *The Life, Public Services, Addresses, and Letters of Elias Boudinot, President of Continental Congress*, Elias Boudinot, Boston and New York, Houghton, Mifflin, and Co., 1896, Vol. I, pp. 260-262).

"You do well to learn . . . above all the religion of Jesus Christ" George Washington to the Delaware Indian Chiefs on May 12, 1779 (Source: *The Writings of George Washington*, George Washington, John C. Fitzpatrick, editor, Washington, D.C.: U.S. Government Printing Office, 1932, Vol. XV, p. 55).

"[D]on't forget to be a Christian. I have said much to you on this head and I hope an indelible impression is made" Jacob Broom, signer of the Constitution to his son, James, on February 24, 1794, from Wilmington, Delaware (Source: From an autographed letter in possession of WallBuilders, P.O. Box 397, Aledo, TX 76008-0397).

"On the mercy of my Redeemer I rely for salvation and on His merits; not on the works I have done in obedience to His precepts." Charles Carroll, signer of the Declaration, written to Charles W. Wharton, Esq., on September 27, 1825, from Doughoragen, Maryland (Source: From an autographed letter in possession of WallBuilders, P.O. Box 397, Aledo, TX 76008-0397).

"I am a real Christian, that is to say, a disciple of the doctrines of Jesus Christ" Thomas Jefferson to Charles Thomson on January 9, 1816 (Source: *The Writings of Thomas Jefferson by Thomas Jefferson*, Albert Ellery Bergh, editor, Washington, D.C., The Thomas Jefferson Memorial Association, 1904, Vol. XIV, p. 385).

"I think the Christian religion is a Divine institution; and I pray to God that I may never forget the precepts of His religion or suffer the appearance of an inconsistency in my principles and practice" James Iredell, U.S. Supreme Court Justice under President George Washington (Source: *The Papers of James Iredell*, James Iredell, Don Higginbotham, editor, Raleigh: North Carolina Historical Commission, 1976, Vol. I, p. 11).

"My only hope of salvation is in the infinite, transcendent love of God manifested to the world by the death of His Son upon the Cross. Nothing but His blood will wash away my sins. I rely exclusively upon it. Come, Lord Jesus! Come quickly!" Benjamin Rush, signer of the Declaration (Source: *The Autobiography of Benjamin Rush*, Benjamin Rush, George W. Corner, editor, Princeton: Princeton University Press, 1948, p. 166).

"I believe that there is only one living and true God, existing in three persons, the Father, the Son, and the Holy Ghost, the same in substance, equal in power and glory. That the Scriptures of the Old and New Testaments are a revelation from God and a complete rule to direct us how we may glorify and enjoy Him" Roger Sherman, signer of both the Declaration and the Constitution (Source: *The Life of Roger Sherman*, Lewis Henry Boutell, A. C. McClurg and Co., 1896, pp. 272-273).

"I shall now entreat . . . you in the most earnest manner to believe in Jesus Christ, for 'there is no salvation in any other.' [Acts 4:12] . . . [I]f you are not clothed with the spotless robe of His righteousness, you must forever perish." John Witherspoon, signer of the Declaration (Source: *The Works of the Rev. John Witherspoon*, John Witherspoon, Edinburgh, J. Ogle, 1815, Vol. V, pp. 276, 278, from "The Absolute Necessity of Salvation Through Christ," on January 2, 1758)

America's Role as a Lighthouse to the World

America has been instrumental in carrying the light of the Gospel of Christ to the darkest corners of the earth. But America has experienced much darkness itself, though not because of a faulty heritage. Rather, it is because liberal-minded men and women diminish, or deny altogether, our Christian heritage. They deny that the fundamentals upon which this nation was built were based on Biblical principles. In doing so, they deny the Creator and His Son, Jesus Christ!

In the name of separation of church and state, the government has seemingly become the adversary of the Gospel rather than the protector of the right to express it. The Ten Commandments have been essentially censored from our public schools because, heaven-forbid, they might corrupt the students! So we live with the legacy of school violence and declining moral and intellectual standards.

Scripture states that, "A house divided against itself cannot stand" (Matthew 12:25). America is divided today. Until the 1960s, most American public policy reflected an understanding of, and respect for, America's Judeo-Christian values and how they influenced our laws. Today politicians use the term "American" values, lest unbelievers and non-Christians be offended. America is divided between extreme liberal and conservative viewpoints. Liberal values are based on the idea that the concepts of right and wrong are opinions. This is in contrast to the Judeo-Christian belief that God defined right and wrong in the Bible. Those who are not learning Biblical values in church and at home believe that anything goes! Values are handled almost like a smorgasbord of ideas, and this approach sways people without a clear value system. Proverbs 12:15 gives solemn counsel about doing this: "The way of a fool is right in his own eyes; but he that hearkeneth unto counsel is wise." And the counselor of Proverbs is no psychic network employee!

It's no wonder that expediency has replaced character. If the inspired words of the Hebrew prophets offend people today, they must be censored in the name of political correctness. Where is the American Civil Liberties Union when this censorship flies in the face of the First Amendment? People who believe in Christ and respect the Bible as God's inspired Word are labeled religious fanatics and the religious right. This is deliberately done to cast doubt on their beliefs — beliefs that they have the freedom to express as Americans.

Labeling is done skillfully and intentionally. For example, people who want to protect the rights of the unborn are called anti-abortion activists, which sounds so insidious as compared to the term pro-choice. Good has become evil, and evil has been artfully portrayed as good.

Consider some contradictions in America's public policy today. The president places his hand on the Bible while taking the oath of office. Yet the Bible, the most widely acclaimed literary book in the history of the world, is banned from public schools. The Ten Commandments hang in Washington's Supreme Court, but they are banned from public schools. Recently, American Civil Liberties Union lawyers sought to remove the motto "With God all things are possible" from the Ohio State Seal. Employees who serve the public are trained to say "Happy Holidays" instead of "Merry Christmas" during the Christmas season because some people might be offended by a tradition that comes out of our own culture! Even nativity displays have been banned from public places around the nation. In the name of political correctness, Christmas vacation is called Winter Vacation and Easter vacation is referred to as Spring break. People who do not believe in the Creator have essentially opted to honor the creation instead.

People questioned where God was when the Columbine shootings took place in Colorado. The sad reality is that God has been banned from public schools. He is officially unwelcome at Columbine and at every other public school in America. The only way He's invited into schools today is within the hearts of His followers.

I must say that we can't blame all of the problems in America on those with liberal viewpoints. The church of Jesus Christ has fallen short of living by God's commandments and of demonstrating the love of Christ. We must be living examples of how wonderful it is to walk with Him.

The Vision of the Eagle

When the Founding Fathers chose the eagle to be America's emblem, it symbolized their vision of American greatness. The eagle is known for its strength and ability to rise above tumultuous storms, thus enduring great turbulence. Is it possible that prophecy refers to a nation whose emblem is the eagle? If so, America's eagle is flying through unprecedented spiritual and political turbulence.

The Book of 2 Esdras is found in the Old Testament Apocrypha. Most of the book records the lamentations of the Hebrew priest Ezra over the fall of Jerusalem. It describes visions that appeared to Ezra in dreams. The archangel Uriel interpreted the visions. The author of the book is unknown, but scholars believe that it was written near the close of the first century. It was translated from Greek to Latin and placed in the appendix of the New Testament by the Council of Trent in the 16th century. One of the visions found in 2 Esdras Chapters 11 and 12 is about a strange, giant eagle. It begins:

> "On the second night I had a dream, and behold, there came up from the sea an eagle that had twelve feathered wings and three heads. And I looked, and behold, he spread his wings over all the earth, and all the winds of heaven blew upon him, and the clouds were gathered about him...And I looked and behold, the eagle flew with his wings, to reign over the earth and over all who dwell in it."

It continues to give more detail about the eagle. From the midst of the eagle's body a voice began to speak. One wing begins to reign, followed by another, then another. Second Esdras continues:

> "There were some of them that ruled, yet disappeared suddenly; and others of them rose up, but did not hold the rule."

The story then describes the creature's twelve feathered wings and three heads. Later, the eagle is positioned among the four ethereal beasts depicted in Daniel's dream (Daniel 7). Finally, the eagle is likened to the Roman Empire.

There are some odd parallels between this vision and America's political history. Prophetically speaking, I will point out several examples. "Two wings...set themselves up to reign, and their reign was brief and full of tumult." This could refer to Abraham Lincoln and John F. Kennedy. Both presidents dealt with contemporary Civil Rights issues. The Civil War could be symbolized by this statement: "In the midst of the time of that kingdom, great struggles shall arise and it shall be in danger of falling; nevertheless it shall not fall then, but shall reign in its former power." The deaths of Kennedy and Lincoln may be symbolized here: "Eight kings shall arise in it, whose times shall be short and their years swift; and two of them shall perish when the middle of its time draws near..." Kennedy was shot in the midst of his first term, and Lincoln perished at the beginning of his second term. In both cases, assassinations happened "in the midst" of their appointed times.

The "rule of the twelve feathers" could refer to the fact that twelve American presidents have served as military generals. The eagle has two sets of wings, a left and a right wing. America's two main political parties are generally referred to as the "left wing" (Democrats) and the "right wing" (Republicans). The eagle's three heads could, by a stretch of the imagination, represent the three branches of government - Judicial, Executive, and Legislative.

Comparing the eagle vision with parts of American history is an example of how one might attempt to discern how the United States could be represented in Bible prophecy. In 2 Esdras, one can find possible parallels with the United States if verses are taken out of context. My primary interest in the vision of the eagle is that it symbolically predicted a future nation whose emblem would be an eagle.

Ancient Roman

Interestingly, eighteen hundred years before this, the eagle was the emblem of the Roman Empire. During the New Testament era, Roman soldiers carried poles called standards. Each standard had a brass eagle affixed to it to signify Roman authority.

Colonial architecture imitated Greek and Roman architecture. The large columns on our federal buildings imitate Greek and Roman construction. Interestingly, ancient Rome had a hill called Capitolina, where the lawmakers met. In Washington, D.C., Congress meets on Capitol Hill.

The Roman Senate directed the political affairs of the empire. The United States Congress meets to pass national legislation. Rome's most powerful figure was one man, Caesar, who headed the entire empire.

America elects one person to be head of our "empire." Roman soldiers were the best trained fighting machines of their day, just as the United Stated military has been called the greatest battle force on earth.

Daniel the Hebrew prophet described Rome as the iron empire in prophecy (Daniel 2:40). The iron (Roman) kingdom became so filled with idolatry and corruption that it began to rot from within and slowly deteriorate. In fact, all the previous empires of Biblical prophecy, including Egypt, Assyria, Babylon, Medo-Persia, Greece, and Rome, were once invincible at their apex of power. If not conquered by an invading power, they died slow deaths in the morgue of immorality.

Romans delighted in watching gladiator fights and racing chariots, while the Greeks enjoyed games like wrestling. Citizens became desensitized to violent entertainment and eventually, like bloodthirsty mobs, yearned to see people fight to the death. The cursed Christians were killed and eaten by hungry animals in the coliseums. This unbridled violence continued as Roman society decayed.

Regarding American entertainment, even some politicians agree that too much violence comes out of Hollywood. The violent spirit of the Greeks and Romans is alive and well in America. Multitudes love wrestling. Proponents of wrestling say, "It's only entertainment." Wrestling now encompasses banging chairs across heads, slamming opponents on tables, and beating opponents with clubs and baseball bats to produce blood for screaming crowds. One wrestler fell from the ceiling and was killed. Several days later, on national television, one of his friends drank two beers to his memory before a frenzied crowd. Violence is seasoned with sex as scantily clad women strut across the platforms, getting jeers and whistles from the predominately male audiences. Wrestling is now the highest rated form of American entertainment. When asked, "Why do they do it?" wrestling show producers reply, "We're just giving the people what they want." What will they give their fans when they scream, "Kill someone for us?" Rome progressed from sports, to violent entertainment, and finally, to killing Christians. Would anyone disagree with me that, as their self-indulgence prospered, their values and policies decayed?

In Rome, Christians were despised. Christians were considered to be demonized, which justified their deaths as political gain. Christians spoke out against sin and they were targeted for mass extermination. Christians hid in the catacombs, a series of underground caverns that stretch for miles under Rome. They lived, worshiped, and buried their dead there.

Yet the games went on as the empire deteriorated.

Before America follows in Roman footsteps, she must listen to the warning in the Book of Obadiah, because sin and cultural decay demand God's judgment.

"Though thou exalt thyself as the eagle, and though thou set thy nest among the stars, thence I will bring thee down, saith the Lord" (Obadiah 1:4).

The Dividing of the Eagle

Many Roman attitudes are resurfacing in American hearts and minds. As Solomon said, "There is nothing new under the sun." A few of these destructive attitudes are:

- increased resistance to the preaching of the Bible;
- increased persecution of Christians and Christian values;
- the love of the "games" is more important than the love of God and His truth;
- commonplace desecration of the Sabbath by not keeping it Holy before God;
- increased corruption that innocent citizens cannot halt.

An eagle has two wings, one head, and one body. America has two major political parties (wings), one president (head) and one body comprised of the people. Since the 1960s, the "left wing" has represented more liberal thinking, while the "right wing" has represented more traditional (or conservative) thinking.

Before the 1960s, both wings often agreed on spiritual matters and moral opinions. During the 1960s, with the hippie movement, the controversy over the Vietnam War, and the removal of prayer and Bible reading from public schools, we saw public policy polarize toward two opposite viewpoints. This polarization has caused great animosity between many groups of Americans.

Generally, Democrats represent the left wing, or the liberal viewpoint. For example, many Democrat leaders support abortion rights and special rights for homosexuals. Many resist allowing prayer in public schools.

The Republican Party is often considered the right wing, or conservative party. A politician who is conservative is generally marked for media criticism. Most Americans can clearly see these divisions.

The Hypocrisy of Liberalism

Extreme liberalism breeds extreme contradictions. When conservative African American Judge Clarence Thomas was nominated for Supreme Court Justice, extreme feminists swarmed all over Washington like buzzards after a wounded carcass. An African American woman stepped forward and alleged that Thomas had made sexual advances toward her. Feminists demanded that the Thomas nomination not be confirmed. Years later, the president had sex with an intern in the oval office during the workday and denied it under oath. Various other women charged him with sexual misconduct; yet, the same feminists who were outraged by Thomas took a Clinton vacation. Some defended the president by saying, "It is simply a weakness in his character."

Environmentalists demand the protection of the rain forests and the spotted owl; yet, how many of them speak up to protect an unborn baby? Poachers are fined thousands of dollars; yet, abortionists are subsidized with government funds to kill unborn children. The double standard has become commonplace.

John Wrote: "Marvel not, my brethren, if the world hates you" (1 John 3:13).

The Christian message is offensive to those who love sin. The Bible teaches that perverted sexual acts are wrong, so it offends the alternative lifestyle crowd. The Bible teaches that God ordains human life and that He knows infants before they are formed in the womb, so this offends the pro-abortion crowd. Bible prophets predict that, during the tribulation, many will die, one third of the world's water will be polluted and one third of the plant life will be destroyed, so it offends the environmentalists. In the Bible, Hebrew prophets rebuked sin, so they were offensive.

Scripture indicates that the ancient Hebrews desired acceptance by their neighbors. So they worshipped foreign idols (Judges 2:11-12), practiced homosexuality (Judges 19:1-30), and allowed their newborn children to be passed through the fire of the idol Molech (1 Kings 11:1-7). They worshiped trees and built groves to honor the earth god (1 Kings 14:15).

Many Americans would feel comfortable around those compromised Hebrews who embraced idolatry, same sex relations, infant murder, and earth worship. These people would be hailed as open minded, tolerant, and politically correct today.

The Hebrew God was not made of wood or stone. He manifested Himself in flashing fire and was seen through His mighty miracles. The power of life and death were in His hands and He parted the Red Sea with His breath (Psalms 18:15). His presence made mountains shake and people tremble (Nahum 1:5). Hebrew prophets fell on the ground, fell into trances and witnessed living creatures near the sapphire throne of the Eternal One (Isaiah 6:1-5). The Cherubim, Seraphim and mighty archangels were heard whispering, "Holy, holy is the Lord." When Abraham heard His voice, he fell in the dust. Daniel fell on his face and John, in Revelation, "fell at His feet as one being dead" (Revelation 1:17). Imagine how God must tremble at a spiritually ignorant professor who attempts to convince young students that God does not exist. That breathing piece of clay is fortunate that God is a loving God, "longsuffering and not willing that any should perish" (2 Peter 3:9).

Hypocrisy and compromise have been rampant since the moral-cultural upheaval of the 1960s. Kids raised without the Bible understood little or nothing about God, prayer, or moral absolutes. As they have grown, they have influenced public policy, education, and the media. Schools are filled with political correctness. Students are taught to question everything their Christian parents taught them. Parents can no longer publicly offer a prayer for protection for their children before a high school football game. Without moral absolutes, kids growing up today are guided by situational ethics. This process allows them to make up their values as they go through life.

Schools in early America did not teach situational ethics. The Ivy League colleges were started by Christians who included Christian values within school curricula. The list includes Harvard (1638), Yale (1701), Princeton (1746), and Dartmouth (1754). These colleges eventually became secular in that they no longer included the teachings of the Gospel. Many Founding Fathers attended these schools before the change. Fifty-two percent of all seventeenth century Harvard graduates became ministers (Source: *The Rebirth of America*). Harvard's "Rules and Precepts" adopted in 1646 reflected its values. Among its precepts were:

- "Everyone shall consider the main end of his life and study to know God and Jesus Christ which is eternal life."

- "Seeing the Lord giveth wisdom, every one shall seriously by prayer in secret seek wisdom of him."
- "Everyone shall so exercise himself in reading the Scriptures twice a day that they be ready to give an account of their proficiency therein, both in theoretical observations of languages and logic, and in practical and spiritual truth."

As professors became more secular and promoted humanism, communism, and atheism, young minds were corrupted with teachings contrary to the Bible (2 Corinthians 11:3). American educators used their platforms to spread their agnostic worldviews, and their students, in turn, promoted the same faithless views.

Warnings to a Faithless Generation

Jesus told a parable about a woman oppressed by an adversary (Luke 18:1-7). She petitioned a judge to intervene, but the judge ignored her. Finally, after she continually called upon him for help, he granted her petition. Christ summarized the parable by asking, "When the son of man cometh, shall he find faith upon the earth" (Luke 18:8)? This seems to be a strange question, considering the spread of Christianity throughout the world. More people profess Christianity than ever before; yet, the very nations that once produced firebrands for the Gospel and sent forth powerfully anointed missionaries are no longer experiencing revival.

Jesus previously taught the disciples that, "Men ought always to pray and not to faint" (Luke 18:1). Christ was warning about the final days when believers will become weary in prayer, and quit before receiving answers. Christ stressed the importance of persistence and patience when waiting for answers to prayer.

Twentieth century history exhibits what can happen to those who do not persevere in prayer. Britain, once a center of European revival, sent famous missionaries like Dr. David Livingstone to the spiritually dark continent of Africa. The Protestant Reformation began with the German, Martin Luther. Holland was the home of Corrie Ten Boom, whose family hid Jews during World War II, only to be killed or imprisoned for their actions. Yet today, much of Europe is virtually paralyzed in unbelief with Christian churches being turned into mosques, and other churches functioning as mere spiritual museums.

Britain, Germany, and Holland stand today as examples of what can happen when Christians grow weary in prayer and turn to unbelief. One missionary said that Amsterdam, Holland might very well be the most morally wicked city in the world. In broad daylight, a man can walk the streets and select a prostitute from a storefront window. The government distributes free drugs to addicts. They simply stop by street corner pharmaceutical trucks equipped to administer their fixes. Amsterdam spawned the hippie movement and has the distinction of being the most liberal city in the world. Sadly, over 16 million people in Holland are infected with AIDS.

Missionary Russell Domingue, having ministered extensively in Amsterdam, heard ministers express their opinions as to why Holland seems to have lost its faith. Apparently, during World War II, many Christians in Holland prayed fervently that the Nazis would not enter their nation. At that time, Christianity was quite strong and many Christians prayed earnestly for the country. Much to their dismay, the Nazis marched into Holland anyway. It seems that this so disappointed the Christians that they lost their spiritual fervor.

Great Britain is another somber example of modern-day spiritual defeat. God greatly blessed the country following the completion in 1611 of the King James English translation of the Bible. English missionaries took the Gospel to Africa, the Middle East and as far away as India. It was said that the "sun never sets on the British Empire." But current day society in Great Britain, as in Holland, is dominated by cynicism, skepticism, and secularism. The "isms" of Humanism and Socialism have choked the Word of God from society, leaving Christian influences weakened.

If Americans stop praying for our nation, we could have a spiritual post mortem similar to Europe. We are the final Gentile stronghold of Christianity in the world. We were blessed spiritually during the World Wars. Of course, our nation was not bombed into rubble. In fact, previous wars have birthed churches that were filled to capacity. Wars provoked our presidents to seek guidance from God. During times of national crisis, our faith in the God of the Bible became our staff and comfort. Our spiritual problem comes from spiritual ignorance. The 1960s produced a generation without truth. Students in public schools are so ignorant about the Bible that they think Jezebel was Ahab's donkey, and the epistles were the wives of the apostles!

However, the Founding Fathers were not ignorant regarding Christianity. They recognized the importance of the Scriptures. George Washington placed his hand upon the Bible while being inaugurated. At the conclusion, he added the words, "So help me God." At that moment, the secretary of the Senate offered to raise the Bible to his lips, but he bowed down reverently and kissed it (Source: *The Lives of the Presidents*).

George Washington said, "It is impossible to rightly govern the world without the Bible." Thomas Jefferson stated that, "The Bible makes the best people in the world." Andrew Jackson said, "That book sir (the Bible) is the rock on which our Republic rests." Abraham Lincoln said, "But for this book we could not know right from wrong. I believe the Bible is the best gift God has ever given to man." President Grant said, "The Bible is the anchor of our liberties" (Source: *Wilmington's Guide to the Bible*). Many American Presidents have made clear and positive statements about the Bible. Ronald Reagan even declared a "Year of the Bible."

John the Baptist called the religious and political leaders of his day a generation of vipers. He asked, "How will you escape the wrath that is coming" (Matthew 3:7)? John was the fundamentalist nightmare of his day. He refused to preach in the dignified, religious synagogues. His church was located in the barren wilderness of Judea. Talk about the wrong side of the tracks! Yet, multitudes came out of the Jordan River dripping wet and repentant. To the religious stiffs, John was a loose cannon. He challenged the religious and social divisions caused by pride. The wealthy despised the poor. The educated oppressed the uneducated. Israel's leaders were divided concerning John the Baptist. They asked if John was of God or of men (Matthew 21:25). This question caused heated debates.

Before the debates cooled, a Nazarene named Jesus began ministering in Galilee and the controversy intensified. Because of Christ's bold message, He was soon unwelcome in some synagogues. This didn't deter His work. The crowds were too large for the synagogues anyway! Poor, common people flocked to Him. The scholars demanded to see His credentials asking, "Where did you go to school? Who gave you the authority to speak and preach" (Matthew 21:23)?

Instead of accepting His miracles as proof of His authority, they built a case against Him. It was *their* authority versus *his* authority — *us* against *them*. The Pharisees (*us*) were very educated and very religious. The common people (*them*) were ridiculed for following Jesus. The Pharisees felt that the unschooled were too ignorant to make spiritual decisions for themselves, thinking that they needed guidance and enlightenment. Jesus was anything but ignorant. At twelve, His wisdom shocked the priest in the Temple (Luke 2:47-49). But Jesus wasn't educated in *their* schools by *their* professors in *their* doctrine!

The arrogant attitude of the Pharisees lives on today. A dear friend of mine who lives overseas corresponds with many wealthy, influential Americans. Once, while he was visiting a billionaire in New York, he said that he would be heading south to visit friends. The billionaire laughed and spoke about the ignorant, uneducated people living in the mountains. My friend asked, "Have you been there?" The man answered "No." My friend replied, "You don't know what you are taking about. They are some of the finest people in America!" The billionaire's views were biased and not factual. The *us* mentality of the Pharisees is exhibited by the media today when they accuse Christians of being narrow minded bigots and imply that if Christians could only see what they see, the world would be a better place. Yet Jesus said, "They are blind leaders of the blind and they will both fall into a ditch" (Matthew 15:14).

Of course people have the right to disagree. This is America! However, societies have declined again and again as a result of sin. God requires much of America because of our heritage. Our current social and political disarray may just be a result of the day we clipped the eagle's wings.

Chapter 2

CLIPPING THE WINGS OF THE EAGLE

The Day We Banned God from America

"Take heed unto yourselves, lest ye forget the covenant of the Lord your God...."

(Deuteronomy 4:23)

When David Barton wrote the book, *America: To Pray or Not to Pray,* he compiled a series of charts that demonstrate the drastic downward spiral of some American institutions, after prayer and Bible reading were banned from public schools in 1963. Divorce rates went up. SAT scores plummeted. Sexually transmitted diseases spread rampantly among teens. More devastating than this, an entire generation was spiritually lost. I can recall this period quite well.

My public school education began in the small Appalachian town of Big Stone Gap, Virginia. Nestled at the base of the mountains in southwestern Virginia, it was a close-knit community of people who were stubborn in spirit and strong in personal conviction. Everybody, whether Baptist, Methodist or Pentecostal, took their faith seriously and raised their children to respect God and country.

My family moved to Big Stone Gap when I was three years old. My father assumed a pastorate, and I began school at age six. I remember rising early each morning, getting my little leather pack with books, and walking across the concrete bridge to school. I also recall, very clearly, seeing my first grade teacher stand in front of the class, reading a story from the Bible and offering a brief prayer to bless the day. Sometimes she asked if one of the students would like to pray. I can remember the feeling of security and safety when I heard the prayer. Being a momma's boy, I missed home, but prayer reminded me of Dad and Mom. It comforted me.

By fifth grade, we had moved to Arlington in northern Virginia. Not only did I experience culture shock, I also noticed something very different about fifth grade. No teacher offered to read the Bible or pray. I finally asked why and the teacher said, "We can no longer do that in a public school." I couldn't believe it! Perhaps the teachers in Big Stone Gap were doing it despite this new law. Being a kid, I hadn't watched the news or paid attention to adult conversation regarding this. In Arlington, things were different. I learned about the atheist who proudly boasted about removing prayer and Bible reading from school. Her name was Madalyn Murray O'Hair.

The O'Hair Factor

O'Hair used her son, William, to demonstrate how an atheist was disrespected by public school prayer and Bible reading. Years later, William Murray wrote this about his mother:

"I was born into a home of near constant rage and violence. My mother never married my father or my brother's father. As a result of my mother's constant angry outbursts she could not hold down a job and she, my brother and I lived with her parents and my unmarried uncle in a small row house in Baltimore, Maryland. My grandfather had never filed an income tax return and most of what he did do during his life was illegal or ill advised. He had no savings. My grandmother read tarot cards and sent out demons by burning human hair. My uncle kept boards of pornography in his room and my mother filled the house with statues of mating animals that she worshipped.

My mother accepted the communist doctrine when I was about ten years old and, from that time on, there were socialist and communist study group meetings in the basement of our Baltimore home. I was taught that, because there was no God, there was no such thing as right or wrong. My mother told me it was better to be a homosexual than to be a Christian. She taught me that the most important things in life were the physical pleasures of drink, food and sex.

For many years I lived the life I was taught. I drank a quart of vodka a day and by the time I was thirty, I had been married twice. I lived only to eat, drink and have what I thought was sexual pleasure. But a time came when the women and the booze no longer gave me the happiness that my atheist mother told me they would bring. I was consuming so much alcohol that it no longer got me high. I started using marijuana and other drugs to supplement the alcohol which had betrayed me."

(Source: www.wjmurray.com 9-25-2000)

William J. Murray, who is now a Christian minister, was a young boy attending public school when his mother set out to remove prayer and Bible reading from public schools in 1959. Her lawsuit, Murray vs. Curlett, was finally heard in court on February 27, 1963. On June 17, 1963, the Supreme Court ruled in O'Hair's favor and reverential Bible reading and prayer were expelled from America's public schools.

I wondered later, "How could one woman accomplish this?" I questioned, "Where was the outcry from Christians who believed in Bible reading and prayer? After all, Christians were the majority — or were they?" Christian reaction was downright anemic. They complained and criticized the decision, but few attempted to challenge it.

Since God was expelled from public schools, thousands of court battles have occurred with the sole purpose of erasing every object, phrase, and symbol of Christianity from America. This decision has put America into a spiritual war zone, essentially separating it from its covenant protection with God. When you are in covenant with God, your enemies are His enemies. An example of God removing a hedge of protection is found in Job 1:10-12. Since 1963, the enemy of God and America has certainly attacked!

The Legacy of Breaking America's Spiritual Covenant

I believe that if they could, Washington, Adams, and most of the Founders would have kicked their way out of their tombs to object to the removal of the Bible and prayer from public schools. Washington said in his Farewell Address in 1796:

"Let us with caution indulge the supposition that morality can be maintained without religion. Reason and experience both forbid us to expect that national morality can prevail to the exclusion of religious principle."

In 1963, the Supreme Court Justices might as well have said to God, "We are rejecting the covenant our fathers had with you." In ancient Israel, when the people rejected their covenant with God, He allowed His hedge of protection to be removed, thus causing great trouble to come upon the land. This was His way of getting Israel's attention. He wanted them to see that they needed to repent and turn their hearts back to Him. Let's look at some of the things that have happened since God removed His hedge of protection from America:

Political Assaults: Five months after the Murray vs. Curlett decision, President John F. Kennedy was assassinated in Dallas, Texas. America, previously victorious in every war, was humiliated in the Vietnam War. We never won it. We merely pulled out our troops and went home. Racial tension festered. Civil Rights leader Martin Luther King was assassinated. The downward spiral continued with the oil embargo, and Richard Nixon's resignation from the presidency. Iran later took Americans hostage for 444 days. A former Israeli intelligence agent told me that Israeli officials told President Carter that they would send a special team into Iran to help release the hostages. President Carter decided to execute a secret mission to free the hostages before the ensuing presidential election. The mission failed and so did Carter in his re-election efforts. Our majestic eagle was wounded over and over again!

An Assault on Values: The removal of the Bible from schools undermined the ability to teach moral absolutes. Rejecting the Bible meant rejecting its principles. Values like honesty, perseverance, faithfulness, and kindness became subject to debate and individual circumstances. For example, if honesty depended on one's situation, the immature students were essentially taught to determine for themselves whether it's right or wrong to live by Godly standards. Talk about having the inmates run the asylum! Here's an example for a class to discuss regarding cheating in school. How do you think a group of fourth graders would respond?

> Situation: Tom's parents are great. They help him with his home-work. He gets an allowance for easy weekend chores. He has his own computer and Internet connection along with a telephone and killer stereo. His parents pay him $25 for every "A" that he gets and he enjoys total privacy when he needs to study. Randy has a part time job after school to help his mom pay the high winter heating bills. He lives with his mom and four younger brothers and sisters. When he gets home after work, he makes dinner for the kids, cleans up and bathes his little brother before bed because his mom works until ten. Exhausted and without time to study, Randy doesn't study for his test in the morning.

The moral guidelines in the Bible are summed up in the Ten Com-mandments: the five "dos" and the five "do nots." Reading the Bible in school planted positive values in the minds of kids. I never remember my teacher forcing me to believe the Bible, but I do remember the comfort I felt when I heard the Bible stories. Imagine if every law in America that is based on Scripture was removed! Anarchy would dominate; theft, killing, and fighting would be uncontrollable. Laws are enforced as a tool to re-strain evil. Likewise, the laws of God's Word act as a restraint against sins like murder, lust, pride, and deception. Without Biblical standards, what is the basis for right and wrong? Humanists will argue that values vary, and that there are no absolutes. Even the Deists saw the Almighty in na-ture and revered the absolute power of the oceans and the result of gravity!

An Assault on our Identity: Teaching creationism was forbidden. With the Bible banished, science was deemed the source of truth. Scien-tific evolution was taught as the origin of our species. It is noteworthy that, before his death, Charles Darwin denied his theory of evolution. Have you ever read that fact in one of your kids' textbooks? According to pure scientific process, a theory needs some evidence to support it. There are many missing links in the evolution theory. If kids think they are a result of a random accident of nature, or that they arose from primordial slime, is it surprising that they have no hope in a God-ordained future? People will let you down. It is not a matter of *if*, but a matter of *when*. But the God of the Bible will never let you down. His mercies are new everyday! Teach kids this, or at least don't prohibit its discussion, and you will see new self-esteem in kids blossoming across the land.

My Grandfather, John Bava, published this poem in one of his books. It mocks the utter nonsense of evolution:

Three monkeys sat in a coconut tree, discussing things that are said to be.
Said one to the other, now listen, you two; There's a certain rumor that can't be true:
That man descended from our noble race, this very idea is a big disgrace.

No monkey ever deserted his wife, starved her babies and ruined her life
And you've never known a mother monk, to leave her babies with others to bunk
Or pass them on from one to another, till they scarcely know who is their mother.

And another thing you will never see: a monk build a fence 'round a coconut tree
And let the coconuts go to waste, forbidding the other monks to taste
Why if I put a fence around a tree, starvation would force you to steal from me.

Here's another thing a monk won't do: go out at night and get a stew
Or use a club, a gun or knife to take another monkey's life
We're fully convinced without any fuss, man has descended, but not from us.

(Source: *Scrapbook of Radiant Gems*, John Bava, page 34)

Since Creationism is a Biblical teaching, it is banned in the name of separation of church and state, even though in some communities about 65% of the youth in public schools also attend church at least occasionally. By the way, separation of church and state is not now, nor has it ever been, a law. It was a concept that our Founders were mindful of because their goal was to protect the free exercise of religion — not to ban religion. However, protecting the free exercise of religion *is* a law; it is the first amendment to the U.S. Constitution. In the name of protecting non-Christians, must we totally eradicate our Christian heritage from every public place and public school? What is wrong with this picture?

An Assault on Morality: So-called modern, enlightened educators appear to believe that condoms are the 21st century cure for all sexually transmitted diseases. It is outrageous to demonstrate in public school classrooms how to conquer the problem of sexually transmitted diseases by stretching condoms over cucumbers! The Bible teaches that people are slaves to sin until they are set free by faith in Christ as Savior. Then they are free to control their choices and behave correctly. In Christ, there is self- control. Abstinence is an act of self-control, but there is little teaching about abstinence. Without moral absolutes, our current system is doomed to propagate the spread of sexually transmitted diseases. When students are taught how to sin safely by having "safe sex," then why would they abstain?

A cucumber sporting a condom never got a teenage girl pregnant, but uncontrolled lust certainly has! Our children need to learn how to live with self-control. Wise choices will stop the problem of pregnancy and the spread of sexually transmitted diseases. These choices may seem old fashioned, but group dating, chaperones, and fulfilling, wholesome activities will save our kids lives. Besides, since condoms fail a percentage of the time, aren't we teaching our kids how to play Russian roulette instead of saving their lives?

During an interview on TBN, evangelist Dave Roever said that the government has spent over six million dollars researching ways to stop AIDS. In conclusion, they discovered the best way was to abstain from sex before marriage and stay married to the same person. This is a six million dollar revelation that can be found in any forty-dollar Bible! If this is the finding, then why is it wrong to teach students in public schools that they should abstain from sex before marriage? Why not just teach the Bible and save tax dollars!

An Assault on the Value of Human Life: Society has taught that any pregnancy can be terminated at any time by abortion. Without respect for life while in the womb, is it any wonder that kids kill each other? Abortion kills unborn babies and their "fetal tissue" is sold for research. This reminds me of what Hitler did to the Jews during the holocaust. Hitler's henchmen considered the Jews to be useless, and many innocent Jews were dissected and used for medical research. Some Nazi soldiers threw babies into the air and skewed them with their bayonets in front of their mothers. Thousands of Jews were used as human guinea pigs in the name of science. Does fetal tissue for medical research sound familiar? The American holocaust is not being played out behind locked doors in Nazi concentration camps. It is being hidden behind closed doors of abortion facilities. It is being sold as a right that our Founding Fathers intended. The loss of respect for life is frightening. If an infant can be redefined as fetal tissue then, in the future, how will senior citizens be defined? Will they be inconvenient, or too expensive, or non-productive?

Ronald Reagan said, "We cannot diminish the value of one category of human life — the unborn — without diminishing the value of all human life." At the heart of respect is basic respect for God and for all the human life that He has created. Teaching that one can redefine life by calling an unborn child a mass of cell tissue devalues all life. Some nations use abortion for population control. In some places, euthanasia is the choice used to eliminate the weak, sick, mentally retarded, and elderly. I believe that some ungodly politicians have not already supported euthanasia simply because they would lose many of their voters! I can see the debate now: "We can save hundreds of millions of dollars under Social Security and Medicare by removing millions of non-productive people from the nation through humane termination. The money saved can be used to invest in the education of our youth." Impossible? Not to those who have no moral and spiritual convictions.

As I learn more about America's extraordinary connection to the Hebrews, it becomes clearer to me why God raised up America. It is also clear that we must uphold the spiritual covenant of our Founding Fathers. God judged Israel for breaking His covenant. Since He is the same yesterday, today, and forever, we can only expect a similar response for America's covenant breaking. God did not unleash His full judgment upon Israel until He first visited them with mercy. His mercy was an expression of His love and was intended to convict their hearts to repentance. Genesis states that, "…the cup of iniquity must become full" before God swiftly unleashes the wrath of His mighty hand (Genesis 15:16). The Ten Commandments were not ten recommendations. If we obeyed them we would be spared from divorce, greed, murder, stealing, lying, and corruption. In the Promised Land, Ancient Israel eventually broke every commandment. Their sins moved the hand of God to unleash His wrath by preparing a plan for Israel to enter into Babylonian captivity.

American captivity is of a different nature. We are not plagued by foreign troops who force us into Siberian slavery. We experience our captivity as an internal void caused by the spiritual darkness that we have without Christ. This void results in unhappiness, depression, despair, ungratefulness, and strife. In other words, our mental prison, caused by spiritual ignorance, leads to spiritual bondage in our lives.

Christians in our nation conquered their problem of internal captivity upon their acceptance of Christ, yet they continue to struggle with sin and its effects in their lives. In addition, they are ridiculed on TV, sued for sharing the Gospel at work, and their jobs are jeopardized if they dare to read the Bible in public school cafeterias on personal time. Yet gangs roam the streets and cause people to live in fear, locked within their homes behind barred doors. Fear stalks America's inner cities after sunset. Our captivity is evidenced by the destructive toll of drug addictions. It is evident in a generation so addicted to lust that premarital sex is considered normal between children. Men think that they are women trapped in male bodies and women want to be men. Sexual liberation has resulted in sexual addiction and bondage. We have lost so many precious lives to these destructive actions. Just as God brooded over Israel, knowing the outcome of their sin, today He laments over His children whose concept of freedom has become so perverted. We must reach this end-time generation of young people with the message of hope and freedom through an experience with Christ.

There is a Promise for the Youth

In our Voice of Evangelism crusades and conventions, many young people rejoice and experience, as the old timers used to say, "A high time in Zion!" Biblical prophets foretold of these days. The Lord promised, "It shall come to pass in the last days that I will pour out my spirit upon all flesh. Your sons and daughters shall prophesy" (Acts 2: 16-17).

Psalms 102:16-18 teaches that the generation that sees Zion (Jerusalem) built up will see the Lord appear in His glory! David wrote, "This shall be written for the generation to come." The Hebrew word "to come" is the word acharon, meaning *the end* or *the finale*. It refers to the last generation on earth that will literally see the return of Christ. The verse continues, "This shall be written for the generation to come (acharon) and the people which shall be created shall praise the Lord" (Psalms 102:18). The generation that sees Jerusalem built up will be the final generation and will also be a generation created to praise the Lord.

The final worldwide revival will have roots among the youth.

Missionaries tell me that as they minister in crusades overseas, thousands in attendance are typically younger than thirty years old! In fact, every great revival in world history has begun among young people. The final revival in America will be no different.

America's New Spiritual Army

As the children rejoiced at the eastern gate when Jesus rode the colt through the city, the offended Pharisees demanded that Jesus quiet down the crowd. Jesus rebuked them saying, "If these do not praise me the rocks will cry out! Have you not heard it said that out of the mouth of babes and sucklings thou hast perfected praise?" Christ quoted from Psalms 8:2, which states, "Out of the mouth of babes and sucklings thou has ordained strength, because of thine enemies that thou mightest avenge thy enemies, that thou mightest still the enemy and the avenger."

It is interesting that Psalms states that praise from the "babes" will avenge "thy enemies." The prophecy speaks of God's enemies. When we praise the Lord, He arises from His Holy habitation and goes after His enemies! Moses said, "Let God arise and let his enemies be scattered" (Psalms 68:1). Notice that it is the "mouths of babes and sucklings" that strengthens God to go after His enemies! In Psalms we learn that incredible spiritual power is released when praise is released from the lips of God's people.

> "Let the high praises of God be in their mouth and a two edged sword in their hand. To execute vengeance . . . to bind their kings with chains and their nobles with fetters of iron."
> (Psalms 149:6-7)

Throngs of protesting youth have toppled some East European Communist nations. In Romania and Bulgaria, thousands of Christian youth prayed, sang and rebuked the spirits that controlled their nations. Consequently, wicked leaders were overthrown and leaders who allowed religious freedom were promoted into high government posts. This end-time spiritual conflict with its attack on social-moral values will be won or lost through prayer or the lack thereof.

In the election of 1980, evangelical Christians prayed, fasted, and voted. Consequently, Ronald Reagan was elected. He inspired the nation to put aside pessimism and embrace hope and patriotism. The Bible that Reagan placed his hand upon at his inauguration belonged to his mother. A special Scripture was marked in that Bible which reads:

> "If my people, which are called by my name, shall humble themselves, and pray, and seek my face, and turn from their wicked ways; then will I hear from heaven, and will forgive their sin, and will heal their land."   (2 Chronicles 7:14)

At a time when Americans are focusing on the global economy, the power of the Internet, and Wall Street, we must be faithful to pray for wisdom and favor for our national leaders and to seek an understanding of America's prophetic destiny.

The birthing of this Republic was not mere chance. God, who sits in the heavens, had a sovereign plan. Right now, standing at the four corners of the throne of God are four living creatures. One has the face of an eagle (Revelation 4:7). I want to focus on the eagle in more detail, and look at God's plan to raise this nation. In the process, we will gain insight into the role of America in end-time Biblical prophecy.

Chapter 3

AMERICA: GOD'S PROPHETIC VINEYARD

Where is America in Bible Prophecy?

"There was another great eagle with great wings and many feathers: and, behold, this vine did bend her roots toward him, and shot forth her branches toward him, that he might water it by the furrows of her plantation. It was planted in the good soil by great waters, that it might bring forth branches, and that it might bear fruit, that it might be a goodly vine."   (Ezekiel 17:7-8)

The vision of the eagle recorded in 2 Esdras contains certain parallels that may refer to the United States. While America is not alluded to directly in Scripture, it may be referred to indirectly. God weaves His prophetic revelations within Scripture by using patterns, types and implications. So we must search for those patterns and references when looking for America's role in prophecy. Let's begin by looking at Isaiah.

"Woe unto the land shadowing with wings, which is beyond the rivers of Ethiopia; That sendeth ambassadors by the sea, even in vessels of bulrushes upon the waters, saying, Go ye swift messengers, to a nation scattered and peeled, to a people terrible from their beginning hitherto; a nation meted out and trodden down, whose land the rivers have spoiled! All ye inhabitants of the world, and dwellers on the earth, see ye, when he lifteth up an ensign on the mountains; and when he bloweth a trumpet, hear ye" (Isaiah 18:1-3).

Some Scholars think that the land beyond Ethiopia referred to in Isaiah is America. The nation in Isaiah's vision was a land "shadowing with wings," or literally a land with buzzing wings that sends ambassadors by the sea. Certainly America, along with many other nations, has sent ambassadors across the oceans. The nation that Isaiah described was "scattered and peeled." The word "scattered" in Hebrew means to *stretch or to be tall*. The word "peeled" in Hebrew refers to *being smooth or bright*. Therefore, Isaiah sees a people who are tall and have a bright complexion.

North Africans are dark skinned, so this nation must be beyond Africa — "beyond the rivers of Ethiopia." Isaiah continued to explain that this nation is "meted out and trodden down." A literal translation would be *mighty and conquering*. Other Bible translations read:

- "a people dreaded near and far that conquers and treads down" (Berkeley translation)
- "a terror far and near; a sturdy race of conquerors" (Moffet translation)
- "terrible from the beginning onwards, a nation mighty" (Rotherham translation)

Since it is located "beyond Ethiopia" and it is well watered by rivers, it is hard to determine what nation the prophet referred to in his day. Continuing to read, a warning is given to the nation. The warning concludes with:

"In that time shall the present be brought unto the Lord of hosts of a people scattered and peeled, and from a people terrible from their beginning hitherto; a nation meted out and trodden under foot, whose land the rivers have spoiled, to the place of the name of the Lord of hosts, the mount Zion." (Isaiah 18:7)

Contemporary Bible scholars are uncertain who Isaiah meant to portray here. It has been speculated that this verse refers to America, but that cannot be proven. There are other theories for us to consider.

America and Jeremiah's Babylon Theory

Jeremiah 50 opens with the prophecy against Babylon (Jeremiah 50:1 and 51:1). He wrote, "Babylon has been a gold cup in the Lord's hand" (Jeremiah 51:7); that "Babylon has suddenly fallen" (Jeremiah 51:8); and that Babylon will become "a heap, a dwelling for dragons" (Jeremiah 51:37). He warned God's people to "Get ye out of the midst of her" (Jeremiah 51:45).

Some prophecy teachers believe that Jeremiah 50 and 51 cryptically refer to America. I disagree, because Jeremiah states that the prophecy is spoken against Babylon. In the sense that Babylon's sins can be compared to the sins of America, there is a lesson to be learned here about repentance, but not a prophetic lesson concerning America.

Jeremiah warned about Israel's seventy years of captivity in Babylon (Jeremiah 25:11). In fact, Jeremiah gave firm warnings about Babylon throughout the whole book of Jeremiah. An accurate comparison of Babylon (in Chapters 50 and 51) to America requires that we also compare the other references in Jeremiah to America. This is literally impossible.

Comparing References to Babylon Made by John and Jeremiah

Jeremiah's prophecy is related to the warnings of the Apostle John concerning Mystery Babylon in Revelation 17 and 18. Regarding Babylon, Jeremiah wrote that the rivers would dry up (Jeremiah 50:38). In Revelation 16:12, John wrote that the Euphrates River would dry up. Ancient Babylon was built on the edge of the Euphrates River and Jeremiah commanded the people to "flee and come out of her" (Jeremiah 51:6,45). John also referred to Mystery Babylon when he wrote, "Come out of her my people" (Revelation 18:4). In Jeremiah's vision, Babylon was a gold cup (Jeremiah 51:7). John repeated the same statement about Mystery Babylon, saying that she has a "golden cup in her hand" (Revelation 17:4). Jeremiah said dragons would dwell there (Jeremiah 51:37). The Hebrew word is tannim and can mean *land or sea monster*. It probably alludes to some type of desert animal dwelling among the ruins. At times, tannim is translated in the original Scriptures as *serpent* or *snake*. Several hundred years later, John said Mystery Babylon would become a habitation of devils (Revelation 18:2). It is interesting to note in Revelation 12 that John described Satan as a "dragon with seven heads and ten horns" (Revelation 12:3, 9).

The comparison continues as Jeremiah cried out, "Babylon is suddenly fallen" (Jeremiah 51:8). And John prophesied seven hundred years later, "Babylon the great is fallen, is fallen" (Revelation 18:2). Because the angel in Revelation 18:2 announced the fall of Babylon twice, with the phrase "is fallen, is fallen" it could suggest two separate destructions of Babylon.

Jeremiah's Babylon was built by King Nebuchadnezzar. It was conquered by the Medes and Persians, and taken by the Greeks and Alexander the Great. Alexander planned to restore the city to its grandeur, but he died unexpectedly in Babylon at age 33. After Alexander's death, Babylon became the capital of the Seleucid dynasty. The temples were eventually moved from the ancient city and a new capital was built at the Tigris River. Babylon became a ghost town. However, it was never destroyed in the manner that Jeremiah predicted — that is, with a destroying wind. John's Mystery Babylon will be destroyed with fire in one hour (Revelation 18:8,10, 17, 19).

I believe that Jeremiah predicted the fall of his current-day Babylon, and at the same time prophesied regarding the Babylon to come later. This could be a dual prophecy, meaning a prophecy regarding Jewish captivity in Babylon in Jeremiah's day, and a prophecy concerning a future Babylon (seen by John in Revelation).

Using the basic laws of Biblical interpretation, I cannot conclude that America is connected to this prophecy of Jeremiah.

Is America the Mystery Babylon in Revelation 17?

The most frequent prophetic teaching about our nation suggests that America is depicted in Revelation 17. Yet again, upon carefully examining the text "line upon line and precept upon precept," the Babylon of Revelation cannot refer to America. This is why:

"And there came one of the seven angels which had the seven vials, and talked with me, saying unto me, Come hither; I will show unto thee the judgment of the great whore that sitteth upon many waters. With whom the kings of the earth have committed fornication, and the inhabitants of the earth have been made drunk with the wine of her fornication. And upon her forehead was a name written, Mystery Babylon the great, the mother of harlots and abominations of the earth. And I saw the woman drunken with the blood of the saints, and with the blood of the martyrs of Jesus: and when I saw her I wondered with great admiration."
(Revelation 17:1, 2, 5, 6)

John's imagery portrays a prostitute riding a beast. In the Bible, a prostitute signifies unfaithfulness to God, or a false religion. Those who see America here compare the Statue of Liberty to the woman on the beast. The woman in Revelation has a gold cup, but Lady Liberty has a torch. The Statue of Liberty stands, yet the harlot rides. Ten kings rule the harlot, yet fifty sovereign states joined together in a federal head rule America.

The woman was responsible for killing the saints and was guilty of the blood of the martyrs of Jesus. America did not exist at the time of Christ's crucifixion and America has protected religious freedom. In John's day, the Roman Empire was guilty of crucifying Christ and murdering thousands of early Christians. We could continue on, but one verse in Revelation 17:18 gives us the ultimate clue as to the identity of the woman who rides the beast:

"And the woman which thou sawest is that great city, which reigneth over the kings of the earth."
(Revelation 17:18)

Rome reigned in John's day. After the decline of Rome, the Roman church continued to set up kings in Europe and literally controlled European politics along with parts of the Middle East. Furthermore, it was clearly Romans who persecuted and executed early Christians, becoming "drunken with the blood of the martyrs." In John's time, apocalyptic writers referred to Rome as Babylon. They did this to avoid Roman persecution for predicting God's judgment against Rome.

Babylon and Rome invaded Jerusalem, destroyed the Temple, and captured the Jews and enslaved them. The destruction of the Jewish Temple in Jerusalem occurred on the 9th of Av, at the time of the Babylonian and Roman invasions.

Daniel's Vision of Empires — a More Plausible Prophecy

I think that a more plausible theory is found in Daniel 7:1-7. The Hebrew prophet Daniel received a vision while he was a captive in ancient Babylon. Using the symbolism of animals, the vision portrays several empires that would rule in the future. Some conclude that one small passage may refer to the United States.

"Daniel spake and said, I saw in my vision by night, and behold, the four winds of the heaven strove upon the great sea. And four great beasts came up from the sea, diverse from one another. The first was like a lion, and had eagle's wings: I beheld till the wings thereof were plucked, and it was lifted up from the earth, and made stand upon the feet as a man, and a man's heart was given to it. And behold another beast, a second, like a bear, and it raised up itself on one side, and it had three ribs in the mouth of it between the teeth of it and they said thus to it, 'Arise, devour much flesh!' After this I beheld and lo another, like a leopard, which had upon the back of it four wings of a fowl. The beast also had four heads; and dominion was given to it. After this I saw in the night visions, and behold, a fourth beast dreadful and terrible, exceedingly strong. It had great iron teeth; it devoured and broke in pieces, and stamped the residue with its feet. It was diverse from all the beasts that were before it, and it had ten horns." (Daniel 7: 2-7)

Notice that these beasts rule in succession: the lion, the bear, the leopard, and finally, the non-descriptive beast with ten horns. Traditionally, scholars point to Daniel 2 and 8 to demonstrate that the four successive empires in Daniel's prophecy are Babylon, Medo-Persia, Greece, and Rome. According to this interpretation, the lion represents ancient Babylon; the bear, Medo-Persia; the leopard, Greece; and the fourth beast, the Roman Empire. The animals in the vision represent specific kingdoms. The entrance to Babylon was flanked with large, winged lions made of stone. Large bears roamed the mountains of ancient Persia. The swiftness of the leopard represented the Greek Empire's incredible ability to conquer when lead by Alexander the Great. In Daniel's vision, the leopard had four wings on its back. When Alexander the Great died, his kingdom was divided between his four generals, signified by the leopard's four wings. The final beast with iron teeth represents the iron kingdom of Rome. It is clear from Nebuchadnezzar's dream in Daniel 2:33 that the legs of iron on the image represent the Roman Empire.

In Daniel's vision, "four kings shall arise." This is future tense. Daniel 7 was written during Daniel's captivity in Babylon. If Babylon is the first beast (the lion) and the four beasts in Chapter 7 shall arise (future tense), then perhaps the vision symbolized a series of end-time empires that would rule in the latter days.

Four Modern Empires of Prophecy

Some scholars teach that these four beasts represent four modern empires that have risen up in the past three hundred years:

- The lion represents Great Britain, whose wings formed the United States.
- The bear represents the nation of Russia.
- The leopard represents the nation of Germany.
- The final beast represents the final kingdom that will rule at the time of the end.

First, consider Great Britain, whose emblem is a lion. Britain was once the mightiest empire in the world. It was said that the sun never sets upon the British Empire. Britain colonized much of the world, including Palestine (present day Israel). Notice that the lion had eagles' wings and the wings were plucked or removed. The lion suddenly stood up and was given a heart like a man. While traditional scholars think this symbolizes Nebuchadnezzar's seven-year nervous breakdown and his recovery in Daniel 4, others believe this speaks of how America was plucked away from the British lion and made to stand alone. America came out of the lion and has been given a heart of a man, or a heart of compassion.

The Eagle's Wings in Daniel's Prophecy

An interesting story in early American history suggests that Daniel 7 influenced the decision to use the eagle as America's national emblem. A Jewish broker named Haym Salomon helped finance the American Revolution. In my personal stamp collection, I have a U.S. postal stamp that says "Contributions to the Cause" with the name Haym Salomon, financial hero *(See fig. A)*. On the back it reads:

Commemorative stamp of broker Haym Solomon, whose financial support prevented the American Revolution from collapsing. **Fig. A**

"Financial hero, businessman and broker Haym Salomon was responsible for raising most of the money to help finance the American Revolution and later to save the new nation from collapse."

The founder of the Institute for Judaic Christian Research in Arlington, Texas has suggested that Haym Salomon contributed to the process of selecting America's seal. Having studied the book of Daniel, Salomon read about the eagle's wings being plucked from the lion. In this, he saw a prophetic picture of how America was plucked away from the British lion; thus, the eagle would be a perfect symbol for America!

After the signing of the Declaration of Independence, a committee was formed to design the seal of the United States. According to the *Federalist Brief,* Thomas Jefferson suggested a seal depicting the children of Israel being led with a pillar of cloud by day and a pillar of fire by night. Benjamin Franklin picked up on the same theme and suggested a seal with Moses dividing the sea and the chariots of Pharaoh being swamped under the waters, with a motto: "Rebellion to tyrants is obedience to God." The Hebrew connection to American independence was very evident in these discussions. Neither of these designs was chosen. Instead, the committee selected the eagle.

The eagle is printed on the back of every dollar bill. Notice the eagle has arrows in one claw and olive branches in the other. The arrows represent war and the olive branches represent peace. The eagle faces the olive branches to communicate that America desires peace. However, the arrows of war are available if needed. In America's modern history, she has been a peace-loving nation, yet she stands ready to defend peace if necessary. The eagle does not wear a crown as do the many coats of arms found in Britain. The crown represents royalty and is omitted from America's seal because America was a land of the people and by the people.

Above the eagle's head is a series of 13 stars surrounded by a circle of clouds. Notice that these 13 stars form the *Magen David*, or the "star of David." This design is found on the Israeli flag and is the emblem of the modern nation of Israel.

Some Christians believe that the pyramid on the back of the dollar bill is related to the occult. I prefer to quote the journals of Congress regarding the meaning of the pyramid:

"A pyramid unfinished of 13 layers of stone. In the zenith, an eye of Divine Providence, surrounded with a glory proper. Over the eye these words, Annuit Coeptis [Latin for "He (God) has blessed our undertakings"]. On the base of the pyramid the numerical letters MDCCLXXVI. Underneath the motto, Novus Ordo Seclorum meaning *A New Order of the Ages* (Source: *Our Flag and other Symbols of Americanism*, Robert Weaver, Alexandria, Virginia, 1972, p.9).

Charles Thomas served as Secretary of the Congress when the seal was approved. He stated that the pyramid signifies strength and duration. The eye and the motto allude to the many single interpositions of Providence in favor of the American cause (Source: *The Story of the Seal*, p.19).

James Wilson, a Justice of the first Supreme Court, noted that "A free government has often been compared to a pyramid . . . it is laid on the broad basis of the people." The eagle's wings that were plucked from the lion could very well represent America. If this is correct, then it was the Almighty who plucked the eagle's wings and formed a new nation that was certain to become a major end time Gentile power.

Who are the Other Three Beasts?

If the Lion represents Britain and the eagle's wings represent America, then what about the other three beasts? Today the bear is Russia's emblem. In Daniel's vision, the bear lies on one side and has three ribs in its mouth. Russia is known for its spread of Communism. The three ribs could represent the three main Communist leaders, Marx, Lenin and Stalin. The bear "devours much flesh." Millions of innocent humans were literally devoured as the Russian bear clawed its way into nations, tearing apart those who resisted. The Russian Revolution of 1917 brought about Communism.

The next major nation after the rise of Communist Russia was Germany. Hitler's Germany influenced the world after the rise of Communism. The leopard is the third beast and the German Nazis were the Third Reich. The army of Germany, as did Alexander the Great centuries before, moved with the speed of a leopard to conquer surrounding nations.

There is a final beast that will arise after the leopard that will be the kingdom of a man called the antichrist. It will be the final beast, the last world empire before the return of Christ.

I think that the interpretation of the prophecy of the eagle's wings representing the United States has some merit. Yet, there is a final theory that I believe refers clearly to America. It is the theory of the transplanted vineyard and will be the theme I want to carry throughout this book.

The Theory of God's Vineyard

The most exciting theory regarding America in prophecy comes from comparing Isaiah 5:1-7 with Matthew 21:33-44. Here we see that God planned to take His chosen vineyard (Israel) and give it to another people, or another nation. The prophet Isaiah penned these words over 2,600 years ago, suggesting this:

"Now will I sing to my well beloved a song of my beloved touching his vineyard. My well beloved hath a vineyard in a very fruitful hill: And he fenced it, and gathered out the stones thereof, and planted it with the choicest vine, and built a tower in the midst of it, and also made a winepress therein: and he looked that it should bring forth grapes, and it brought forth wild grapes. And now, O inhabitants of Jerusalem, and men of Judah, judge, I pray you, betwixt me and my vineyard. What could have been done more to my vineyard, that I have not done in it? Wherefore, when I looked that it should bring forth grapes, brought forth wild grapes? And now go to; I will tell you what I will do to my vineyard: I will take away the hedge thereof, and it shall be eaten up; and break down the wall thereof, and it shall be broken down; And I will lay it waste: it shall not be pruned, nor digged; but there shall come up briers and thorns: I will also command the clouds that they rain no rain upon it. For the vineyard of the Lord of hosts is the house of Israel, and the men of Judah his pleasant plant..." (Isaiah 5:1-7)

Hundreds of years later, Jesus took the parable of the vineyard written in Isaiah 5 and revealed additional information concerning a new vineyard that God would raise up. Christ's parable about these future events is recorded in Matthew 21:33-43.

"Hear another parable. There was a certain householder, which planted a vineyard, and hedged it round about, and digged a winepress in it, and built a tower, and let it out to husbandmen, and went into a far country: And when the time of the fruit drew near, he sent his servants to the husbandmen, that they might receive the fruits of it. And the husbandmen took his servants, and beat one and killed another and stoned another. Again he sent other servants more than the first: and they did unto them likewise. But last of all he sent unto them his son, saying, they will reverence my son. But when the husbandmen saw the son, they said among themselves, this is the heir; come, let us kill him and seize upon his inheritance. And they caught him, and cast him out of the vineyard and slew him. When the Lord thereof of the vineyard cometh, what will he do unto those wicked husbandmen? They will say unto him, He will miserably destroy those wicked men, and will let out his vineyard unto other husbandmen, which shall render him fruits in their seasons...Therefore say I unto you, the kingdom of God shall be taken from you and given to a nation bringing forth the fruits thereof. (Matthew 21:33-43)

Israel was the true vineyard of the Almighty. Continual disobedience to God brought judgment upon the vineyard. The Hebrew prophets foresaw a time when God would remove the hedge and allow the vineyard to be trampled down. This happened twice, once in 606 B.C. with the invasion of the Babylonians, and once in 70 A.D. with the invasion of the Roman tenth legion. The difference between the two is that, after the

Babylonian invasion, the Jews returned to repossess the land. After 70 A.D., the Jews were dispersed for over 19 centuries. Thus these prophetic words came to pass:

> "And the vineyard which thy right hand hath planted, and the branch that thou madest strong for thyself. It is burned with fire, it is cut down: they perish at the rebuke of thy countenance."
>
> (Psalms 80: 15,16)

Some Old Testament Hebrew prophets were rejected and others were slain by their own people because their rebukes were so strong. Christ warned, "Upon you shall come all the righteous blood from Abel to Zacharias whom ye slew between the Temple and the altar" (Matthew 23: 35). The parable in Matthew 21 reiterates how God sent prophets to the vineyard of Israel and the people of Israel slew the prophets. Jesus announced that God would transfer His vineyard and give it to a nation that would "bring forth fruit in its season."

Most scholars believe this nation was the same nation that Moses, Hosea, and other prophets foresaw, "a nation and a people who were not" that God would one day raise up for His name. This nation is the same holy nation the Apostle Peter described when he wrote, "You are a chosen generation, a royal priesthood, a holy nation..." (1 Peter 2:9). This new nation is the church, the Body of Christ! When the workers in the vineyard killed the son, Jesus, the vineyard was given over to others. God raised up Gentiles to carry the Gospel of Christ to the nations of the earth after Christ's death was approved by religious Jews. Since Americans have supported sending the light of the Gospel around the world, our nation could represent the end time "transplanted vineyard." Let's explore the prophetic history of America and look for the vineyard.

Transplanting the Vineyard - The Early Beginnings of America

Christopher Columbus is generally considered to be the discoverer of America. Actually, the native Indians were here long before Columbus arrived, and the Vikings came to America centuries before the Pilgrims.

First, I'd like to focus on the Vikings. They were a collective band of Nordic people — Danes, Swedes, and Norwegians — who traversed the seas from about 800 to 1100 A.D. Called the Viking Age, this period has long been associated with piracy, plunder, and barbarism. This is now being recognized as a gross simplification. It seems that they were more interested in trading than in raiding. As commerce developed in various regions, the Vikings assimilated into local populations. A century and a half after settling Normandy, their Franco-Viking descendants conquered England. England would one day be America's birth mother.

The Vikings introduced new forms of administration and justice, such as the jury system (or the right to be judged by one's peers). Even the word "law" came from a Norse word. The Anglo-Saxons and Normans (Franco-Vikings) eventually conquered England in 1066. By 1215, the Magna Carta was signed by the King and representatives of the common people. It formally expressed a form of representative government that protected personal rights and limited the King from imposing tyrannical laws upon the people. The Magna Carta became the basis of English Common Law in which our Founding Fathers were schooled. This is clearly apparent when studying the text of the Declaration of Independence and the U.S. Constitution. In fact, the Bill of Rights guaranteed personal freedoms first articulated in the Magna Carta.

The Magna Carta's preamble listed its participating parties, including God! The system of government ratified by the Magna Carta required an agreement between the King and representatives of the people. It limited the King from practicing tyranny that violated specific personal rights. All parties entered the covenant before God. Part of the Preamble follows:

> "John, by the Grace of God, King of England, Lord of Ireland, Duke of Normandy and Aquitaine, and Earl of Anjou, to his Archbishops, Bishops, Abbots, Earls, Barons, Justiciaries, Foresters, Sheriffs, Governors, Officers, and to all Bailiffs, and his faithful subjects, — Greeting. Know ye, that We, in the presence of God, and for the salvation of our own soul, and of the souls of all our ancestors, and of our heirs, to the honor of God, and the exaltation of the Holy Church and amendment of our Kingdom, by the counsel of our venerable fathers, Stephen Archbishop of Canterbury, Primate of all England, and Cardinal of the Holy Roman Church, Henry Archbishop of Dublin, William of London, Peter of Winchester…and others our liegemen; have in the First place granted to God, and by this our present Charter, have confirmed, for us and our heirs for ever" (Source: the British library's online

information server http://www.bl.uk/index.html).

The Declaration of Independence reflects the same theory of government. The Bill of Rights is actually derived from specific personal freedoms defined in the Magna Carta.

His Beloved Son Discovers the Vineyard

Around 986 A.D., a Viking explorer en route to Greenland, Bjarni Herjolfsson, was driven off course by a storm. He is believed to be the first European to see North America. Until it was visited by the Icelandic explorer Leif Ericson, the land was not explored. Ericson is believed to have been one of the first Europeans to set foot on North American soil. Shortly before this, he was converted to Christianity in Norway. Upon traveling to Greenland to convert its Viking settlers to Christianity, he lost his way and came upon the North American shore. After completing his mission in Greenland, he wanted to return to the North American shore for exploration.

He purchased Bjarni Herjolfsson's ship and, based on his records, retraced Herjolfsson's voyage. He sailed south along the coast of Labrador and Newfoundland. He called this area Vinland, or Wineland, because of the number of grapes growing there (the vineyard). The name Leif means *beloved* and Eric means *the ever powerful*. So his full name means *the beloved son of the ever powerful*. He actually reached Vinland on October 9, 1000 A.D., but the exact location of his landing remains undetermined. Some scholars think that it was Newfoundland in Canada, while others point to Nova Scotia or New England. Leif later lent his ship to his brother for further exploration of Vinland. In 1004 A.D., his brother was killed by natives. It appears that about 1,000 years after Christ's birth, God was already preparing to raise a new nation, America.

Thorfinn Karlsefni was an Icelandic trader who led the first known pre-Columbian attempt by Europeans to settle in North America. On a trip to Greenland in the first years of the 11th century, he met and married Ericson's widowed sister. Thereafter, he led a group of colonists to Vinland with the intent to establish a permanent colony. However, the local Indians banished the settlers after three years and the Vikings were unable to settle their new vineyard.

Although the Vikings failed to settle America, I believe their early efforts point to God's preparation of the end-time vineyard described by Jesus. America's Hebrew connections seem to indicate that the United States has been God's end-time spiritual Israel until the "times of the Gentiles" is fulfilled. When the "times of the Gentiles" comes to an end, God will return His spiritual mantel to Israel.

Long before America was settled, the physical nation of Israel was destroyed. Christians and Muslims fought in the area that the Romans called Palestine. Over time, the city of Jerusalem fell into the hands of the Byzantines, the Muslims, the Maramalukes, the Crusaders, the Ottoman Turks, the British, and finally back into the hands of the Hebrews.

Prophetically, God's plan for Israel will be completely fulfilled in the time known as "Jacob's trouble" or the "great tribulation." Before this could transpire, Israel had to be rebirthed as a nation. Since America was to play a role in the reestablishment and preservation of the nation of Israel, God established America as a superpower long before Israel's restoration in 1948. Amazingly, God used Jewish people to assist in the discovery and establishment of the American vineyard. The first would be an Italian Jew named Columbus.

Chapter 4

AMERICA'S REMARKABLE PROPHETIC HISTORY

Columbus and His Hebrew Connection

"For the execution of the journey to the Indies, I did not make use of intelligence, mathematics, or maps. It is simply the fulfillment of what Isaiah had prophesied. All this is what I desire to write down for you in this book."   (Christopher Columbus)

Christopher Columbus is believed to be an Italian Jew. The details of Columbus' journey expose an interesting Hebrew link between America and ancient Israel.

Christopher Columbus — the Christ Bearer

In his diaries, Christopher Columbus wrote that he was compelled to sail west by the "inspiration from the Holy Spirit." He continued, "It was the Lord who put into my mind (I could feel his hand upon me) the fact that it would be possible to sail from here to the Indies." This was more important to Columbus than finding a trade route to the East or finding gold.

Opinions about Columbus vary. Some think he was a hero, others believe he was a villain responsible for genocide. Some events in Columbus' life portray him poorly. However, my objective is to identify his role in God's plan for America and its Hebraic connection.

Although Christopher Columbus (Christoferens Columbo in Italian) was born in Genoa, Italy, I believe there is evidence to suggest that his lineage was of Spanish-Jewish origin. Columbus' paternal grandfather was a *converso* who had changed his name from Colon to Columbo. Conversos were Jews who had, by choice or necessity, converted to Christianity. Apparently, in the midst of the Spanish Inquisition, Columbus was raised a Christian, perhaps to survive Jewish annihilation. His use of the Spanish form of his name in his diaries and letters and certain oddities associated with his voyages to the New World, lend credence to the idea that he was Jewish. Colon was considered a Spanish-Jewish name. The name Columbo is synonymous with the name Jonah, which means *dove*. Compare Jonah's story in the Bible to the events surrounding Columbus.

Jonah was the first Hebrew prophet sent to a Gentile nation (See the book of Jonah). Columbus, having been tempted by the lust for gold, found his fleet being tossed at sea by a violent storm on his return from the New World. The storm was so strong that he recommended that the crew appease God with a sacrificial vow. One from among them was to vow to make a pilgrimage to a particular monastery if they survived. Columbus took 39 beans and marked a cross on one of them. Using the beans, they drew lots. The first time Columbus drew the marked bean. They drew three more times, and Columbus drew the marked bean twice more. The odds of this happening are minuscule (Source: *The Light and the Glory*, Peter Marshall). This experience was similar to Jonah's. God was trying to get Columbus' and Jonah's attention!

Jonah's mission was to go to Nineveh, a Gentile nation, and be a light unto them. When Jonah strayed, God intervened with a storm. Likewise, Columbus' mission was to open the door to the New World. This New World would house the Gentile nation that would send the message of Christ to the world.

Hebrew Clues Regarding Columbus' Heritage

In letters to his son Diego, Columbus put a mark in the upper left corner of the paper that resembles the Hebrew letters bet and hei. These letters denote the Hebrew blessing b'ezrat haShem, meaning *with the help of God*. The use of bet hei is a blessing that Jews often place in the upper left corner of a letter to a loved one. In Columbus' papers, this mark appears only in letters to Diego. In one letter to Diego that was also to be read by the king and queen, the mark was missing — implying that Columbus did not want the monarchs to see this potentially incriminating evidence regarding his Jewish heritage.

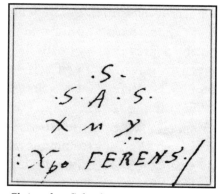

Christopher Columbus sometimes signed his name in a peculiar triangular form. Some think this may allude to his Jewish heritage.

During the last years of his life, Columbus worked to put his affairs in order. Unusual symbols began to appear in his writings that suggest he was familiar with Jewish mysticism. For example, he began to sign his name in a triangular fashion, asking that his descendants continue to use this signature. This strange signature is believed to be a cryptic substitute for the Kaddish, the mourner's prayer. If Columbus was Jewish, the Spanish Inquisition would not allow his sons to say Kaddish for their father when he died. Thus Columbus supplied his sons with a signature that would serve that purpose.

"Listen o isles to me and harken ye people from far; the Lord hath called me from the womb; from the bowels of my mother hath he made mention of my name. And now saith the Lord that formed me from the womb to be his servant, to bring Jacob again to him, though Israel be not gathered, yet shall I be glorious in the eyes of the Lord and my God shall be my strength. And he said, It is a light thing that thou shouldest be my servant to raise up the tribes of Jacob and to restore the preserved of Israel; I will also give thee for a light to the Gentiles that thou mayest be my salvation unto the end of the earth." (Isaiah 49:1,5,6)

Columbus' idea of traveling west seems to have solidified in 1484 when he worked as a cartographer. He was 33 years old. This is the year in a man's life that the Italians call *anno de Christo*, the year of Christ, which, according to tradition, is reserved for revelation. The name Christopher means *Christ bearer*. Columbus thought this was a sign, believing that God selected him for a divine purpose. Columbus felt that he had received a revelation directly from God to sail west. He felt that he was given the task of bearing Christ to the ends of the earth, fulfilling what the prophet Isaiah predicted. Interestingly, the prophecy of Isaiah referred to a "light to the Gentiles" and "restoration of Israel." Later in his diaries Columbus likened himself to Moses, the man who led the Jews to the Promised Land. Perhaps Columbus felt that part of his mission was to assist in the restoration of the Jews to their ancient homeland.

After moving to Spain, Columbus began using his old family name Colon, according to his son and biographer Don Ferdinand Colon. This may have been a signal to the conversos in Ferdinand and Isabella's court. There were many conversos in the royal court, including one Don Isaac Abravanel, who traced his ancestry directly to King David. Colon, the old family name, was the name with which Columbus was presented to Ferdinand and Isabella. The conversos' support helped make Columbus' expedition possible.

The Expedition and the 9th of Av on the Hebrew Calendar

When Columbus was given an audience with the Spanish monarchs, a trade route to the Indies and riches may not have been his only goal. Near the end of his life, Columbus wrote, "Gold is most excellent, a valuable thing and whoever possesses it does whatever he wants with it in the world…Jerusalem and Mount Zion will be rebuilt by a Christian." It is possible that Columbus wanted to find a trade route to finance an expedition to the Holy Land and expel the Muslims. It is also possible that he saw the need for gold in order to finance the reconstruction of the city and possibly the Temple itself.

In his studies, Columbus calculated the age of the world to be 5241 years by using the Hebrew calendar (1480-81). He wrote, "From the destruction of the second house according to the Jews to the present day . . . are 1413 years." This meant that Columbus' date for the destruction of the Temple was 68 A.D., a date often cited by Jews, as opposed to 70 A.D., the date used by Christians. Furthermore, Jews often refer to the Temple as the second house. Columbus apparently saw some significance in the destruction of Jerusalem and the Temple and felt that he would play a part in the restoration of the holy city.

On March 30, 1492, King Ferdinand and Queen Isabella signed a decree to expel the Jews from Spain. Until that time, Spain had been one of the few safe havens for Jews. As mentioned earlier, many Jewish converts were in the royal court, including Luis de Santangel, Ferdinand's Budget Minister. Now, there seemed to be no place for the Jews to go. Oddly, this date coincided with key events in Israel's history. According to tradition, when Cyrus the king of Persia was crowned, his coronation made it possible for Jewish exiles to return to Israel and rebuild the city of Jerusalem for the Holy Temple. Exactly one year later, Ezra left Babylon intending to assist with the reconstruction. Was it coincidence that the Jews found themselves wandering once more, longing for a homeland without torment? If Columbus was Jewish, it must certainly have crossed his mind. I think that the same "coincidence" surely crossed the mind of God.

On April 30, 1492, one month after the edict of expulsion was signed, it was read publicly. The same day, Columbus received the order to prepare for his expedition. Initially, Columbus' request to sail westward had been declined. Had it not been for the persuasion and financial support of Santangel and Abravanel, Columbus' voyage would not have originated in Spain. Ironically, the expedition these Jews helped make possible took place the same day they were ordered to leave the country they had served.

The year 1491- 92 corresponds to the Hebrew year 5252, written as הרנב. The Hebrew numbers can translate to the phrase har nov, meaning *mount of fruit*. According to Strong's Concordance, har is a shortened form of harar, which is from an unused root meaning *to loom up*. Nov(fruit) is from noov, meaning *to germinate, flourish, to bring forth* (Matthew 21:43). It seems that this year signified a time to rise up and bring forth fruit. America, the nation that would bring forth fruit, was about to be established!

On August 2, 1492, thousands of Jews departed from Spain. One of their ports of departure was Palos, the same port from which Columbus had intended to depart. Columbus originally planned to set sail on August 2, 1492. Faced with throngs of despairing, heartbroken people at Palos that day, Columbus decided to delay his voyage by one day. Were the

Jewish refugees the only reason Columbus decided to wait?

Jews gathered at the ports, clutching whatever possessions they had been allowed to keep along with dirt from the earth. That day, the 9th of Av, commemorated the destruction of both Temples. For centuries, this day had been observed as a day of mourning. On August 2, 1492, the 9th of Av took on a whole new meaning. According to Jewish tradition, to undertake any enterprise on the 9th of Av is considered bad luck. Consider some of the following events that transpired in Hebrew history on the 9th of Av:

- The twelve scouts sent out by Moses returned with a bad report.
- The Exodus generation was condemned to die.
- Nebuchadnezzar set fire to the first Temple.
- Romans destroyed the second Temple.
- Romans plowed up the Temple Mount to convert it to a Roman colony.
- The last independent outpost of the Bar Kokhba rebellion fell to the Romans.
- King Edward of England expelled all Jews in 1290 A.D.
- The last group of Jews left Vienna in 1670 after expulsion from Austria.
- The Turkish government banned the immigration of Russian and Romanian Jews into Palestine in 1882.
- World War I began, precipitated by the assassination of Archduke Francis Ferdinand.
- A decree to expel Jews from parts of Hungary was issued in 1941.

August 2, 1492 symbolized that Jews were not welcome in the world. As Christopher Columbus gazed upon his despairing countrymen, perhaps in his heart he had a secret desire to find a safe haven for them. For whatever reason, Columbus decided to delay his voyage until the next day.

The Voyage and the Hebrew Feast

On August 3, 1492, Columbus received communion and set sail aboard his flagship, the Santa Maria. Martin Vicente and Francisco Pinzon commanded the Nina and the Pinta, the two ships that accompanied the Santa Maria. Columbus began his diary with: "In the name of our Lord Jesus Christ." Later in the diary, he noted that his departure coincided with the expulsion of the Jews. The date of his departure was the 10th of Av on the Hebrew calendar. Historically, on this date both Temples were burned.

Columbus planned his voyage very carefully. He included some Jews in his crew. The most famous of these was Luis de Torres. Columbus hired him to be an interpreter because he expected to find a remnant of the lost tribes of Israel at his destination. The physician, the mapmaker, and the officer in charge of nautical instruments were also Jewish.

"Save now this nation, once firm as a rampart, and clear as the sun; she is exiled, a wandering one" (Jewish prayer for the Intermediate Days of Sukkoth).

Trouble plagued the journey and many of the crew wanted to turn back. Columbus faced failure and on Tuesday, October 9, the Pinzon brothers met with him to discuss turning back before a mutiny. Columbus agreed that if land was not sighted within three days, they would turn around. This date on the Hebrew calendar was 18 Tishri 5253. This critical meeting took place in the middle of the Jewish Feast of Tabernacles, or Sukkot. This feast commemorates Israel's wandering through the wilderness with no place to call home. God instructed Israel to dwell in booths during this feast to remember the nights that they slept under the stars. Under the night stars, Columbus and his men wandered through the waters of destiny during Sukkot even as Israel wandered through the wilderness.

"As thou didst save together God and nation, the people singled out for God's salvation, so save thou us... They passed between the deep divided sea and with them for their guide, the light from thee so save thou us! Establish us as thy chosen vineyard and make us as a tree planted by the streams of water ... plant us we pray upon a faithful sod" (Portions of prayers recited on Hoshanah Rabbah).

Around 2:00 a.m. on Friday, October 12, as the three days were nearly over, Rodrigo de Triana (possibly a Jew) sighted land. What happened at that point is very interesting. In the book *Columbus' Jewish Roots,* it is said that, when he spotted land, he spoke to another Jew in Hebrew saying, "I,I" (island, island). The other Jewish sailor replied, "V'annah?" (and where?). Triana replied, "Hineh" (there).

On Hoshanah Rabbah

This day began the 71st day of the voyage. In the Bible, seventy represents restoration. Israel was in Babylon 70 years and returned to the Holy Land in the beginning of the 71st year. It was also 21 Tishri on the Hebrew calendar, the day of Hoshanah Rabbah. Hoshanah, a Hebrew phrase means *please save now* and Rabbah means *many.* The Hebrew liturgy for this day was composed of prayers that plead with God to be saved. In the ancient Temple, as well as in synagogues today, worshipers took the four species and marched around the court of the Temple seven times reciting Psalms 118. On this day, the Divine judgment of man, which began on Rosh Hashana and climaxed on Yom Kippur, concluded. Thus, Hoshanah Rabba is a minor Yom Kippur (a Day of Atonement).

Wearing a scarlet doublet, Columbus went ashore with several others. As Columbus stepped onto the shore, he knelt on the sand and prayed:

"Oh Lord Almighty and everlasting God, by Thy Holy Word thou hast created the heaven and the earth and the sea blessed and glorified be Thy name and praised by Thy majesty which hath designed to use us, thy humble servants that Thy Holy Name may be proclaimed in this second part of the earth."

His prayer concluded by christening the island San Salvador. San Salvador means *Holy Savior.*

The Thread of Shemini Atzeret

The day after the discovery of the New World would have been Shemini Atzeret, or the eighth day of Convocation (22 Tishri). Traditionally, this day is accepted as the day that Solomon dismissed the people from the Temple dedication celebration. This is recorded in 1 Kings 8:66.

Coincidence or not, the discovery of the New World corresponds to a significant event in Jewish history. Perhaps a new Temple was being symbolically dedicated!

In Israel, this day is also called Simchat Torah, or rejoicing in the Torah. At this time there is much celebration as the Torah scroll is rolled back to the beginning of Genesis. In the beginning, God created the heavens and the earth. Is it possible that Columbus could have had this day in mind when he prayed on the shores of San Salvador?

The timing of the discovery was incredible. God was beginning to create a new world. As a point of interest, the very first letter in the book of Genesis is the Hebrew letter beit. The symbol for this letter is a house. The word beit (house) is often used to refer to the Jewish Temple. I think it was possible that God, on this important Jewish date, was beginning construction on a new house, a new Temple, a new dwelling among a new chosen people. The above-mentioned Hoshanah Rabbah liturgy supports the idea that the prayer is for God to plant the Jews on a fruitful sod and to establish them as His chosen vineyard.

There is a tradition on Hoshanah Rabbah (21 Tishri) of baking bread with a hand on top of it. The hand symbolizes that God sealed His decision made for that time. The hand is also said to represent the document or the verdict of that decision. "And it shall come to pass in that day that the Lord shall set his hand again the second time to recover the remnant of his people, which shall be left ... from the islands of the sea. And He shall set up an ensign (a flag) for the foreign nations and shall assemble the outcasts of Israel and gather together the dispersed of Judah from the four corners of the earth" (Isaiah 11:11, 12). It seems that, on Hoshanah Rabbah in 1492, God indeed made a decision and set His hand to recover his people.

Part of that decision included a Jewish man from Italy sailing west into the unknown to discover a new land. This new land would, in the endtimes, become the world's economic, military, and political superpower. More importantly, it would become a nation that would carry the Word of God to the world and offer a safe haven for the Jews. As you will see, America's connection to Israel and the Jewish people is not merely political and economic. It is a spiritual link that symbolically connects America to the Hebrews and the land of Israel as certainly as an umbilical cord connects a baby to its mother.

God's People Needed a Safe Haven

God inspired the discovery of the New World knowing that, 446 years later, the greatest assault on His chosen people would erupt in Europe as the Nazis coerced millions of Jews into death camps.

During World War II, America was the safest place on the face of the earth for the Jews. God ensured that the natural seed of Abraham would not be annihilated. He also blessed the world by using America to thwart the demonic hordes of Nazi troops as they sought world domination.

Another example of America's prophetic importance regarding the Jews is the fact that America supported Israel's official rebirth as a nation in 1948. All too often, Israel's neighbors resent America for her support. They consider our connection to be political and economic, and do not comprehend that the Almighty divinely designed the bond between these two nations. Many remarkable prophetic parallels continue to unfold as we look at early American history.

Chapter 5

HEBREW PARALLELS ASSOCIATED WITH EARLY AMERICAN HISTORY

The Hebrew Connection Continues Early in American History

Columbus, an apparent Italian Jew, died before he realized that the continent he discovered would house the most powerful Gentile nation on earth. He would never see the Hebrew influence on America's early history. By 1503, Columbus still thought that he had discovered remote parts of Japan and China. It seemed that his assignment from God was finished. It is interesting that Columbus compared himself to Moses, and Moses did not enter the Promised Land to which he led the people of Israel.

What did Columbus' voyages accomplish? They paved the way for colonization of North and South America, partly in an effort to spread the Gospel. Although many natives were forcibly converted, there were some caring men who truly wanted to help the natives. These men founded missions and schools such as San Antonio, San Diego, and San Francisco. In these missions, they taught the natives about the one true God of the

Bible. Many of these men died at the hands of the natives they hoped to convert. Fifteen hundred years earlier, Jesus said, "Verily, verily I say unto you, except a corn of wheat fall into the ground and die, it abideth alone: but if it die, it bringeth forth much fruit" (John 12:24). I believe these men and others who followed in their footsteps were the "corns of wheat" or "seeds" that God used to sow His new vineyard. Columbus discovered the site for the new house, and the martyred missionaries built the foundation. Many would follow to build the house itself, and open the door for millions to enter into freedom and safety.

The Naming of America

For several years after Columbus' discovery, no one realized that a new continent had been discovered. Columbus sailed along the South American shore, never realizing the vastness of this land. In 1499, Amerigo Vespucci, an Italian who helped outfit Columbus' voyages, began making journeys across the Atlantic. Vespucci made a total of three journeys. The first of these followed the coast of what is now Venezuela, while the second and third voyages took him to the coastline of Brazil. It was on one of those journeys that Vespucci penned the words, "These regions, we may rightly call Mundus Novus, a new world, because our ancestors had no knowledge of them ... I have found a continent more densely peopled and abounding in animals than our Europe or Asia or Africa." Even though he never formally commanded an expedition, Vespucci was credited as being the first to recognize that Columbus' discovery was actually another land, previously unknown.

At this time, a German mapmaker named Waldseemuller was about to publish a new map of the world. Having read Vespucci's letters, he decided that since Amerigo Vespucci had discovered a fourth part of the world, it should be called America, after him, since Europe and Asia got their names from women. In 1507, the name America appeared on a map for the first time. Soon after, the idea of calling the New World America spread. The name Amerigo in Italian means *rich in wheat*.

English Colonization

"And it shall come to pass in that day, that the Lord shall set his hand again the second time to recover the remnant of his people, which shall be left ... from the islands of the sea. And he shall set up an ensign for the nations, and shall assemble the outcasts of Israel and gather together the dispersed of Judah from the four corners of the earth."   (Isaiah 11:11,12)

The Spanish concentrated on converting the Indians of Central and South America. They also took their gold and enslaved them. The English began, timidly at first, exploring North America. In 1497, an Italian named John Cabot sailed from Bristol, England aboard the Matthew. Cabot was commissioned by the English King, Henry VII, and on June 24, 1497, landed on Newfoundland, claiming it for the English. This marked Britain's first efforts at colonizing the New World. Humble as it was, it was to forever impact the world. It would be 110 years before a permanent English colony would be established.

Britain's Hebrew Heritage

Earlier we discussed the Vikings and their relationship to the British. The Vikings assimilated into Franco communities and it was their descendants, the Normans, who conquered England in 1066 A.D. Now let's discuss another affiliation with the British — their relationship with the Jews.

For centuries, people have pondered what became of the lost tribes of Israel. Legends and theories have arisen, but still no one but God knows what became of them. I do not want to imply that any legend or theory is a fact, and I do not want to validate the theory that the Anglo-Saxons are one of the lost tribes. However, I do want to mention several interesting topics as they relate to this book. First, I'd like to consider why God selected Britain as the nation that would birth the United States.

The first possible reference in the Bible to Great Britain is the name Tarshish. Tarshish was a great-grandson of Noah, whose descendants migrated to Western Europe, Spain, and the British Isles. There was a city in southern Spain called Tartessus, which was often visited by Phoenician merchants. Some think that this town was ancient Tarshish. It was known for its tin trade (Ezekiel 27:12). There were tin deposits in Great Britain. Great Britain was originally called Britinnia, due to its tin mines located in Cornwall, England. Ezekiel 38:13 mentions Tarshish and the young lions thereof. This terminology infers that the mother lion is Tarshish. The fact that Britain's emblem is the lion supports the claim that Tarshish is Britain.

Judges 5:17 informs us that the tribe of Dan owned ships. Because they lived on the Mediterranean coast, the Danites were likely expert mariners. Dan's tribal inheritance included the port city Joppa. The Danites were later forced to migrate north, where they occupied Bashan, or the Golan Heights, as we know it today. Moses prophesied that "Dan is a lion's whelp - he shall leap from Bashan" (Deuteronomy 33:22). The word leap can mean to *gush out*.

Irish history refers to a group of people known as the Tuatha de Danaan. Tuatha means *People of God*. Dunn in the Irish language means *judge*. Coincidentally, this also is the meaning of the name Dan. Scholars speculate that, during the Assyrian invasion of the northern kingdom, a small group of people from the tribe of Dan fled in boats (leapt from Bashan) and landed in Britain. If Britain was the Biblical Tarshish, then the Danites would have known this escape journey to be possible, and Britain would have become a safe haven for God's people. This could explain why God selected Britain to be a great power and the mother of America. I am not saying that this migration story is undeniably true, but in light of this book, it becomes an interesting piece of the puzzle.

The Hebrew Meaning of Britain

The Israelites were known to be covenant people. The Hebrew word brit means *covenant*. In Hebrew ish means *man*. Therefore, the word British means *covenant man* in Hebrew. This may be more than a coincidence. Many British, especially in the area of England, believe that their nation was settled by some of the lost tribes. This idea may not be too far fetched.

According to early Jewish American history, after the Jewish expulsion from Spain on March 31, 1492 many Jews fled to Britain. In 1502, a Jewish man named Juan Sanchez de Saragossa was awarded a royal trading license to promote trade and settlement in the New World. Research indicates that some of those who followed Cortez to Mexico were converted Jews seeking freedom in the New World. Some fled to current day Texas and New Mexico, areas that were to become part of America. So Jews had settled on American soil over 100 years before the landing at New Amsterdam in 1654.

Interestingly, there would have been no Jews in the early English colonies because of a 400-year-old law that forbade Jews from settling in English lands. Rabbi Manasseh Ben Israel of Amsterdam addressed Oliver Cromwell, Lord Protector of England, with a fervent messianic argument. It stated:

> "England must allow Jews to live on its soil, or else the D-day of judgment day will never come for the Christians or the Jew...Before all (prophecies) be fulfilled the people of God must first be dispersed into all places and countries of the world."

The ban on Jews was lifted and Jews were eventually allowed to settle in the new colonies.

Elizabeth and Raleigh — More Unusual Parallels

> "But the angel said unto him, fear not, Zacharias: for thy prayer is heard; and thy wife, Elizabeth shall bear thee a son, and thou shalt call his name John. And thou shalt have joy and gladness, and many shall rejoice at his birth. For he shall be great in the sight of the Lord, and shall drink neither wine nor strong drink; and he shall be filled with the Holy Ghost, even from his mother's womb. And many of the children of Israel shall he turn to the Lord their God. And he shall go before him in the spirit and power of Elias, to turn the hearts of the fathers to the children and the disobedient to the wisdom of the just; to make ready a people prepared for the Lord.   (Luke 1:13-17)

Let's look at the meaning of John's parents' names — Zechariah and Elizabeth. Zechariah means *God remembers* and Elizabeth means *God's oath*. What was the oath? God promised as far back as the Garden of Eden that He would send a deliverer who would reconcile Himself with man so God could once again commune with mankind (Genesis 3:15). The fruit of Zechariah and Elizabeth's union was John the Baptist — Jesus' forerunner. Jesus the Messiah was born of a young virgin named Mary. By dying on the cross, Jesus fulfilled God's promise of reconciliation to mankind. Today our faith in Jesus' blood sacrifice as payment for our sins reconciles us to God. One day we will see the complete fulfillment of His promise when we literally see Him face to face! This will be the soon-coming Messianic kingdom!

America seems to fit into God's plan to establish the Messianic kingdom by allowing its people to propagate the Gospel and support his special people, Israel. If this is true, we should not be surprised to learn that there are parallels in American history with the story of Elizabeth and Zechariah.

In the mid-to-late 1500s, Queen Elizabeth I of England was known as the Virgin Queen. Until this time, England had been very hesitant to follow up on Cabot's initiative. England had been intimidated by the Spanish and did little to explore the New World. Elizabeth I changed this policy and initiated spiritual and material expansionism. Vessels flying Elizabeth's ensign traveled as far away as present-day San Francisco and several points in between. However, efforts to colonize always fell short. (Note: Elizabeth's cousin was Mary Queen of Scots, mother of King James I. James is the English version of Jacob/Israel.)

In 1578, Sir Walter Raleigh, Elizabeth's favorite courtier, sailed with his half brother Sir Humphrey Gilbert to America. It was probably this voyage that stimulated Raleigh's plan to found an English empire in the New World. On the Hebrew calendar, this year means to *stretch out*, *to extend* — apparently just what Raleigh planned. This year can also mean *to initiate* or *launch something* as well as *to send a plague*. Raleigh's materialistic motives seemed to have plagued many English expeditions.

In 1585, Raleigh, authorized by Elizabeth I, sent out an expedition of 100 people to settle on Roanoke Island, in present day North Carolina. The group included a Bohemian Jew named Joachim Ganz. Ganz was sent to prospect for minerals but this expedition was short-lived. In 1587, Raleigh sent out another expedition of over 100 men, women, and children. This colony could have survived had England successfully supported it. At the time, the Spanish invaded England. The English won, but this distraction delayed sending support to the colony for over two years. When Raleigh finally sent ships to Roanoke Island, they found nothing but the word "CROATOAN" carved on a tree. To this day, nobody knows what became of the Lost Colony. The Lumbee Indians of North Carolina claim that the colonists' blood runs in their veins. Coincidentally, 1587 on the Hebrew calendar means *the desolation, the ruin*.

Raleigh and the English learned a valuable lesson about New World colonization. A better job of supplying the new outposts was required if colonies were to survive. Though she never saw an English colony survive in the New World, Elizabeth I was responsible for reawakening English efforts to colonize. She and her courageous explorers prepared the way for growing English influence, including its freedom-based views of government. I believe that, through the efforts of Elizabeth I and Sir Walter Raleigh, God remembered His oath to plant a vineyard that would yield spiritual fruit one day.

Jamestown or Jacobstown

"Propagating the Christian religion to such people as yet live in darkness and miserable ignorance of the true knowledge and worship of God, and may in time bring the infidels and savages living in these parts to human civility and to a settled and quiet government..." (Source: Preamble of Virginia Company Charter, King James I).

This preamble indicates that the purpose of the Virginia Company was indeed noble as its authors proclaimed their desire to take the Gospel of Christ to the natives. They promised the settlers that they would enjoy "all liberties ... to all intent and purposes as if they had been abiding and born within this our realm of England." Americans today owe a debt of gratitude to those who supported freedom. Although the charter articulated the promise of freedom and the goal of taking Christ to the natives, other selfish ambitions manifested almost immediately upon landing on the banks of the James River.

In December 1606, three ships left England for the New World carrying 144 men. Among them was a minister named Robert Hunt. In May 1607, they sailed into the Chesapeake Bay and up the James River for about forty miles. Finally, on May 14, 1607, they landed on the spot that they named Jamestown. It is fascinating that the first English colony in America was founded on the very same day on which the modern nation of Israel would be founded 341 years later, on May 14, 1948.

King James or King Jacob

The settlement was named Jamestown after His Majesty, King James I. This was the same King James who commissioned the translation of the Bible into English, hence the 1611 King James Bible. The name James is the English version of the name Jacob, or in Hebrew *Ya'akov*.

Jacob, the son of Isaac, was the father of the twelve tribes of Israel. My studies confirm that Jacob's life was full of schemes and acts of deceit. His name means *supplanter*. Yet, God promised Jacob that the covenant made with his fathers, Abraham and Isaac, would be fulfilled through him. God even changed his name to Israel, which means *prince of God* or *ruling with God*.

In 1626, Captain John Smith wrote a history of Virginia and New England. The cover page of the book had sketches of the three English monarchs who commissioned its exploration. The sketches depicted Queen Elizabeth I, King James I, and King Charles I. Instead of using their English names, however, their names were written in Latin. James was referred to as "Jacobus" and this clearly identifies James I as a namesake of Jacob, or as he was later called, Israel. Because of this name association, we could claim that the first English colony in the New World was named after Israel, the father of the twelve tribes of Israel.

Just as the twelve tribes issued forth from Israel (Jacob), twelve of the thirteen original colonies came from Virginia (Virginia was chartered through James/Jacob). During the early days of American settlement, all of the eastern shore of North America was referred to as Virginia. However subdued, the Hebrew thread is seen woven within American history.

Jamestown — The Supplanter

Just as Jacob of the Bible deceived and manipulated those around him, the people of Jamestown did the same to their Indian neighbors. Threats, robberies, and even a kidnapping stain the legacy of those early settlers. It resulted in starvation, cannibalism, and death. On several occasions, the people of Jamestown faced starvation. Instead of asking the Indians for help they demanded it and, in some cases, seized it.

God had allowed the colony to settle in an area where the natives would have been willing to teach the colonists how to plant, fish, and become self-sufficient. But the colonists' attitude was arrogant. They expected the Indians to serve them so they could turn their attention to the more pressing matters of looking for gold. Ironically, this is the same serpent attitude that bit Columbus. The only time the English became concerned about the lack of food was when it was too late to do anything. No doubt God wanted to use them to further His purpose, but their unwillingness to conform to His will and to practice His principles frustrated the plan. Matters degenerated quickly to the point that the colonists cannibalized their own dead.

At one point, the colonists kidnapped Chief Powhatan's daughter, Pocahantas. They held her for ransom and demanded that Powhatan give them food. This was their method of survival. Instead of working to provide for themselves, they took what belonged to others. They should have been planting and preparing for the winter, but according to John Smith, their time was spent looking for gold. Ironically, there was no gold

The death rate in Jamestown swelled to 90%. In May of 1610, they decided to abandon the settlement and return to England. This could have aborted God's plan for America except for the timely arrival of the new Governor, Lord De la Warr, who made the colonists return to the settlement. Eventually discipline, a work ethic, and church services were instituted. These practices helped Jamestown survive and 20 years later it became self-sufficient. During those years, the tobacco industry was established and became profitable. Once again, the Englishmen decided that it would be more profitable for others to do the work. In 1619, Jamestown received its first African slaves and put them to work in the tobacco fields. The issue of slavery and the cavalier English attitudes would explode some 250 years later, as brother fought against brother in America's Civil War.

God allowed Jacob to endure difficult times in his life. These difficulties were often caused by his deceitfulness. As an old man, Jacob himself was deceived regarding his favorite son, Joseph. Joseph's jealous brothers sold him into slavery and told Jacob that a wild animal had killed him. To create evidence for the deception, they smeared blood on Joseph's coat and took it to their father. Jacob mourned the loss for years — never knowing that he had been told a lie. Joseph obtained great favor while in Egypt and became the second most powerful man in the land. When famine came, Jacob's sons journeyed to Egypt to buy food. They encountered Joseph who eventually forgave them saying, "But as for you, ye thought evil against me; but God meant it unto good, to bring to pass as it is this day, to save much people alive" (Genesis 50:20).

Virginia also survived and grew into a wealthy colony. But America was to pay a great price for the colony's treacherous policy of slavery. The lessons learned at Jamestown were critical for America. Even as Jamestown struggled to survive and grow, another group of colonists was preparing to embark on a voyage to the New World.

An Interesting Look at Dates

"And it shall come to pass in that day, that the Lord shall set his hand again the second time to recover the remnant of His people, which shall be left ... from the islands of the sea. And He shall set up an ensign for the nations, and shall assemble the outcasts of Israel and gather together the dispersed of Judah from the four corners of the earth.   (Isaiah 11:11, 12)

The Hebrew word for ensign is nes. This word can also be interpreted to be *the sail of a ship.* The word nes comes from a word nasas that means *to gleam from afar* or *to be conspicuous, like a signal.* It suggests the idea of a flag fluttering in the breeze, to raise a beacon, a standard bearer. When assigning numerical values to the Hebrew letters, the Hebrew numeric value is 110. One hundred and ten years after Columbus' discovery of the New World, a lesser-known event occurred. This event is important in light of the following information.

Exactly 110 years after Columbus landed at San Salvador, an English explorer named Bartholomew Gosnold, discovered the Cape Cod peninsula where current day Massachusetts is located. The date of the discovery was May 15, 1602. On May 15, 1948, Israel officially became a nation. Through these dates, we are reminded of the America-Israel connection. Gosnold's discovery may allude to the raised ensign mentioned in Isaiah. The United States does stand out among the nations as a beacon for the Gospel and for freedom. Where did we inherit this love of the Gospel and of freedom? I think that it was from our English forefathers.

On his voyage, Gosnold sailed along the North American coast from Maine to the Narragansett Bay to what is now called Rhode Island. He named Cape Cod and some of the islands in Nantucket Sound, including Martha's Vineyard and the Elizabeth Islands. When he returned to England, Gosnold promoted the establishment of colonies in the areas that he had explored, and he supported the merchants who obtained a charter from King James I to colonize Virginia. Gosnold was assigned the command of the Godspeed, one of three English ships that comprised the 1606 Jamestown expedition. Exactly five years after his discovery of Cape Cod, Gosnold stood on the banks of the James River aiding in the construction of the first permanent English colony in America, Jamestown, a place named after James I.

The Pilgrims and the Hebrew Letter Beit

The Hebrew letter beit is composed of three lines resembling a square, yet open on the left side. From the perspective of the Torah, the top line of the square faces east, the right side faces south, the bottom side faces west, and the open side faces north (Source: *The Alef-Beit,* Rabbi Yitzhak Ginsburgh).

The Hebrew letter ב, pronounced "beit," is the first letter used in the Hebrew Bible in Genesis 1:1. The first word is b'reshit. Rabbis have wondered why God began creation with the ב, which is the second letter of the Hebrew alphabet instead of the first letter א (pronounced alef). Rabbis say one reason might be because a beit represents a house. All through the Bible, God's interaction with man has been an effort to establish and maintain a relationship whereby God might dwell among men. "And let them make me a sanctuary that I may dwell among them." The Hebrew word for sanctuary is mikdash. The Temple in Jerusalem came to be known as the bet mikdash, meaning *the house of sanctuary,* where God would dwell among the children of Israel. If the interpretation of the Bible that teaches that America will serve as God's vineyard is correct, then God must have a dwelling place, or a house, there.

Deuteronomy 12:5 states, "But unto the place which the Lord your God shall choose out of all your tribes to put his name there, even unto his habitation shall ye seek, and thither thou shalt come." So God chose a specific place in Israel to place His home. The place of His habitation was in Jerusalem upon the Temple Mount. Looking at an aerial photograph of the Old City, you will discover that the three valleys near Jerusalem form the Hebrew letter ש (shin). According to rabbinic Judaism, this letter represents the name of God. God literally placed His name in the landscape where He would dwell among His people. Would you be surprised to learn that this same landscape shows up in America?

Cape Cod and the Letter Beit

If you look at a map of Cape Cod, starting at the tip of Provincetown where the Pilgrims first landed, and follow it around to Plymouth, you will find that the peninsula forms the letter beit, or a house *(See fig. B).* Notice that the open side of this geographical beit is on the north side. We mentioned earlier that Gosnold explored a small island just off the coast of the

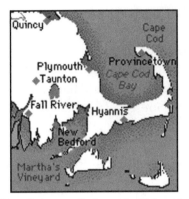

Cape Cod naturally forms the Hebrew letter beit. In Hebrew, "beit" means "house."
Fig. B

peninsula. This particular island had vines growing on it, so he named it Martha's Vineyard after his daughter. It is separated from Cape Cod by Vineyard Sound. It seems that God chose this particular geographic area, a vineyard, to start building His house. Here we see the first fruit of the prophetic vineyard.

"Except the Lord build the house, they labor in vain that build it: except the Lord keep the city, the watchman waketh but in vain" (Psalm 127:1).

Building the House

Eighteen years after Gosnold's discovery and thirteen years after the founding of Jamestown, the Pilgrims (intending to settle at the mouth of the Hudson River) were blown off their course at sea. On November 9, 1620, they landed about one hundred miles north of their intended destination, at Cape Cod. After much debate and prayer, they decided that perhaps God had led them to this spot and that He did not want them to proceed to the Hudson. So, on November 11, 1620, they dropped anchor in the waters of the Cape.

Settling there presented a legal problem. Since Cape Cod was outside of the jurisdiction of the Virginia Company, the Pilgrims would not be under English jurisdiction. Some of the people on the Mayflower were not Pilgrims and they would be unwilling to conform to the Pilgrims' strict adherence to Biblical Law. A solution was needed, and the result was the "Mayflower Compact." This document provided for equality and government by the consent of the governed. It was based on the theory of English Common Law that resulted from the Magna Carta. The same principle of government was articulated in the Declaration of Independence and later reflected in the United States Constitution. The Compact was signed on

November 11, 1620.

William Bradford, who later became governor of the colony, wrote of their landing at Provincetown: "Being thus arrived in a good harbor and brought safe to land, they fell upon their knees and blessed the God of heaven, who had brought them over the vast and furious ocean, and delivered them from all perils and miseries thereof, again to set their feet on the firm and stable earth, their proper element. And no marvel if they were thus joyful." This is remarkable in light of all the hardships they had endured. One hundred and two people had been stuffed between decks somewhat like sardines. The conditions were miserable, at best. They endured sickness and mockery from the crew. After arriving at Provincetown, Bradford's wife fell overboard and drowned. Although there were hardships, there were also miracles.

While they were in the middle of the Atlantic, a fierce storm arose and snapped the crossbeam that supported the ship's mast. The situation was grave. The Pilgrims did the only thing they knew to do — they prayed! At this time, William Brewster, one of the elders, remembered that a large iron screw from his printing press was on board. A search ensued to find the screw. Once found, it was used to support the sagging crossbeam in its proper position. Everyone praised God for deliverance from a sure death.

On December 21, 1620, after scouting for the best place to settle, a group of ten men stepped onto Plymouth Rock and made history. One might wonder if, as they stepped onto the rock, they thought of the Scripture, "Upon this rock, I will build my church" (Matthew 16:18). As they looked around, they saw an area that was perfect for habitation. There were four sources of water nearby, the harbor was deep enough to receive large ships, and the land was already cleared. It looked like it had been used for planting corn. It was as if someone had cleared it, used it, and then left it for them. Coincidentally, this day was the second day of Chanukah, the Jewish celebration of the rededication of God's house in Jerusalem. God's vineyard was growing and His house was about to take shape.

The Miracles of the Plymouth Plantation

The harsh New England winter set in quickly upon the Pilgrims. By the time the Mayflower returned to England in April 1621, only half of those who made the voyage were still alive, yet they wanted to stay in the

New World and did not return with the crew. They worked to construct a blockhouse that also served as a meetinghouse. Eventually, at the founding of each new community, one of the first structures to be built was the meetinghouse. They believed that their covenant with God and with their fellow men was the basis of their colony. Apparently, this is exactly what God wanted from them, because miracle after miracle attested to God's favor.

One of the strangest events regarding this new settlement involved their acquaintance with the Indians. One day, as the men were meeting in the blockhouse, one Indian approached the compound. To their amazement, he spoke English. His name was Samoset and he was a chieftain among the Algonquin tribe that lived in Maine. He had learned English from men on fishing expeditions off the coast of Maine. When asked about the local Indians, Samoset told a story that shocked the Pilgrims. According to Samoset, the territory the Pilgrims were occupying had belonged to a hostile tribe known as the Patuxets. They had cleared the land, but about four years before the Pilgrims had arrived, a mysterious sickness swept through and killed all of the tribe. The neighboring tribe, fearing some supernatural reason for this devastation, would not venture near the area. So the land the Pilgrims were occupying did not belong to anyone. It seems that God had dispossessed the previous owners in favor of the Pilgrim believers.

The Lord had done the same thing for Israel many years before. In the book of Joshua, the Lord told Israel through Joshua: "I sent the hornet before you, which drove them out from before you, even the two kings of the Amorites; but not with thy sword, nor with thy bow. And I have given you a land for which you did not labor, and cities which ye built not, and ye dwell in them; of the vineyards and oliveyards that ye planted not do ye eat. Now therefore fear the Lord, and serve him in sincerity and truth..." (Joshua 24:12-14).

The Pilgrims discovered that the nearest tribe was the Wampanoags, who were some distance away. Their chief was Massasoit, who was probably the only chief along the Northeastern seaboard who would befriend the white men. The hand of God was evident as He provided the ideal place for the Pilgrims to live.

Incredibly, one Patuxet named Squanto had been in England while his tribe fell victim to the mysterious illness. He spent years in England and returned to his native land with, of all people, Captain John Smith.

After Smith left, other Englishmen came and captured many Indians, including Squanto, with the intention of selling them into slavery. A friar rescued Squanto and introduced him to Christianity. After several years of Christian instruction, Squanto returned to his native land, only to discover that his tribe had been wiped out. Sad as this may have been, Squanto had seemingly been chosen by God to help the Pilgrims in their first years at Plymouth. Bradford wrote that Squanto was a special instrument sent by God for their good, beyond their expectation. Squanto taught them how to fish, plant maize, hunt deer, refine maple syrup, and select the proper herbs for medicines. It was this kind of friendly relationship that led to the first Thanksgiving — a remarkable contrast to the behavior of the Jamestown colonists. This story is also very different from what students are taught today in our public schools about the Pilgrims and the first Thanksgiving!

The first person on record (other than an Indian) to use the word "American" with reference to a European colonist was Cotton Mather, a Puritan minister. The Puritans, as distinguished from the Pilgrims, began to immigrate to the New World in 1628. Their trading company, under the jurisdiction of the Monarchy, eventually developed into a theocracy. The Puritans have been mercilessly criticized for their strict adherence to the Bible. The Puritans, probably more than any other group that settled in America, defined what God was looking for in a people and a nation. They also influenced our American system of government. Is it coincidence that the American Revolution began in the area where the Puritans settled? They felt they had been given a divine opportunity to construct a colony that existed and thrived on Biblical principles. Their philosophy of living the Christian life in the New World was covenant based – that is, a covenant between God and man.

This covenant nature of living together was expressed in 1776 in the Declaration of Independence. Its closing statement declares: "And for the support of this declaration, with a firm reliance on the protection of Divine Providence, we mutually pledge to each other our lives, our fortunes, and our sacred honor." Many of the men who signed the Declaration of Independence were Puritan descendants. The Hebrew name for the United States of America can be translated to mean *lands of the covenant*.

The City of Salem

John Endicott, born in Cornwall, England, joined with six other men to obtain the grant of the Massachusetts Bay Charter. In 1628, Endicott's expedition landed in the New World. Endicott and the group of about 100 people named their settlement in honor of the ancient city that became Jerusalem. In Genesis 14:18, Abraham met Melchizedek in the city of Salem, which was near the place where God established His covenant with Abraham. Salem later became the city of Jerusalem, the capital of Israel. By naming their settlement Salem, Endicott's men commemorated the first covenant between God and mankind.

The founders of Salem considered themselves to be the spiritual heirs of the Old Testament, or new Israelites. Understanding this, it was only suitable that they should name their first settlement Salem, after the Holy City of God (later called Jerusalem). They likened their leaving England and crossing the Atlantic to Israel leaving Egypt and crossing the Red Sea. At the dawn of the American Revolution, one colonial assembly referred to the American people as "God's American Israel."

John Endicott served as governor until John Winthrop arrived in 1630. Winthrop and about 900 colonists went to Salem first and then moved on to settle Charlestown. During the American Revolution, the battle of Bunker Hill was fought at Charlestown. The colonists continued to explore the land and later established the city of Boston, located at the mouth of the Charles River. It was in Boston Harbor that the famous Boston Tea Party took place. It demonstrated the colonists' beliefs that they were being unfairly taxed without being represented in English government. This was not the kind of freedom that they were promised in their charter. It was tyranny!

Cotton Mather, the famous Puritan minister, referred to Winthrop as Nehemias Americanus, the American Nehemiah. In the Bible, Nehemiah was the man who led Israel back from captivity to the Promised Land and began rebuilding the walls of Jerusalem and the Temple. Winthrop saw New England as a religious and political refuge. In his letters, he referred to it as a city on a hill (Matthew 5:14) and the New Jerusalem. Winthrop became God's assistant in building the new vineyard of the Lord, America.

For the Love of Hebrew

Many of the Puritan ministers were well versed in the Hebrew language. Cotton Mather wrote, "I promise that those who spend as much time morning and evening in Hebrew studies as they do in smoking tobacco will quickly make excellent progress in the language." William Bradford, a Pilgrim, also studied the Hebrew language. Bradford intimated that he studied Hebrew intensely so that when he died he would be able to speak the "most ancient language, the Holy Tongue in which God and the angels spake."

The original Jewish language is Hebrew. It is interesting that some of America's founders considered making Hebrew the official language of America. The language seems to have played an important role in the development of early New England. Hebrew is found on the seals of schools such as Columbia and Dartmouth. Harvard University, founded by the Puritans in 1636, considered Hebrew to be a critical part of higher learning. From Harvard's beginning, Hebrew was taught by the presidents, of whom it was said that some were better Hebraists than the Jews. John Endicott wanted to make the Mosaic Law the basis of law in Massachusetts. Many of the young men wore earlocks, reminiscent of the earlocks prescribed by the Mosaic Law and worn by Orthodox Jews today. The main reason that the Salem Witch Trials of 1692 occurred was because of the Puritan's attempt to enforce the Mosaic Law. The Law of Moses says that you must not "suffer a witch to live" (Exodus 22:18). It is safe to say that the Hebrew Scriptures were at the heart of Puritan society. Hebrew, the language of Israel, was emphasized in the new vineyard, America.

The Puritans wanted to found a New Israel in the New World, a city set on a hill. As they sought to do this, they constantly taught that, unless the Lord builds the house, those that build it labor in vain. Their colony developed to such an extent that, in 1691, they were given a new Charter that incorporated an area from Plymouth all the way to Maine. Puritan beliefs greatly influenced the Declaration of Independence and the United States Constitution. Both of these documents have their roots in the Bible.

A Second Exodus

The Puritans had tried to purify the Church of England from within, but were met with resistance. For years, Puritan ministers pleaded with English Church officials to fix corrupt practices. Oddly, from autumn of 1628 to 1629 was the Hebrew year 5389. Upon correlating the numbers to the Hebrew alphabet, they spell the Hebrew word hishaphet which means *to judge or plead*. It was during this time that the Great (Puritan) Migration began. You will recall that the Jewish exodus from Egypt resulted from God's judgment upon Egypt and its tyrant, Pharaoh. Pharaoh's decrees caused the Hebrews to want to leave. In 1628, William Laud was appointed bishop of the Church of England. Laud began immediately to aid King Charles I in suppressing the Puritans. This settled the issue of whether or not the Puritans should remain in England. It was this oppression that caused the Puritans to want to leave. Just as Pharaoh's oppression in Egypt drove the Hebrews to the Promised Land, oppression by the Church of England drove the Pilgrims to their new Promised Land.

Peter Marshall wrote in his book *The Light and the Glory*, "Today we can see what lay ahead of them ... and sense just how extraordinary was the timing of the Puritan exodus. If Laud had not come to power and abetted the King in his drive to bring the Puritans to heel ... there might not have been a Puritan exodus in sufficient numbers to seed America with spiritual freedom." Persecution brought forth a new people into a new nation.

Charles I consented to let the Puritans start a colony. Soon after, he was confronted with discontented subjects who pleaded with him to curtail his power. Charles reluctantly consented. However, in 1629, he dissolved Parliament and ran the country by himself, without representation of his subjects. Civil War resulted and Charles I was executed. Perhaps the Hebrew year 5389, meaning in Hebrew *to judge or to plead*, had predicted this.

The Pruning of the Vineyard

The law of God requires that every vineyard be pruned (Leviticus 25:3). If the Plymouth and Massachusetts Bay Colonies were the fruitful vines of the new vineyard, then God required them to be pruned. In 1636, members of the Massachusetts Bay Colony, Roger Williams and Thomas Hooker, founded the colonies of Rhode Island and Connecticut. Both colonies supported religious freedom and the governmental codes instituted in Massachusetts. The vineyard was pruned and yielded new branches. Connecticut's state motto is: "He who transplants still sustains." The motto refers to a vineyard, since the state seal has three grapevines representing a vineyard!

Often in ancient Israel, God's people strayed from His laws, bringing war and captivity upon themselves. When the Puritans compromised their Biblical principles, trouble erupted. In 1675-76 the Indians, who had lived in harmony with the settlers, began turning upon them. Chief Metacomet of the Wampanoag tribe led King Phillip's War. Metacomet, or Phillip as he was referred to, was the second son of Massasoit. Massasoit was the Indian chief who had befriended the settlers fifty years before. The war was bloody, but its result accomplished two things. It caused the churches to be filled with praying, repentant people, and it taught the settlers how to fight a war.

As with ancient Israel in the times of Judges, various Canaanite tribes inhabited Israel and fought the Hebrews. The Hebrews cried out to God for help. In reality, The Lord allowed these tribes to remain in the land to teach the people about war (Judges 3:1-2). The settlers, through fighting the Indians, learned secrets of warfare that would later be used during the American Revolution.

A Strange Tale About Concord

There is a strange story about King Phillip's War and the town of Concord. It is said the town was named Concord to reflect the peaceful way in which the settlers acquired new land from the Indians. During the war, many New England towns were attacked and burned, but Concord was spared. The Indians feared Concord's minister, Edward Bulkely, and his relationship with the Great Spirit. The historical records of Sudbury tell of an Indian who didn't think the Indians would prosper if they burned Concord. He believed that the Great Spirit loved the people of Concord and told them not to go there, because they had a great man who prayed. Because of this man of God, the city of Concord was spared. Exactly one hundred years later, Concord would be the place where the "shot heard around the world" would be fired. The shot exploded near the home of another great man of God, William Emerson, the great-grandson of Edward Bulkely.

A Rebellion was Building

While New England fought, another problem developed in Virginia. Because of the Navigational Acts of 1651 and 1660, the farmers were forced to trade only with English businesses at prices established by the English. The outrageous prices levied by officials were only part of the problem. The governor, Sir William Berkeley, had a monopoly on the fur trade. One hundred years later, these same Navigational Acts resurfaced at the start of the American Revolution.

Toward the end of 1675, the Indians began raiding plantations in Virginia. While Berkeley made a half-hearted attempt to stop the attacks, the colonists formed an army making Nathaniel Bacon its leader. Bacon defeated the Indians twice and occupied Jamestown, the capital of the colony. Governor Berkeley felt that Bacon rebelled against the English Crown and marched against him. Bacon burned Jamestown in 1676. The following month, he stood near Yorktown and met Berkeley's soldiers. One month later, Bacon died of malaria, thus ending the rebellion. One hundred years later, another rebellion would change the destiny of America.

The Prophetic Significance of the Indian Wars

Some historians think that Bacon's Rebellion was the forerunner of the American Revolution. This war and King Phillip's War are interesting for several reasons. First of all, there is a 100-year cycle. One war started in 1675 and lasted into 1676. One hundred years later, the American Revolution began in 1775 and American Independence was declared in 1776.

Secondly, both wars taught the settlers how to fight like the Indians. The British wore heavy clothing and stood in formation in an open field. The Indians wore light clothes and hid to ambush the enemy. These Indian tactics helped the Americans win the Revolutionary War.

Thirdly, King Phillip's War was fought in Puritan New England. It was there that the American Revolution began. Bacon's rebellion was fought in Virginia and actually ended in Yorktown. One hundred years later, the American Revolution ended in the same spot. These cycles and patterns are more than just a coincidence. A close study of the American Revolution continues to reveal the Israel-American connection with its profound Hebraic patterns and parallels.

Chapter 6

THE AMERICAN REVOLUTION AND THE CHILDREN OF ISRAEL

The Hebrew Parallels in the American Revolution

The children of Israel journeyed into Egypt as a free people. They had the favor of Pharaoh and the protection of Joseph, a Hebrew (Genesis 47). As years passed, Joseph died and the Hebrew population grew, becoming a threat to the Egyptians. To stop the threat, Pharaoh enslaved the Hebrews (Exodus 1:7-12), and they cried out to God for deliverance (Exodus 2:23-25).

In comparison, by the year 1775, the colonists were crying out to God and to one another for freedom from the lion of Britain. It was Patrick Henry who cried out, "Give me liberty or give me death" (Source: Address to the House of Burgesses-March 23, 1775, Patrick Henry). The desire for independence from England welled up in the hearts of Americans.

In Egypt, Pharaoh oppressed the Hebrews. In America, a tyrannical government oppressed the colonists. The British imposed the Navigation

Acts, the Stamp Acts, the Townshend Duties, and the Intolerable Acts. The laws were intended to make the independent-minded colonists submit to the king. George III wrote to Lord North, Prime Minister of Great Britain, "The dye is cast...the Colonies must either submit or triumph."

In Egypt, God sent Moses to tell Pharaoh, "Let my people go" (Exodus 5:1). When the British were pressuring the colonists, Puritan ministers began preaching a message of liberty and freedom from Britain. Colonists were told to protect their right to participate in their government. Soon the king dispatched troops to Boston, the seat of American patriotism, to suppress rebellion in the colonies. The king denied representation of the colonists in Parliament.

In response to Moses' proclamation, "Let my people go," Pharaoh heaped more burdens upon the Hebrews. He felt that he could suppress their spirits and cause them to forget their desire to leave Egypt. In a similar fashion, the king believed that he could force the colonists into subjection. In both Egypt and America, the tyrants were wrong!

In March of 1770, the Boston Massacre occurred. In December of 1773, Boston colonists, dressed like Indians, raided British ships and dumped expensive tea into the harbor. This Boston Tea Party became a triggering point for the war. The colonists believed that God had brought them into their Promised Land, and now a new Pharaoh named King George III oppressed them like the Hebrews in Egypt. Moses and Aaron faced the leader of the strongest nation on earth and, with God's help, saw a great deliverance. One of the Founders suggested that our national seal depict Israel crossing the Red Sea and Pharaoh being drowned in the waters. Here, another prophetic parallel unfolds. Just as Israel was delivered from Egypt during Passover, America initiated her liberation during the same Jewish feast of Passover!

America and the Passover Connection

> "And thus you shall eat it: with your loins girded, your shoes on your feet, and your staff in your hand; and ye shall eat it in haste: it is the Lord's Passover." (Exodus 12:11)

As noted in this book, many important events in America's history have coincided with Jewish festivals and special days in Hebrew history. One such parallel involves the creation of the Minutemen. As tension built in the colonies, British General Thomas Gage sent soldiers to seize munitions that were stockpiled in Sommerville, Massachusetts. Caught off guard, the colonists met in Worchester, Massachusetts, on September 21, 1774 to organize companies of Minutemen, who were to ride the countryside to warn of approaching British forces. September 21 was the 16th of Tishri, the Feast of Tabernacles. The Feast of Tabernacles commemorated Israel's wanderings in the wilderness. The next consecutive Hebrew feast is the Passover, which would take place in the spring of the following year. On another Jewish feast day, America was making itself ready to "separate from Egypt!"

According to Scripture, on the fourteenth day of the Hebrew month Nisan, the Hebrews prepared the Passover meal in Egypt. Late that night, as they sat eating in their homes, the destroyer went through the land of Egypt and killed all firstborn.

April 14,1775 corresponds to the Hebrew date Nisan 14, 5535, the day when Jews prepared for Passover. On April 14, 1775, orders arrived for British Commander Thomas Gage to move against the rebels and arrest their leaders. Captain Oliver De Lancy executed the orders. De Lancy led the 17th Light Dragoons, a cavalry unit. The insignia upon their helmets depicted a huge skull and crossbones, which symbolized their mission. Thousands of years before, as the Hebrews prepared for Passover, the destroyer (or death angel) made its way across the land. Is it a coincidence that De Lancy's arrival fell on the eve of Passover, or is this yet another American connection to the Hebrews?

On April 15, the first day of Passover, the Provincial Congress fled Concord after being warned by Paul Revere that the British were coming. On Easter Sunday, Revere rode to Lexington to warn John Adams, John Hancock, and others. On April 18, British patrols scoured the countryside to find colonial informants. One of these patrols encountered a farmer from Lincoln, Massachusetts. The colonial farmer heard them coming and mistook them for countrymen. He asked, "Have you heard anything about when the regulars are coming?" Upon hearing this, a British soldier slashed the farmer across his head with a sword and took him prisoner. The poor man was finally released after being told to keep quiet lest his house be burned and he would again be taken prisoner. This was the first American blood shed at the onset of the Revolution. The man's name was Josiah Nelson, and here we find another parallel.

The Josiah Connection

> "And behold, there came a man of God out of Judah by the word of the Lord unto Bethel: and Jeroboam stood by the altar to burn incense. And he cried against the altar in the word of the Lord, and said 'O, altar, altar; Thus saith the Lord; Behold, a child shall be born to the house of David; Josiah by name; and upon thee shall he offer the priests of the high places that burn incense upon thee, and men's bones shall be burnt on thee."   (1 Kings 13:1-2)

Another parallel develops regarding the story of King Josiah. In this story, Jeroboam, fearing the loss of his kingdom to Jerusalem, instituted false idol worship in Bethel and Dan so that his subjects would not have to travel to Jerusalem. Three times a year, Jewish males were required to go to Jerusalem to worship. These times marked three festivals: Passover, Pentecost, and the Feast of Tabernacles. One of these three festivals was probably approaching when Jeroboam started considering his predicament. We can determine which one by looking at the context of the story. The Bible tells us in 1 Kings 12:33 that Jeroboam "devised of his own heart and ordained a feast unto the children of Israel" on the fifteenth day of the eighth month.

To identify the eighth Hebrew month, we must understand that in Judaism there are two calendars. The civil calendar begins with the month Tishiri, making the eighth month Iyar, which follows the Passover season. However, in Exodus 12:2, God told Moses that "this month shall be unto you the beginning of months: it shall be the first month of the year to you." The month referred to here is Nisan, which is the first month of the religious calendar. So, starting with Nisan, the eighth month would be Cheshvan, the month that follows the Feast of Tabernacles season. So, it was either the approach of Passover or Tabernacles that provoked Jeroboam to establish his own religious holiday. Josephus, the Jewish historian, identifies the Feast of Tabernacles as the holiday during which Jeroboam sought to keep his subjects away from Jerusalem. It was at this time of year that the prophet came and delivered his ominous tidings (Source: *Antiquities*, Book 8, Chapter 8, Section 4).

According to *Wilmington's Guide to the Bible*, this prophecy took place around the year 931 B.C. Josephus identifies the unnamed prophet to be Jadon (Source: *Antiquities,* Book 8, Chapter 5, Section 5). In Hebrew, the name Jadon means *thankful*. The name comes from the word meaning *hand* or, *to stretch out the hand*. If Josephus is correct, this is very significant. The object of the prophecy, Josiah, whose name means *founded by God*, was born around the year 649 BC — 282 years later!

Josiah, the boy king, was born to King Amon and his wife Jedidah. The name Amon means *a multitude*. It comes from either a root meaning *a tumult* or a root meaning *faith, belief, or training*. This particular root also means *amen*. It is interesting that the name Amon is synonymous with the name of the Egyptian sun god. Amon, the Bible says, was a wicked leader who forsook the Lord God of his fathers. Some of his servants conspired against him and slew him in his own house (2 Kings 21:23). Due to a revolution, Josiah, meaning *founded by God,* came to power when he was only eight years old.

Josiah broke a long series of wicked rulers. Before and after him, there existed immorality and darkness. J.G. Greenhough wrote: "Josiah's good reign was like a brilliant sunset, before the final darkness comes on." The Bible says that when he was sixteen, he began to seek after God. At twenty, he began purging Jerusalem and Judah of idolatry. At age 26, he began restoring the temple. During the restoration, a copy of the Law of Moses was found. After hearing the words of the Law, Josiah reinstituted the Law of Moses as the law of the land, basing the government on the Torah. Not long after this, Josiah destroyed the altar and burned the high place at Bethel that Jeroboam had built, fulfilling the prophecy. The Bible continues:

"And as Josiah turned himself, he spied the sepulchers that were there in the mount, and sent, and took the bones out of the sepulchers, and burned them upon the altar, and polluted it, according to the word of the Lord which the man of God proclaimed, who proclaimed these words. Then he said, 'What title is this that I see?' And the men of the city told him: It is the sepulcher of the man of God, which came from Judah, and proclaimed these things that thou hast done against the altar of Bethel. And he said, let him alone; let no man move his bones. So they let his bones alone, with the bones of the prophet that came out of Samaria. And all the houses also of the high places that were in the cities of Samaria, which the kings of Israel had made to provoke the Lord to anger, Josiah took away, and did to them according to all the acts that he had done in Bethel.

And he slew all the priests of the high places that were there upon the altars, and burned men's bones upon them, and returned to Jerusalem. And the king commanded all the people, saying, Keep the Passover unto the Lord your God, as it is written in the book of this covenant. Surely there was not holden such a passover from the days of the judges that judged Israel, nor in all the days of the kings of Israel, nor of the kings of Judah." (2 Kings 23:16-22)

Notice that Josiah completely fulfilled the prophecy and, in doing so, discovered the sepulcher of the man who had prophesied about him. Instead of desecrating his tomb, Josiah honored him by allowing it to remain. Furthermore, the Bible indicates the general time frame of this event. As soon as Josiah returned to Jerusalem, he instructed the people to keep the Passover. Therefore, the fulfillment of this prophecy happened around the time of Passover.

The Prophetic Implications

As I mentioned earlier, Josiah Nelson became the first man to shed his blood for the American Revolution. Let's look at him as a symbol of the American Revolution. By doing this, we can compare the story of Josiah the King with the American Revolution.

The name Amon (Josiah's father) means *faith*, *training* or, it can mean *multitude*. It is also associated with Amon, the Egyptian sun god. Originally Amon was the Theban god of reproduction, thus the association with the meaning *multitude*. Later it was associated with Ra, god of the sun, and became known as Amon-Ra. Amon-Ra was the most revered of the Egyptian gods.

Apparently, the Hebrew King Amon forsook the faith and training of his ancestors and lived like those who worshiped Amon-Ra. King Amon became so evil that his own subjects killed him in his house. You might say they revolted! Only then was Josiah allowed to ascend to the throne.

As I have suggested, aspects of the American Revolution can be compared to Israel's exodus from Egypt. Egypt's chief deity was Amon, the sun god. As Americans, we owe our love of liberty, law, and the Gospel to our English forefathers. Their faith and example shaped our nation in its infancy. However, there arose a Pharaoh who knew not Joseph and his name was King George III. Just as Amon was overthrown in his own house, British subjects revolted against their tyrannical king. It was at this point that the sun began to slowly set on the British Empire. The Americans, personified by Josiah, began the ascent to the throne. Josiah means *founded by God.* I believe that God founded America and that the Revolution symbolized the construction of His house in the midst of His end-time vineyard.

Josiah's prophecy was delivered 282 years before he was born. If we compare America to Josiah, at what point was America's prophecy proclaimed and who spoke it?

"I said that some of the prophecies remained yet to be fulfilled. These are great and wonderful things for the earth and the signs are that the Lord is hastening the end. The fact that the Gospel must still be preached to so many lands in such a short time — this is what convinces me" (Source: *Book of Prophecies*, Christopher Columbus)

"Establish us as thy chosen vineyard and make us as a tree planted by the streams of water ... plant us, we pray, upon a fruitful sod." (Source: portions of prayers recited on Hoshanah Rabbah)

Remember that Columbus saw himself as a tool functioning to fulfill prophecy. He believed that his expedition had accomplished God's will and that he had been God's instrument in spreading the Gospel and in liberating Jerusalem. Consider also that the day he stepped foot in the New World was Hoshannah Rabbah. On this day, the Jews pray, "Establish us as His chosen vineyard ... Plant us ... on a fruitful sod." Remember that Columbus saw his discovery as a last day fulfillment of God's plan to take the Gospel to the nations. Knowing these facts about Columbus, we could see him as the personification of the prophet that spoke to Jeroboam. As mentioned earlier, 282 years after the prophet spoke to King Jeroboam, Josiah, whose name means *founded of God,* was born. According to Josephus, a man named Jadon delivered the prophecy at the end of the Feast of Tabernacles. Jadon comes from a word meaning *to extend a hand.*

Hoshannah Rabbah, the day of Columbus' discovery, falls on the first day after the Feast of Tabernacles. This holiday is considered a minor Yom Kippur because of God's resolve to seal His decisions from the High Holy Days season. To illustrate God's seal, a hand is baked upon the holiday bread. The theme of God setting His hand is linked to the prophecies concerning the return of the Jews to the land of Israel.

> "And it shall come to pass in that day, that the Lord shall set his
> hand again the second time to recover the remnant of his people,
> which shall be left...from the islands of the sea. And he shall set up
> an ensign for the nations, and shall assemble the outcasts of Israel,
> and gather together the dispersed of Judah from the four corners of
> the earth."   (Isaiah 11:11,12)

So the timing of Columbus' discovery and the festival theme of
God's extended hand (the meaning of Jadon) symbolize the prophecy of 1
Kings 13.

October 12, 1492 corresponds with the Hebrew date 21 Tishri, 5253.
If we add 282 years to this year, it brings us to the Hebrew year 5535. On
the Gregorian calendar, this year corresponds to the fall of 1774 until the
fall of 1775. This means that April 19, 1775, the first day of the Revolution,
would have been during this Hebrew year! Furthermore, the Bible says
that Josiah fulfilled the ancient prophecy at about the time of Passover.
The first shots of the Revolution were fired during the seven days of
unleavened bread known as Passover.

After Jadon delivered the prophecy, he began his return to Jerusalem
by a different route, obeying the word of the Lord saying "eat no bread,
nor drink water, nor turn again by the same way that thou camest. So he
went another way and returned not by the way that he came to Bethel" (1
Kings 13:9, 10). However, the prophet, being coaxed by another "prophet,"
fell into disobedience and was killed, though not consumed, by a lion.

Likewise, Columbus was coaxed by greed and fell into
disobedience. Spain, the nation he represented, followed suit and killed,
persecuted, and sold into slavery those they intended to convert. In the
name of Christianity, Spain dominated New World exploration for a century.
That changed in 1588 when Great Britain (the lion) defeated the Spanish
Armada. This defeat did not totally destroy Spain, but it helped to bring
about its decline. Spanish coffers, previously filled with gold from the
New World, were depleted. In 1588, Britain was established as the chief
naval power of the Old World and the dominant power in the New World.

Although the United States was born in April 1775, it would not
officially realize its freedom until September 3, 1783. In 1783, Great Britain
recognized the independence of the colonies in the Treaty of Paris. After

only eight years of struggle, America assumed her role in the destiny of nations. In like manner, Josiah became king not at his birth, but when he was eight years old. The Bible indicates that Josiah reigned for thirty-one years. This means that he died at the young age of 39. Thirty-nine years after the Revolution began, America, having survived another war with Britain, signed the Treaty of Ghent. This treaty forever ended America's conflict with Britain.

Josiah's reign was seen as a bright spot wedged between the dark reigns of evil Jewish kings. At just sixteen, Josiah began seeking the God of his ancestors. During his reign, Josiah re-instituted the Law of Moses as the law of the land. He was responsible for restoring the Temple to its previous glory and ridding the land of false gods, false prophets, and places of idol worship.

In the same manner, America has been a bright spot in a relatively dark history of the world. We have led the fight for freedom and human rights, and we have spread the Gospel of Christ around the world. In 1791, sixteen years after the Revolution began, we ratified a document called the United States Constitution. This Constitution ensured American liberties and served as a model for future societies. Remarkably, the first ten amendments to the Constitution are known as the Bill of Rights. They corresponded to the Ten Commandments outlined in God's Law. This is yet another example of how our form of government is based on the Bible. We can observe Josiah's story being illustrated throughout American history.

Another interesting event happened in 1791. Plans were started that year to build a capital city which was to be built along the banks of the Potomac River. George Washington personally selected the sight at the head of the navigable Potomac where it meets the Anacostia. Virginia and Maryland donated land for the site. It was called Columbia to honor Christopher Columbus. Remember that Josiah would not allow the bones of the prophet to be disturbed. To the contrary, the king honored the prophet's memory. To this day, the memory of Columbus is honored in America's capital district.

One of Josiah's greatest accomplishments was the restoration of the disregarded House of God. I believe that the American Josiah continued to restore God's house as well. In its infancy, America based law and order upon the statues from the Bible. The Pilgrim and Puritan fathers had so influenced American society and government that 100 years later, their descendants still relied upon the only credible form of government and self-rule they had ever known. In essence, they continued to build on the foundation laid by their forefathers.

The Temple in Jerusalem had long since been destroyed and Jews were scattered throughout the world; therefore, it seems that God began constructing for Himself another house in America. In 1838, an American named John O'Sullivan wrote, "The far-reaching future will be the era of American greatness...the nation of many nations is destined to manifest to mankind the obedience of Divine principles to establish on earth the noblest temple ever dedicated to the worship of the Most High." As you will see later in this book, Mr. O'Sullivan was more precise in his editorial than even he could have imagined.

Other Prophetic Utterances

In September 1768, the Boston Gazette stated, "If an army should be sent to reduce us to slavery, we will put our lives in our hands and cry to the Judge of all the earth...behold how they come to cast us out of this possession which thou hast given us to inherit. Help us, Lord, our God for we rest on thee, and in thy name we go against this multitude." This provides great insight into what the residents of Boston thought about the prospect of war with Britain. Apparently, they felt that God was on their side and would fight on their behalf.

Earlier in April 1768, the New York Gazette noted, "Courage, Americans. The finger of God points out a mighty empire to your sons. The savages of the wilderness were never expelled to make room for idolaters and slaves. The land we possess is the gift of heaven to our fathers, and Divine Providence seems to have decreed it to our latest posterity...the day dawns in which the foundation of this mighty empire is to be laid, by the establishment of a regular American Constitution...before seven years roll over our heads, the first stone must be laid." This is an amazing statement since exactly seven years later in April 1775, the first shots of the Revolution were fired at Lexington-Concord.

The Shot Heard Around the World

"By the rude bridge that arched the flood, their flag to April's breeze unfurled. Here once the embattled farmers stood, and fired the shot heard round the world" (Source: Portion of the Concord Hymn, Ralph Waldo Emerson).

Around 10:30 p.m. on April 18, 1775, the British detachment of about 700 men boarded their boats. About the same time that the British left their barracks, Paul Revere and William Dawes were apprised of the British movements and were sent to spread the news to outlying areas. Dawes took the land route, while Revere crossed the river to Charleston.

There was a full moon in the sky that night, and when Revere passed the British ship, the HMS Somerset, his boat should have been easy to spot. However, on this night, the moon didn't rise to the east as it normally did; instead, it moved to the south and hung very low on the horizon. This enabled Revere's boat to be miraculously obscured in the shadow of the moon, thus allowing him to escape the blockaded city of Boston. Revere and Dawes were eventually caught, but not before they were able to successfully announce the British advance.

After midnight, word spread among the colonists in Lexington about the British. The first person to answer the call was Reverend William Emerson, the great-grandson of Edward Bulkely. He was the man in Concord that the Indians feared during King Phillip's War one hundred years earlier. They believed the Great Spirit would punish them if they attacked Concord because of Bulkely's relationship with God. Now, one hundred years later, his descendent rushed to defend his community.

The first armed colonial force to arrive at Concord was the Lincoln militia. As the British advanced, the militia crossed the North Bridge to Puckatasset Hill. A small British force pursued them across the river. The rest of the British remained in town and burned several buildings. When they saw the smoke, the 400-man militia advanced toward town. At approximately 9:30 a.m., they squared off, separated only by the North Bridge. The British fired first and killed two militiamen. The militia fired back, killing three British soldiers and wounding others. The rest of the British ran all the way back to Boston.

Many of the people who fought in the war were Puritan descendants. Their forefathers were strong-willed people who loved and trusted God, and lived in a committed covenant relationship with Him. They recognized that it was God who had provided for them since they first came to America. It was God who gave them this land for a purpose, and nobody was going to deny their right to live freely on this land. I believe that their view of being in covenant with God, destined by His plan, was the true motivation for the men at Lexington and Concord.

The Historical Significance of Nisan 19th

The fight at Concord lasted only two or three minutes; yet, the result of the battle lasts to this day! Lexington and Concord signaled the birth pains of a new nation. As the Americans pursued the retreating British, they were, in a spiritual sense, personifying the waters of the Red Sea overcoming the armies of Pharaoh who had gone to pursue the children of Israel. In fact, it was miraculous that the entire force was not killed or taken prisoner.

According to the Hebrew calendar, April 19, 1775 was Nisan 19. The Jewish commentator Rashi indicated that this is the date in Jewish history when Pharaoh set out in pursuit of Israel. So here at the North Bridge was the birth of the American exodus.

Another peculiarity in Jewish history occurred on April 26, 1655. This day was also Nisan 19. On that day, the Dutch West India Company refused to grant permission to Governor Peter Stuyvesant to exclude Jews from New Amsterdam (present day New York). Therefore, Nisan 19 signifies a banner day in Jewish history, especially for American Jews. This marked the end of official efforts to bar Jews from North America and allowed Jews to prosper and multiply in the New World. To this day, more Jews live in the United States than in the nation of Israel. Is it a coincidence that, on this same day, Nisan 19, the nation destined to be the greatest nation in the world revolted against its Pharaoh?

America has been a haven for Jews. It helped bring about the birth of modern Israel — a rebirth made possible only after the defeat of Adolf Hitler. America was instrumental in ensuring that defeat. Hitler was born on April 20, 1889 and that date and year also corresponds to the Hebrew date Nisan 19!

The Stone of Stumbling

I have already stated this, but it warrants being repeated. I believe that America is unquestionably God's end-time vineyard. America was destined to "bring forth fruit" by taking the Gospel to the nations. America was also destined to realize "the times of the Gentiles" by temporarily evangelizing the world until God's chosen messengers, the Jews, resume the mission.

"Escaped from the house of bondage, Israel of old did not follow after the ways of the Egyptians. To her was given an express dispensation; to her were given new things under the sun. And we Americans are the peculiar, the chosen people — the Israel of our time; we bear the ark of the liberties of the world...God has predestined, mankind expects, great things from our race; and great things we feel in our souls...We are the pioneers of the world, the advance guard sent on through the wilderness of untried things, to break a new path in the New World that is ours"
(Source: *White Jacket*, Herman Melville).

"Jesus saith unto them, "Did ye never read in the Scriptures, the stone which the builders rejected, the same is become the head of the corner: this is the Lord's doing, and it is marvelous in our eyes? Therefore I say unto you, The kingdom of God shall be taken from you, and given to a nation bringing forth the fruits thereof. And whosoever shall fall on this stone shall be broken: but on whomsoever it shall fall, it will grind him to powder"
(Matthew 21:42-44).

Notice that Jesus identified the stone that the builders rejected as the same stone that causes some to fall and be broken. This is the stone that Peter referred to in his epistle.

"Unto you therefore which believe he is precious: but unto them which be disobedient, the stone which the builders disallowed, the same is made of the head of the corner, and a stone of stumbling, and a rock of offense even to them which stumble at the word, being disobedient; whereunto also they were appointed. But ye are a chosen generation, a royal priesthood, a holy nation, a peculiar people; that ye should show forth the praises of him who hath called you out of darkness into his marvelous light: which in times past were not a people, but are now the people of God: which had not obtained mercy, but now have obtained mercy" (1 Peter 2:7-10).

Peter calls those who believe in the stone of stumbling a "chosen generation, a holy nation...which in times past were not a people but are now the people of God" (1 Peter 2:9-10). If this can apply to an individual believer, it could apply to a nation that puts its trust in Jesus, the stone of stumbling. Actually, Peter quoted Exodus 19:5-6. In Exodus, God decreed these same words to Israel at Mount Sinai forty-seven days after leaving Egypt. So originally the status of being a "chosen generation" was given to an entire nation. Israel was to provide a light to the rest of the world and teach the nations about the one true God. After the destruction of the Temple, this mission was taken from Israel and given to a nation that would temporarily act as the "chosen generation, a peculiar people, a holy nation."

Remember that America, like Israel, was birthed during Passover. There are also connections within the parable of Matthew 21 and the stone of stumbling in 1 Peter 2:8. They link the nation that will render fruit with the stone of stumbling. I'll explain. The first shots of the American Revolution were fired in the Hebrew year 5535, which translates to the Hebrew word ha takalah, and according to the *Shilo Hebrew-English Dictionary* means *the stumbling block*!

Jesus predicted that He would become the stumbling stone and this certainly happened. Presently in the Jewish community, if a Jew becomes a believer in Christ as his or her Messiah and Savior, that believer is often excommunicated from the synagogue and from his or her family. Most Jews believe that Jews cannot be Christian and Jewish at the same time. To them, a conversion to Christianity is an act of rejecting Judaism.

I have a Jewish friend from Israel who confessed his faith in Christ. He was removed from the family will and told never to come into the house again. Christ became a stumbling stone. America forever coupled herself with the stone of stumbling in order to become a holy nation. This is our prophetic heritage. To deny that America was founded as a Christian nation and built upon Biblical principles is to be simultaneously ignorant and spiritually blind!

Summary of the Hebrew Thread

Below is a list of Hebrew threads that, when woven together, form the garment of the American Republic. They took place between Columbus' arrival in the New World and the end of the American Revolution.

- The Hebrew language: Sir William Bradford, the second governor of the Plymouth Colony, said that the Hebrew language was the language in which "God and the angels spoke to the holy patriarchs of old time."

Bradford wrote in Hebrew at the beginning of his books. The Founding Fathers considered making Hebrew the official language of the colonies. Hebrew was typically taught at the early Ivy League Universities (Source: *History of the Plymouth Colony*, Sir William Bradford).

- Israeli and American national documents, the Torah and the Constitution, respectively, are both based upon Scripture.

- In England, the Pilgrims were called "separatists." Abraham, the first Hebrew was called out of Ur to separate himself from the land of his fathers.

- Both Abraham and the Pilgrims came into a land that was already inhabited by other people. Both were to possess the land and attempt to teach its natives about God.

- Israel and America were each divided between the north and the south at one time in their history.

- Jerusalem was and is the Hebrew capital. It belonged to no tribe and was the center of the thirteen tribes. Washington, D.C. is the American capital. It is separate from the states, yet still the center of government.

- The city of Jerusalem was actually built during the reign of Israel's second king, King David. David built his house on the mountains of Zion. In 1800, the White House was completed in time for America's second president, John Adams.

- Israel was founded with thirteen tribes and America was founded with thirteen colonies.

- Saul, the first king of Israel, and George Washington, America's first president, were both a head taller than the average man. Neither King Saul nor George Washington actually wanted to be the leader.

- When George Washington ran for the presidency, the only man suggested to run against him was a man named Israel!

- There is also visual evidence representing the spiritual connection between America and Israel. It is seen in the layout of current day America and in the Washington, D.C. Mall. This visible perspective affirms once again the Divine design of our nation.

Chapter 7

HEBREW PATTERNS IN AMERICA AND THE NATION'S CAPITAL

Patterns of the Tabernacle and the Tribes of Israel

"Whatever is, has already been, and whatever will be has been before; and God will call the past to account."
(Ecclesiastes 3:15, NIV)

Bill Cloud and I wrote a book titled *Living in the Final Chapter*. In it we wrote, "There exists a principle in the Bible which teaches that significant events of today almost always have a historical precedent. Moreover, it is God Himself who establishes the pattern in the beginning and who causes it to be repeated in the future."

Powerful examples of this truth are found within the seven Feasts of Israel. Notice that the very crucifixion of Jesus fits the pattern of the Feast of Passover in great detail:

The Old Testament Passover	The Crucifixion of Jesus on Passover
— Lamb was taken into house on the 10th of Aviv	— Jesus entered the Temple on the 10th of Aviv
— Lamb was young male, without blemish	— Pilate found no fault in Christ
— Lamb was examined for 4 days	— Jesus was tested by leaders for 4 days
— Lamb was slaughtered on the 14th of Aviv	— Jesus was crucifed on the 14th of Aviv
— Lamb was killed at 3:00 p.m.	— Jesus died at 3:00 p.m.
— Lamb was tied to a wooden pole	— Jesus was crucified on a wooden cross

Another pattern is revealed in the Feast of Pentecost. The Christian church was birthed on the very day of Pentecost (Acts 2:1-4). The first Pentecost occurred in the wilderness with Moses and Israel. Exodus 19 gives the details of how God came down on the mountain and spoke to Moses. God gave Moses the Law. Below are some comparisons between the first Pentecost in Israel, and the day of Pentecost when the Christian church was born.

The Pentecost in Moses' Time (Exodus 19)	The Pentecost in Peters' Time (Acts 2)
— God spoke in 70 languages so all could hear	— They spoke in the tongues of 16 nations
— God's voice issued forth as a flame of fire	— Tongues of fire descended upon them
— The mountain shook and quaked	— A sound came like a rushing mighty wind

These are two of many examples where prophetic events of the past are repeated thousands of years later. More prophetic patterns appear when comparing the symbolism within the layout of the wilderness Tabernacle, a map of modern America, and a diagram of the Washington, D.C. Mall.

In Biblical prophecy, symbolism is used to literally represent people or things. For example, a lamb can represent Christ (Revelation 5:5-7), a serpent commonly symbolizes Satan (Revelation 12:9), and a horn on a beast can represent a king or a kingdom (Revelation 17:12). Through prophetic symbolism the Bible interprets itself. One symbol that represents God dwelling among His people is the tabernacle of Moses. It was constructed in the wilderness, and hundreds of years later King Solomon placed it in a magnificent Temple in Jerusalem.

Both the tabernacle and the Temple consisted of three chambers: the outer court, the inner court, and the Holy of Holies. Paul wrote that, "Our bodies are the temple of the Holy Spirit" (1 Corinthians 3:16). Every human has a body, soul, and spirit because we are created in the image of our triune God (1 Thessalonians 5:23). When comparing the tabernacle and the Temple to our bodies, we discover that the outer court represents the body, the inner court represents the soul, and the Holy of Holies represents the human spirit. Each of the three areas of the tabernacle and the Temple contained sacred furniture:

- The outer court had two pieces: the brass altar and the laver of water.
- The inner court had three pieces: the menorah, the table of shewbread and the golden altar.
- The Holy of Holies had one piece: the Ark of the Covenant.

The Old Testament is full of symbolism, along with the prophetic books of Daniel and Revelation. Daniel and Revelation deal with the time of the end and contain many prophecies to be fulfilled in the time before Christ's return. The tabernacle in the wilderness was a portable tent in which God's presence dwelt while the Hebrews received the Law of God (Torah) and prepared to organize a nation (Israel). The actual position of the sacred furniture in the Temple is important in terms of understanding the prophetic significance of the United States.

The Position of the Sacred Furniture

Notice the drawing of the inside of Moses' tabernacle (*See fig. C*). The only entrance was situated on the east, where the tribe of Judah camped. Moving from east to west, let's look at the position of the sacred furniture. The first item of furniture was the brass altar, where the animal sacrifices were offered. Three fires continually burned upon this altar. Two were used as backup in case the main fire went out.

The second piece of furniture was the brass laver. This was a large round bowl made of brass that, in Solomon's day, held over 30,000 gallons of water. The priest washed himself and the sacrifices here before entering the inner court.

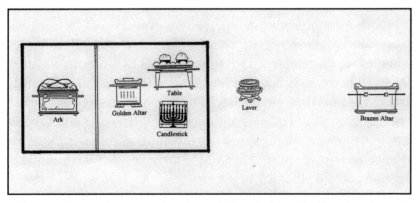

A diagram showing the rectangular shape of Moses' tabernacle. This also shows the position of the holy furniture in the Wilderness Tabernacle. **Fig. C**

Three pieces of furniture were located in the inner court. To the south was a candelabra with seven branches, called a menorah. Olive oil was placed in the shafts of the menorah and it was used to light the inner court. Directly across from the menorah to the north was the table of shewbread. On this table were placed twelve pieces of bread prepared for the priest from grains harvested from the land.

Continuing westward was the golden altar. The golden altar was situated just before the large veil in the Temple that separated the inner court from the Holy of Holies. Hot coals of fire and special incense made by the priests were placed on this altar. The coals and the incense represented the prayers of the saints going up before God to heaven.

Traveling westward in a straight line, past the golden altar, the priest had to pass through a giant veil. This veil divided the inner court and the Holy of Holies. The Holy of Holies was the most important room in the tabernacle (and the Temple), and it contained the most important piece of furniture, the Ark of the Covenant. In the Holy of Holies, God came down and visited with the High Priest once a year on the Day of Atonement. The Day of Atonement was known as Yom Kippur. The entire tabernacle was a dwelling place for the Lord. Each of the six pieces of furniture had a unique purpose and substance. For example:

The Furniture	The special substance that set it apart
— the brazen altar	— *Fire* was the main substance
— the brass laver	— *Water* was the main substance

— the menorah	— ***Oil*** was the main substance
— the table of shewbread	— ***Wheat and grains*** were the main substances
— the golden altar	— ***Coals and spices*** were the main substances
— the Ark of the Covenant	— ***Gold*** was the chief substance

The tabernacle visibly represented the Heavenly Temple, where the Almighty is worshiped. The earthly tabernacle was where the Lord visited His people and spoke directly to Moses and Aaron. Each piece of furniture had a specific spiritual function. Just as the man-made tabernacle provided a dwelling place for the Lord, America was to be a new spiritual tabernacle that welcomed the Holy Scriptures and the Presence of the Lord. The Almighty would have freedom to perform His will through and in His new vineyard!

The Tabernacle in America

Another remarkable pattern appears when we superimpose a diagram of the tabernacle over a map of the United States. The tabernacle was rectangular with the furniture positioned at precise, predesignated locations. To begin, draw a rectangular box around a map of America. Then reproduce a diagram of the tabernacle within the rectangle. Be sure to place each piece of furniture precisely. You will see that the places on the American map that lie beneath each piece of furniture have a similar spiritual significance.

The only entrance to the tabernacle was on the east. When the colonists came across the Atlantic, they landed on America's eastern coast and began building. So, in a similar way, America's historic entrance is on the east. If we place each piece of furniture on the map in the same position as it was in the wilderness tabernacle, we find an amazing pattern that occurs only in America. It will not happen with any other nation on earth! Each piece of Tabernacle furniture with a specific purpose and substance correlates to the area of America beneath it (*See fig. D*).

Moving from east to west, the brass altar is over the area of Tennessee and the edge of Kentucky and Virginia. Fire was the central feature on the brass altar. This area of America experienced dynamic revivals before and after the Civil War that impacted the nation. Great revivals burned in Kentucky throughout the 1800s. Many people do not

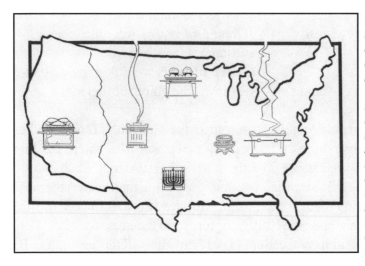

The furniture of the tabernacle overlaid onto a map of the continental United States of America. The position of the holy furniture and the corresponding regions within the US suggest that our nation was uniquely and divinely established by the God of Israel. The US seems to be God's modern-day wilderness tabernacle. **Fig. D**

realize that the first major outpouring of the Holy Spirit that birthed a major denomination was just outside of Cleveland, Tennessee. In 1896, near Murphy, North Carolina, a group of Baptists were baptized in the Holy Spirit. From their experience, the Christian Union was formed, which became the Church of God, headquartered in Cleveland, Tennessee. In fact, the oldest continuing Pentecostal church in the United States is a large, thriving congregation located in Cleveland, Tennessee. The fires that fell in this area correlate to the fire on the brass altar in the tabernacle.

If we continue in a straight line, the next piece of furniture is the brass laver filled with water. On a map of America, the laver would be positioned over the area where the Mississippi River flows. The mighty Mississippi is recognized as the waterway of America. It propels huge barges with shipping materials and provides irrigation for thousands of farms. The main substance in the laver was water and America's waterway is situated beneath the laver on the diagram.

The next piece of furniture is the golden candlestick called the menorah. Its main substance was oil. Not surprisingly, the tabernacle menorah is over Texas and Oklahoma, which are America's two major oil-producing states! The oil in the menorah was used to light the seven branches of the candlestick. The oil from Texas and Oklahoma is used to produce energy. In early America, lanterns containing oil were used to light colonial homes.

Looking north, we see the table of shewbread where bread made from Israeli-grown wheat was placed. In the diagram, the table of shewbread appears over the states of Nebraska, Kansas, and the Dakotas. These farming states are called America's breadbasket.

Continuing on, the golden altar lies over the region of Colorado. The main substances on the golden altar were hot coals of fire and the incense. The incense used in Moses' time was red and contained eleven different types of spices. Some of the incense from the ancient Temple was discovered in Qumran, Israel along with the Dead Sea scrolls. The incense had a deep red color and contained ten of the eleven spices of the Temple incense. The state of Colorado was named after the Colorado River. Spanish explorers named the river Colorado because it means *reddish colored*. Hot coals had to be used on the altar to burn the incense, and Colorado was known for its coal deposits.

Continuing past the golden altar toward the Holy of Holies, we have to pass through the veil. The veil is over America's continental divide! The continental divide is an imaginary line that marks the highest regions in the country. It is clearly seen on any map of America and on any satellite picture.

The Holy of Holies is the most important area of the tabernacle. It contains the golden Ark of the Covenant. This ark is over the area of Nevada and California. Both of these states, especially California, were noted for the discovery of gold. The state of California was founded in the late 1800s because of the gold rush.

The Almighty designed a dwelling place in the wilderness and determined the size and exact location of each piece of furniture. This mobile dwelling place was to be God's dwelling place among His chosen people. Here they would bring offerings, worship the Almighty, and hear God's Word through Moses and Aaron.

How sovereign that America is the only nation on earth whose geography symbolically correlates with the layout of the wilderness tabernacle! America is a nation that has financed the preaching of the Gospel around the world. Its worship has literally reached heavenly satellites because of freedom and the faith of its people.

Throughout Scripture, God used symbolism to reveal His mysteries and His greatness. Another interesting example is found by comparing the emblems of the tribes of Israel with those found on federal buildings in the Washington, D.C. Mall.

Emblems of the Twelve Tribes in Washington, D.C.

Just as the Israelites left behind religious oppression in Egypt and crossed the Red Sea en route to the Promised Land, our forefathers crossed the sea to a land of religious freedom. The Israelites traveled in an orderly fashion. They journeyed in four groups, each comprised of three tribes. Each group was assigned a position east, west, north or south of the tabernacle (*See Fig. E*).

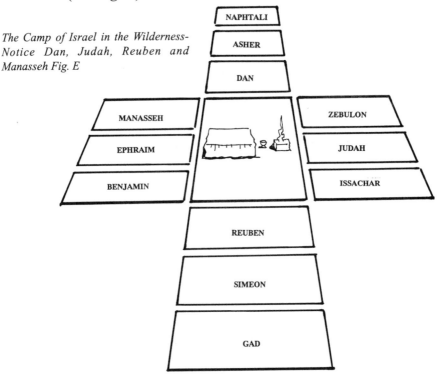

The Camp of Israel in the Wilderness- Notice Dan, Judah, Reuben and Manasseh Fig. E

For example, Judah was to the east, Reuben was to the south, Dan was to the north and Manesseh was to the west. To the east, Judah was the largest camp with 186,400 men (Numbers 2:9). To the south, Reuben was the second largest camp with 151,450 men (Numbers 2:16). To the north, Dan had 157,600 men (Numbers 2:31). To the west was Manesseh (along with Ephraim and Benjamin) with 108,100 men (Numbers 2:18-24). Each tribe had a specific emblem that became its seal of national identity. Judah's emblem was a lion, Reuben's was a man, Dan's was an eagle, and Manesseh's was an ox or a bull.

There were thirteen colonies in early America and there were thirteen tribes in ancient Israel. During David's reign, Jerusalem became the capital of Israel and it was located in the center of the nation. Washington, D.C. was purposely situated in the center of the states, halfway between Massachusetts and Georgia. Jerusalem was built on a foundation of white Jerusalem limestone and the stones of its protective outer wall were originally white. Pierre L'Enfant, an engineer and the main designer of Washington, D.C. said, "I see white buildings glistening in the sun. I see wide avenues and tree-lined parks. In the exact center of the city, on Jenkins Heights, I see the Capitol. This will be the home of the Congress, the men who make the laws of our new nation."

In ancient Israel at the Temple dedication, animals were offered as a sacrifice and eaten by the people while they rejoiced! When the cornerstone of the capitol was put down in 1793, citizens came to watch George Washington place it. After the ceremony, a 500-pound ox was killed, prepared, and served to the guests (Source: *The Story of the Capital,* Marilyn Prolman).

As more federal buildings were erected, the area became known as the Washington Mall. The arrangement of the buildings is noteworthy. To the north was the White House, to the east was the Capitol, to the south was the Jefferson Memorial, and to the west was the Lincoln Memorial. The Washington Monument was built in the center of the mall. Bill Cloud shared an interesting perspective with me about the layout of the primary monuments in the Washington Mall. There is a parallel between the layout of the Mall and the layout of the wilderness camp of Israel.

The Emblems of the Camp

Situated at the north of the wilderness camp was the camp of Dan, whose emblem was the eagle. To the north of the Washington Mall stands the White House. The man occupying the White House is the President, whose official seal is the eagle, the same emblem of ancient Dan!

Situated to the east of the camp was Judah, whose emblem was the lion. To the east of the Mall stands the Capitol. In front of the Capitol is a statue of Ulysses S. Grant, who is memorialized upon a horse, overlooking a beautiful fountain. Surrounding this fountain are four stone lions that represent the authority of the lawmakers. Judah's emblem was a lion, and the tribe of Judah was known as the lawgiving tribe (Genesis 49:10). Out of the tribe of Judah came the eternal lawgiver, Jesus the Messiah, who will one day literally govern the nations.

To the south was Reuben, whose emblem was a man. The Thomas Jefferson Memorial sits to the south of the Washington Mall. Jefferson was a Deist and a Unitarian. He believed in a Creator who retreated after creation was finished and left the affairs of men to themselves. He believed that only the good nature of men and their reasoning could be trusted. Jefferson was a Humanist thinker. His memorial shares the same relative position as Reuben in the wilderness camp, and Reuben's emblem was a statue of a man. It was Reuben who forgot God's laws and tried to act upon his decision making and strength.

To the west of the wilderness camp was the tribe of Ephraim, whose emblem was a bull or an ox. The Lincoln Memorial stands on the western part of the Mall. Lincoln was the only president who shared his first name, Abraham, with the founder of the nation of Israel. God told Abraham, "I am your shield and reward" (Genesis 15:1). God revealed that He would bless Abraham in times of conflict. God also promised Abraham that he would become a great nation and that Abraham's seed would be delivered out of Egyptian bondage. To confirm God's covenant, Abraham took animals and divided them in the middle. Afterward a "deep sleep fell upon him and a horror of great darkness fell upon him" (Genesis 15:12). God shielded Abraham Lincoln's nation from destruction as it was split between the north and south. A "horror of darkness," the Civil War ensued. Abraham, the father of Israel, survived his test and Abraham Lincoln saw the end of the horrible Civil War.

Joseph's sons were Ephraim and Manesseh. In his youth, Joseph's own brothers sold him into slavery. In the time of Lincoln, slavery was the spark that ignited the Civil War. During the Civil War, two brothers, the north and the south, fought each other. Ephraim and Manesseh were divided in Israel. Ironically, the first battle of the Civil War was at Bull Run, in the area of Manassas, Virginia. In the English translation of the Bible in Revelation 7:6, the tribe of Manesseh is called *Manassas*! Bull Run, Manassas, and a division between brothers all interconnect in Abraham Lincoln's day, thus the Lincoln Memorial.

In summary, the eagles (Dan and the White House) are to the north, and the lions (Judah and the Capitol) are to the east. The emblems of the man (Rueben and the Jefferson Memorial) sit to the south, and the bull or ox (Manses and the Lincoln Memorial) sits to the west (*See fig. F*).

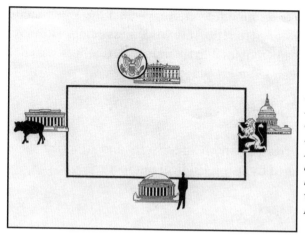

The tribe emblems of the wilderness camp can be found in or around the four land-marks bordering the National Mall. The Capitol Building has a lion, the Jefferson Memorial has a man, the Lincoln Memorial has a connection to an ox and the White House is home to the President, on whose emblem is the eagle.
Fig. F

The four major tribal emblems coincide uniquely with the four main federal buildings located in the Washington Mall. These four emblems — the eagle, the lion, the ox, and the man — are the same images found on the living creatures that worship God in His heavenly throne! The layout of the wilderness camp symbolized God's throne room. The same emblems surround God's Tabernacle. Likewise, in Washington, these emblems surround the Washington Monument, dedicated to the memory of the father of our nation. Interestingly, the original plans for the Washington Monument designated it to be a temple!

Israel and America Were Both Divided

Both Israel and America were once split into northern and southern realms. David and Solomon each ruled forty years, totaling eighty years before Israel was divided into North and South. America's Civil War started in 1861. Eighty years prior in 1781, George Washington and the Continental Army surrounded Cornwallis at Yorktown, and Cornwallis surrendered. Washington's envoy to Cornwallis was named Benjamin Lincoln. It was Lincoln who handled the terms of the surrender that marked the official birth of America. Eighty years later, Abraham Lincoln worked to preserve the nation from collapse.

The Cross on the Mall

An aerial view of Israel's wilderness camp formed the shape of a cross. Additionally, an aerial view of the Washington Mall forms the shape of a cross. It is difficult to determine for certain whether the Washington, D.C. Mall was purposely designed to reflect the wilderness camp. However, throughout this book, the many remarkable Hebraic and American parallels and cycles seem to have been Divinely planned.

Strange Prophetic Numbers and Cycles

There is another series of patterns that Israel and America share. These patterns are determined by using Biblical numbers.

1. The thirteenth year

Some consider thirteen to be a number that represents bad luck. Some hotels do not have a thirteenth floor. But the number thirteen represents a very important year in the life of a Jewish male. On the thirteenth year (plus one day) of a Jewish male's life, he is inducted into manhood through a ceremony called a Bar Mitzvah. The only record of Christ's youth is when He debated the scribes and doctors in the Temple at the age of twelve (Luke 2:42-47). It was customary at that age for young men to begin discussing the Law and questioning their elders as they prepared for their transition into manhood.

Israel actually had a total of thirteen tribes, although we usually hear the number twelve. Jacob had twelve sons, yet his son Levi did not receive an inheritance of land and wealth because he and his descendants were to live and serve in the Temple. Joseph's two sons were Ephraim and Manesseh. They were counted among the twelve sons of Jacob. So technically, there were thirteen tribes that entered the Promised Land.

Early America had thirteen colonies in the same way that Israel had thirteen tribes. Originally there was one colony called Virginia, the Old Dominion, named after the Virgin Queen Elizabeth I. Over time, the colonies formed states like Massachusetts (in New England), Pennsylvania (in the Mid-Atlantic), the Carolinas, and Georgia.

The number thirteen was used symbolically at times in American history. For example:

- There were 13 colonies.
- There are 13 stripes on our flag.

- The number 13 is also used symbolically regarding America's one dollar bill:
- There are 13 steps on the pyramid
- There are 13 letters in "Annuit Coeptis," the Latin above the pyramid
- There are 13 letters in "E Pluribus Unum"
- There are 13 stars above the eagle
- There are 13 plumes of feathers on each span of the eagle's wing
- There are 13 bars on the shield
- There are 13 leaves on the olive branch

2. The thirtieth year

Jesus began His ministry at the age of thirty (Luke 3:23). The Israelite priests were from the tribe of Levi. Levites were chosen to lead in spiritual matters and present offerings to the Lord in the tabernacle. Levite men could enter the priesthood at the age of thirty (Numbers 4:3). Thirty was considered to be an age of spirituality and spiritual maturity.

Thirty years after the Declaration of Independence was signed, a great revival took place in America. Between 1800 and 1810, revival spread throughout the east coast and all of the states. Just as Levite priests first entered God's Presence at age thirty, our nation first began experiencing powerful revival at the tender age of thirty.

.

3. The number fifty

Fifty is an important number in the Bible and in Judaism. At the age of fifty a priest could retire (Numbers 4:39). Every fifty years marked a time of Jubilee in Israel. The silver trumpets were blasted as liberty was proclaimed throughout the land. During the year of Jubilee, people were released from their debts and from slavery because, according to the Law, Hebrews were never to oppress one another. God also instructed that the stranger was not to be oppressed. The year of Jubilee was also a time of great increase as God blessed the land with bountiful crops (Leviticus 25:1-55).

Historically, America has opened its doors to strangers (or foreigners). It is not by chance that America has fifty states. Immigrants from around the world came to America, the land with fifty states, to find rest and release from oppression.

In 1701, William Penn signed Pennsylvania's Charter. Fifty years later, a commemorative bell was cast. Known as the Liberty Bell, it has served as one of America's most beloved symbols of freedom. Before the bell was cast, a Quaker named Isaac Norris selected a portion of Scripture from Leviticus 25:10 to be inscribed on it. It read: "Proclaim liberty throughout the land unto all the inhabitants thereof." This passage is found in the same Leviticus chapter that proclaims the year of Jubilee! In 1835 the bell was cracked and it never rang again. Thirty-eight years later in 1873, the beginning of the passage from Leviticus was inscribed on the bell. It read: "And ye shall hollow the fiftieth year and proclaim liberty to all the inhabitants through the land."

The Statue of Liberty has been a profound symbol for millions of immigrants who came to America through Ellis Island seeking freedom from oppression. Just as those who obeyed the Torah were given spiritual liberty and blessing, those who would pledge allegiance to America and its Constitution were guaranteed the right to experience liberty!

In Hebrew, "The United States of America" means *The Covenant Lands of America*. Just as ancient Israel was the "Land of the Covenant," America is also "The Land of the Covenant." Consider this:

- Both Israel and America were founded upon God's Word, the Bible.
- Both Israel and America were given responsibility to teach the Word to the nations.
- Both Israel and America share parallels that do not exist between other nations.

Even the election cycle of the American presidency has a Biblical basis. In the book of Numbers, the twelve tribes were to be counted. The people were to "Declare their pedigrees after their families, by the house of their fathers, according to the number of the names, from twenty years old and upward by their polls" (Numbers 1:18). This polling, or numbering, established the number of men in each tribe. Today, on the second Tuesday in November, every four years Americans go to the polls to vote. The person receiving the highest number of electoral votes wins the presidency.

The Hebraic patterns within America and Israel continue to be revealed in the Civil War.

Chapter 8

A NATION DIVIDED -
THE SPLIT BETWEEN
THE NORTH AND SOUTH

Hebrew Parallels with the Civil War and Israel's Divided Kingdom

"Every kingdom divided against itself is brought to desolation, and a house divided against a house falleth." (Luke 11:17)

Yet another interesting parallel is uncovered when we compare the division of Israel into two kingdoms with the American Civil War. When God brought the Hebrews out of Egyptian bondage, there were 600,000 men in the nation (Exodus 12:37). Upon adding the wives and children, most scholars estimate the total Hebrew population at the time of the exodus to be about 3,000,000. When the Constitution was signed, the American population was about 3,000,000 (Source: *Lee's Brief History of the United States*, Susan Lee, 1896).

Author Susan Lee wrote, "There were about 500,000 slaves who were found in all colonies, though much more south of the Potomac." When the Hebrews left Egypt, among them was a "mixed multitude" (Exodus 12:38). This group assimilated into the nation of Israel as it sought freedom in the Promised Land. By the time of our independence, we were also a mixed multitude of people whose emphasis was upon freedom.

David was the second king of Israel. He came from the tribe of Judah, the tribe of the "lawgiver" (Genesis 49:10). David ruled Israel for forty years and then his son Solomon ruled for another forty years. Together they ruled for eighty years. After Solomon died, his son Rehoboam took control of Israel. It was Rehoboam who caused a split in Israel, resulting in the formation of the northern and southern kingdoms (1 Kings 12:1-27). The split began eighty years after David became king. Eighty years after the British surrendered at Yorktown, the American Civil War began, which temporarily created the North and the South!

Splitting Over the Yoke

The motives causing division in Israel and America were prophetically similar. Rehoboam was King Solomon's son. He succeeded his father as king and sought the advice of both young and old regarding how to rule. The older men complained that Solomon had placed them under "a grievous yoke" (1 Kings 12:4). They were compelled to perform much heavy labor. They were tired of the heavy yoke and the high taxes. Then the young king sought counsel from the young men who grew up with him. They said, "Tell the people their yoke will be heavier and you will chastise them with scorpions" (1 Kings 12:11). When Rehoboam continued to place "a grievous yoke" upon the people, rebellion divided the nation into north and south. The people were tired of being treated like slaves.

"So Israel rebelled against the house of David, unto this day" (1 Kings 12:19). Rehoboam took 180,000 men from the tribes of Judah and Benjamin to fight against the house of Israel. Brother was fighting brother (1 Kings 12:21). God was grieved and warned him by saying, "You shall not go up nor fight against your brethren, the children of Israel, for this thing is from me" (1 Kings 12:24). The king refused God's instruction and armed the men of Benjamin and Judah for war (2 Chronicles 11:12).

Two Capitals and Two Kings

Ten tribes seceded from Israel and eleven states seceded from the United States before the Civil War. Two kings were appointed in Israel — one over the northern kingdom and one over the southern kingdom. Rehoboam was the king of the south and Jeroboam was the king of the north. The northern kingdom had seceded. On February 8, 1861, seven states formed the Confederate States of America and established a provisional Congress. The following day, Jefferson Davis became their president while Lincoln remained the Union President. Essentially, during the Civil War, America had two presidents (or kings).

The divided Israel had two capitals. The original capital was Jerusalem, where Rehoboam reigned. The second capital was established in Dan within the Northern Kingdom where Jeroboam reigned. Notice the strange parallel. As with ancient Israel, America was divided into north and south. It had two separate presidents and two capitals. Washington, D.C. was the capital of the north and Montgomery, Alabama (later Richmond, Virginia) was the capital of the south.

During most of Lincoln's administration, there was fighting between the North and South. The Bible tells us that the fighting between the northern and southern kings continued, "And there were wars between Rehoboam and Jeroboam continually" (2 Chronicles 12:15).

The Two Southern Generals

The south had two famous generals who frequently defeated the north in battle. One was Robert E. Lee and the other was Thomas Jonathan "Stonewall" Jackson. Lee was asked by Lincoln to serve as a Union general, but he declined. When asked about slavery, he replied, "If I owned the four million slaves in the south, I would sacrifice them all to the Union, but how can I draw my sword upon Virginia, my native state?" Lee also said, "The future is in the hands of Providence, but if the slaves of the South were mine I would surrender them all without a struggle to avert the war." Generals Lee and Jackson were both prayerful men who sought God to bring revival among their soldiers (Source: *Personal Reminiscences, Anecdotes, and Letters of General Robert E. Lee*, D. Appleton and Co., 1874, p. 138).

Lee was so concerned about his soldiers' eternal souls that one biographer wrote, "One almost feels that he cares more about winning souls than battles, for supplying his army with Bibles than with bullets and powder." Jackson and his army won victory after victory against the Union. When asked how he managed to be so calm in battle, he replied, "Captain, my religious belief teaches me to feel as safe in battle as in bed." He prayed often and gave God glory for his smallest successes. He even tried to avoid marching or fighting on the Sabbath day.

According to historians, Jackson prayed that God would baptize his army with The Holy Spirit. His personal letters indicate that he ordered religious services to be conducted. During the winter of 1862 and 1863, while the Confederate army camped near the Rappahannock, a great revival broke out. It is estimated that over 150,000 Confederate troops were converted to Christ during the war!

Lincoln's Prayer That Changed the War

When Rehoboam was king, the Egyptians prepared an invasion of Judah and Jerusalem. Scripture indicates that the princes of Israel and the king humbled themselves. And when the Lord saw they were humbled, He said, "I will not destroy them, but I will grant them some deliverance; and my wrath shall not be poured out upon Jerusalem" (2 Chronicles 12:6-7).

History recounts that there was great confusion amongst several Lincoln appointed Union leaders. In various places, Union armies lost battles, including one in Fredericksburg, which is not far from Washington. Lincoln began to question why the South was so successful in battle. Apparently he realized that prayer, fasting, and faith were the key to seeking God's answer. Consequently, on July 2, 1864, Congress adopted a resolution similar to an Old Testament prophetic lamentation. It called upon citizens to "confess and repent of their manifold sins, implore the compassion and forgiveness of the Almighty, and beseech him as Supreme Ruler of the world not to destroy us a people." Israel's leaders had spoken a similar prayer when it was divided many years before.

Finally, in the summer of 1864, General Sherman, Admiral Farragut, and Grant made inroads into the South and they began winning major victories. These victories helped Lincoln's re-election. It seems the real turning point in the war favoring the North came after a major decree made by President Abraham Lincoln. He was concerned about why the North had lost so many battles. He concluded that it was the nation's sins of slavery and pride. Lincoln called for a national Day of Humility, Fasting and Prayer. On April 30, 1863, Lincoln stated:

> "It is the duty of nations as well as of men to own their dependence upon the overruling power of God; to confess their sins and transgressions in humble sorrow, yet with assured hope that genuine repentance will lead to mercy and pardon." He concluded by saying, "It behooves us, then, to humble ourselves before the offended Power, and confess our national sins, and to pray for clemency and forgiveness."

After the people observed this decree, it seemed that the Union began winning the war. Two days after the decree, General Stonewall Jackson was accidentally shot and killed by one of his own men. The battle at Gettysburg came soon after but, without Jackson and Divine Providence, the South was never to succeed.

Lincoln later revealed his personal prayer for the battle at Gettysburg. He knew that if Gettysburg were lost, the Union would be dissolved. Lincoln shared:

> "I went to my room one day, and I locked the door, and got down on my knees before Almighty God, and prayed to him mightily for victory at Gettysburg. I told him this was His war, and our cause His cause, but we shouldn't stand another Fredericksburg or Chancellorsville. And I there and then made a solemn vow to Almighty God, that if He would stand by you boys at Gettysburg, I would stand by Him. After that a sweet comfort swept into my soul."

It is written in 2 Chronicles 12:7 that, when God saw the princes and the king of Israel humbling themselves, He declared: "They have humbled themselves; therefore I will not destroy them, but I will grant them some deliverance and my wrath shall not be poured out upon Jerusalem." Abraham Lincoln was one of America's most humble presidents. Had another been in the White House, our nation could have been dealt a fatal blow.

As with ancient Israel, America was divided over a "yoke." Israel's "yoke" was harsh rule and a heavy tax burden, while America's "yoke" was slavery. God promised Israel that one day He would reunite the divided nation into one (Ezekiel 37:16-19). God not only saved America, but He reunited our nation through the prayers and leadership of humble, praying men. The evidence of His grace is that we were able to come together after such devastation. After four years of war, Lincoln said he had no hatred in his heart for the people in the South. He said, "Judge not that ye be not judged. They are just what we would be if in their position."

During his second inauguration in March 1865, Lincoln delivered the greatest speech of his life. He stepped forward and kissed a Bible that was opened to the fifth chapter of Isaiah and he began his speech. Carl Schurz wrote, "No ruler had ever spoke words like these to his people. America had never before had a president who had such words in the depths of his heart." Lincoln's closing remarks were:

> "Fondly do we hope — fervently do we pray — that this scourge of war may speedily pass away. Yet, if God wills that it continue until all the wealth is piled by the bondman's two hundred and fifty years of unrequited toil shall be sunk, and until every drop of blood drawn with the lash shall be paid by another drawn with the sword, as was said three thousand years ago, so still it must be said, the judgments of the Lord are true and righteous altogether. With malice toward none and with charity for all; with firmness in the right, as God gives us the right, let us strive on to finish the work we are in; to bind up the nation's wounds; to care for him who should have borne the battle, and for his widow, and for his orphan — to do all which may achieve and cherish a just and lasting peace among ourselves and with all nations."

No one knew that this humble man would become one of America's greatest presidents. During Lincoln's speech, he quoted Isaiah chapter 5, which includes reference to a new vineyard — the same Scripture on which the theme of this book is based. Apparently, Lincoln believed that the prophecy referred to America's Civil War. Two months later, the same speech was repeated at Lincoln's funeral in Springfield, Illinois. The vineyard had survived. More wars were to come and additional presidents would die premature deaths. Those deaths would fall upon presidents elected on a zero year and would be called the "zero cycle."

Chapter 9

THE ZERO CYCLE AND THE DEATHS OF AMERICAN PRESIDENTS

Is there an Ancient Indian Curse on America's Leaders?

"As the bird by wandering, as the swallow by flying, so the curse causeless shall not come."
(Proverbs 26:2)

One hundred years after Lincoln's death, author Gordon Lindsey questioned, "What about the new president? Will he also die in office?" Lindsey was referring to the strange cycle called the "zero curse" and how it impacted American presidents. He stated, "If this cycle of the presidents continues, then the president elected in 1960 will die sometime between 1961 and 1969." Lindsey was correct. The president-elect was John Kennedy, whose life ended abruptly in Dallas, Texas at the hands of an assassin.

This "zero cycle" was first noted after Roosevelt's death. The information was published, but few paid attention until after Kennedy's death. The topic resurfaced again after the assassination attempt on Ronald Reagan, who had been elected in 1980, another year containing a zero. I once asked Louis Mason, a dear friend and former Secret Service Agent who was with Reagan during his administration, if the Secret Service Agency was aware of the zero year cycle. Louis replied that a few of the Christian agents had heard of it but, to his knowledge, it was never discussed in detail.

The "zero cycle" or "zero curse" appears to have started after the death of those who fought in the Revolutionary War. Three early presidents who had signed the Declaration of Independence all died on July 4. John Adams and Thomas Jefferson both died the same day, July 4, 1826, exactly fifty years after the Declaration was signed. James Madison passed away on July 4, 1831. William Harrison, elected president in 1840, rode in his January inaugural parade and afterward got a cold that developed into pleurisy. He died about 30 days after his inauguration and was the first president to die in office.

Abraham Lincoln's Dream

Twenty years later, Abraham Lincoln was elected. While living in Springfield, Illinois, Lincoln befriended Rev. James Smith, pastor of a Presbyterian Church. Smith recalled Lincoln's conversation before he became president. He had lent Lincoln the book, *The Christian Defense.* After reading it several times Smith said, "From then on Mr. Lincoln attended church regularly, even the prayer meetings and the revival meetings."

At his farewell speech in Springfield, Lincoln said, "Unless the great God who assisted him (speaking of General George Washington) shall be with me and aid me, I must fail; but if the same Omniscient Mind and Almighty Arm that directed and protected him shall guide me and support me, I shall not fail. I shall succeed" (Source: *America's Presidents and Destiny*, Gordon Lindsay).

Lincoln believed that dreams could predict future events. The day after his election, he went home and sat down before a bureau that had a swinging mirror. As he looked into the mirror, he saw a reflection of himself that had one body and two heads. One head was very pale. He jumped up and the vision vanished. When he sat down again he saw the same image, this time much clearer. He told Mrs. Lincoln what he saw and she interpreted it to mean that he would be elected for two terms. The pale face represented his second term through which he would not live (Source: *Lincoln the Unknown,* Dale Carnegie).

At the end of the Civil War, Lincoln had another dream. He saw himself in a coffin with thousands of people weeping. He felt that his death was certain. On Good Friday April 14, 1865, an actor named John Wilkes Booth shot Lincoln to death at Ford's Theater. His fatal head wound rendered him unconscious for about nine hours before his death.

He seemed to have been unappreciated until after his death. Even his own Republican Party spoke of electing another president. Lincoln's Emancipation Proclamation announced the end of slavery according to law. But it would be over 100 years later, after Kennedy's death, that the intolerant practice of racism would begin to crumble.

James Garfield - Wrong Place at the Wrong Time

Twenty years later, James Garfield was elected president. At the Republican Convention in 1880, not one vote was cast for him on the first ballot. In the next four, he received one vote. He disappeared during the fourteenth through the eighteenth ballots. He got one vote in the 33rd ballot. Then things changed, and he ended up winning the nomination by a landslide! Three months later, after being elected president, Garfield was shot at the railway depot in Washington by a despondent office seeker named Charles Guiteau. The terrible "zero cycle" had struck again.

William McKinley and the Pan American Exposition

William McKinley was elected in 1900 and became the 25th President. At the Pan American Exposition in Buffalo, New York, vast crowds sought to shake his hand. Concerned about his safety, George Cortelyou, the president's personal secretary, unsuccessfully tried to cancel the event. Leon Czlogosz stood in line wearing a dark suit with a bandage on his right arm. No one noticed the .32 caliber revolver hidden within the bandage. While face-to-face with McKinley, Czlogosz fired at point blank range and the president slumped as panic broke out. McKinley did not die instantly, but an immediate operation resulted in a gangrenous wound that killed him.

The Cycle and the 1920 Election

The cycle continued with the election of Warren G. Harding in 1920. Harding, the 29th president, surrounded himself with unscrupulous men who were willing to sell national resources to the highest bidder. Harding's administration was considered to be one of the most corrupt in America's history. For example, Albert B. Fall, Secretary of the Interior, was convicted of bribery for accepting $100,000 from Edward Dohoney in connection with the Elk Hills Naval Oil Reserve in California.

In 1923, Harding set out on a speaking tour. As it progressed, people noticed that he seemed to be aging before their eyes. When he returned home, he suddenly became violently ill and died. Rumors spread that he had been poisoned. Other rumors suggested that Mrs. Harding had something to do with his death because she refused to have an autopsy and immediately had the body buried. There was no evidence to prove the rumors. Harding became the fifth president in a row who had been elected on a zero year to die while in the White House.

Roosevelt and His 666 Votes

After receiving 666 votes in his first nomination, President Roosevelt was elected president in 1932. Because of his popularity, he ran for a third term in 1940 and a fourth in 1944 but he died during his fourth term. The president was stricken while sitting for an artist in Warm Springs, Georgia. Interestingly, Roosevelt ran against Wendell Wilkie in 1940. If Wilkie had won, would he have survived the presidency? Wilkie suffered a heart attack and died on October 8, 1944. Consequently, whoever was elected in 1940 would not have lived through his full term! After six zero year presidents died in office, some wondered what would occur during the next zero year election.

The Death of John F. Kennedy — Elected 1960

The 1960 race between Richard Nixon and John Kennedy was one of the closest elections in history. Nixon served under Eisenhower as Vice President and Kennedy served as a senator from Massachusetts. Although there were severe voting irregularities and alleged fraud in Illinois, Kennedy triumphed, becoming the first Catholic president in American history.

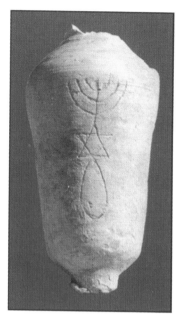

While archaeologists debate the age and authenticity of the "messianic seal," it nevertheless is becoming a popular emblem among Christians who love their Hebraic roots. **Fig. 1**

The so-called Messianic seal seen etched on this stone vase. Written in paleo-Hebrew on the bottom of the vase is "oil of the spirit." **Fig. 2**

The grotto on Mount Zion where the pottery was allegedly discovered. **Fig. 3**

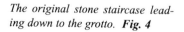

The original stone staircase leading down to the grotto. **Fig. 4**

This large room connects to another cistern by following the tunnel in the background. **Fig. 5**

This area is a series of cata-combs, many now closed off and sealed. **Fig. 6**

This is the area where, in 1969, Tech Otheeos is said to have dis-covered the pottery engraved with the so-called "messianic seal." **Fig. 7**

This Orthodox school on Mount Zion was built over the site of a church commissioned by the mother of Constantine. *Fig. 8*

A small portion of a mosaic floor located in the basement of the Orthodox school. This is a remnant of the ancient church built by Constantine's mother. *Fig. 9*

Perry with his friend Israel from Jerusalem. It was Israel who prayed with Perry in his office when the prophetic word came forth.

On November 29, 1998, Perry Stone met then Texas Governor George W. Bush at the Western Wall in Israel.

The future President stopped to meet our tour group of over 150 people. Many of them encouraged him to run for President.

Gimel   Vav   Resh

Gore

Beit   Vav   Shiyn

Bush

The name "Gore" transliterated into Hebrew.

The name "Bush" transliterated into Hebrew.

The Hebrew letters have been reversed to read from left to right!

Several weeks before his death, he met with Evangelist Billy Graham. In a television interview on Larry King Live, Graham recounted how Kennedy had asked him if he believed in the literal return of Jesus Christ. When Graham replied that he did Kennedy said, "Why don't we hear about this in the Catholic church?" Graham sensed that Kennedy was hungry for spiritual knowledge and that he was searching for deeper spiritual truth.

The Haitian Curse Against Kennedy

Three succeeding Kennedy generations have been stricken with tragedy. Joseph Kennedy, Jr. was killed in a military plane crash, John Kennedy was murdered in Dallas, and Robert Kennedy was assassinated in California. Ted was humiliated by an incident in Chappaquidik, and John Kennedy, Jr. died in a plane crash. This has led many to ask, "Is there a curse on the Kennedy family?"

Allegedly, there was a curse placed upon John Kennedy after his blockade of the island of Haiti. Haiti was controlled by Papa Doc, a dictator and professed witch doctor. According to a former missionary to Haiti, Papa Doc claimed that he and a group of witch doctors came together and cast a deadly voodoo spell on Kennedy. In this act, a voodoo doll represented Kennedy and sharp needles were driven into the doll in symbolic areas of attack. The needles were allegedly placed in Kennedy's head. An evil spirit was commanded to find a Kennedy assassin. Several weeks later, an assassin shot Kennedy in the head. The Bible makes it clear that occult curses have no power over people who are engaged in a covenant with God (Numbers 23:1-30). I don't want to judge Kennedy's personal religious faith, but being religious is different from being born again and entering a covenant relationship with God through Jesus Christ. Religion cannot protect you, but a covenant relationship with God can!

Two weeks before his trip to Dallas, Kennedy sensed that his life was in danger. His own secretary warned him not to go to Dallas because she did not feel good about the trip. Kennedy disregarded the feeling and went anyway. On that beautiful day in Dallas, the assassin waited in the book depository window for the presidential motorcade to turn the corner and provide a clear shot. In 1960, we saw yet another beloved president fade into eternity when the cycle struck again.

I have toured the book depository in Dallas. It now houses a museum on its sixth floor. It is an eerie place as people often stand in silence remembering the assassination. You may have heard the following information about the parallels between the deaths of John F. Kennedy and Abraham Lincoln. Without a doubt, history does repeat itself.

- Lincoln was elected in 1860 and Kennedy in 1960 — 100 years apart.
- Both of their Vice Presidents were named Johnson: Andrew Johnson and Lyndon Johnson.
- Andrew Johnson was born in 1808 and Lyndon Johnson in 1908 — 100 years apart.
- John Wilkes Booth (Lincoln's assassin) was born in 1839 and Lee Harvey Oswald (Kennedy's assassin) was born in 1939 — 100 years apart.
- The names Lincoln and Kennedy each contain seven letters.
- The names John Wilkes Booth and Lee Harvey Oswald each contain fifteen letters.
- The names Andrew Johnson and Lyndon Johnson both contain thirteen letters.
- Both Vice Presidents were southern Democratic Senators before being elected.
- Both presidents had contested elections.
- Both were involved with Civil Rights.
- Both presidents were U.S. Congressmen before becoming presidents.
- Both were shot on a Friday.
- Both were fatally shot in the head.
- Both were shot in the presence of their wives.
- Both experienced the death of a child while they were in the White House.
- Lincoln had a secretary named Kennedy, and Kennedy had a secretary named Lincoln.
- Both secretaries warned the presidents not to go to the places where they died.
- A southern radical shot each president.
- Lincoln was shot from a theater and the assassin hid in a warehouse. Kennedy was shot from a warehouse and the assassin hid in a theater.

- Both assassins were killed before they stood trial.
- Lincoln was shot in Ford's Theater and Kennedy was shot in a Ford Lincoln limousine.

In preparing for her husband's funeral, Jackie Kennedy searched through the White House library for information concerning the death of Lincoln and how to prepare for the death of a slain president. Kennedy lay in state in the Capitol rotunda where a statue of Lincoln overlooked the coffin. Kennedy was buried in Arlington National Cemetery just across the river from the Lincoln Memorial.

Ecclesiastes 1:9 may explain why there are so many parallels between the lives and deaths of Lincoln and Kennedy. Solomon wrote, "The thing that hath been is that which shall be; and that which is done is that which shall be done: and there is no new thing under the sun." Just as the seven Feasts of Israel have a prophetic fulfillment, history seems to run in cycles. This is demonstrated by the many parallels that Lincoln and Kennedy shared.

The Attempt on Ronald Reagan's Life in 1980

When Reagan was elected in 1980, I was aware of the "zero cycle." Because of his age, I thought that he might die of natural causes while in office. At the time, I was unaware of the prophecy in 1970 regarding his presidency. Nonetheless, I prayed for his success and protection.

I was ministering in Asheboro, North Carolina when reports of an assassination attempt on his life flashed on television. I recall my heart feeling like it had dropped into my stomach. I stayed glued to the television awaiting news, stunned with surprise and disbelief. Soon the videotape of the attempted murder was shown. A bullet had missed Reagan's heart by an inch. His life was spared and he completed two terms in office.

Was it luck that saved Reagan's life? Nancy was so frightened that she began to consult astrologers to seek safe times for Reagan to travel. God prohibits astrology and says that it has no power over life or death (Deuteronomy 4:19, 17:3-4). The real secret to Reagan's safety was prayer! I remember speaking to Christian musician Phil Driscoll about the "zero cycle" in the mid 1980s. He told me about Reagan's secretary, who was a Spirit-filled Christian. She prayed in the Oval Office and interceded for the president every morning. He also told me that there were a large number of Christians on Reagan's staff who prayed for him regularly.

Scripture teaches that people can win spiritual battles as they walk out their prophetic destiny. For example, Paul wrote to young Timothy when he was having difficulty being accepted as pastor of a large church. Paul reminded Timothy that, "With the prophecy that went before you, war a good warfare" (1 Timothy 1:18). If one is certain of God's prophetic destiny, then prayer and intercession will thwart the enemy's efforts to stop its fulfillment. This is especially important with regard to our nation's highest leaders. A prayer strike force should ask God to form a hedge of protection around spiritual and political leaders in our nation.

How Long Can a Curse Continue?

In Scripture, a spiritual curse can result from God's disfavor. He can lift His protective hedge or permit the enemy to rise up against a nation or a person. Scripture teaches that a curse can continue for several generations. When Joshua conquered Jericho, he pronounced a curse upon any person who rebuilt the wicked city. Joshua spoke the curse, "...Cursed be the man before the Lord, that raiseth up and buildeth this city Jericho: he shall lay the foundation thereof in his firstborn, and in his youngest son shall he set up the gates of it" (Joshua 6:26). After its destruction, Jericho sat in ruins until 400 years later when Ahab instructed Hiel to rebuild it. As Hiel began to rebuild the city, his oldest son died. When the project was completed, his youngest son died.

> "In his days did Hiel the Bethelite build Jericho: he laid the foundation thereof in Abiram his firstborn, and set up the gates thereof in his youngest son Segub, according to the word of the Lord, which he had spoken by Joshua the son of Nun."
> (1 Kings 16:34)

If the "zero cycle" results from a verbal curse, its cause must be identified and then it must be broken. President Reagan broke the "zero cycle" while in office. I believe it was because of his personal commitment to Christ, along with much fervent prayer during his term in office. Reagan gave special honor to the Bible and sought the counsel of several godly ministers. Every leader needs Spirit-filled Christians to surround him or her with continual prayer, to expose the plans of the enemy, and to keep a hedge of protection around the leader and his or her family.

Individuals who know about the "zero cycle" commonly ask three questions:

- Why does this cycle manifest about every twenty years in years that end in zero?
- Why has it impacted Presidents of the United States?
- Who or what may be responsible for this curse?

Cursed by Shedding Innocent Blood

I have spent much time researching the correlation between the "zero cycle" and American presidents. I now believe that the zero cycle may be a result of how our Founding Fathers treated the Native American Indians.

With all of its greatness, we must be aware that America's early history is blood stained. Although we have fought to defend freedom, to stop the spread of atheistic Communism, and to deliver nations from terrible dictators, much innocent blood was shed on American soil. Multitudes of Native American Indians were slain at the hands of early, gold-seeking settlers from Europe. Columbus, who called the natives "Indians" since he thought he had landed in India, was tempted by their golden ornaments. Rumors of gold spread throughout Europe, causing Spanish explorers like Hernando Cortez (1519) to come to Mexico in search of gold. Cortez killed thousands of Aztec Indians, shipping their gold to Spain. The English and French sent ships to South America, Mexico, and North America in search of lost cities and hidden gold. Any Indian attempting to defend his village from the intruders met with the swift punishment of death.

I will add that there were missionaries to the Indians, such as John Eliot (1631), Roger Williams (1636), David Brainard (1700), and John Wesley (1735) who were committed to teaching the Gospel of Christ's love to the Indians. While white men invaded the territory and chased Indians from their land, some Indians befriended the missionaries. The struggle between the new Americans and the Native Indians continued through the birth of America and its early presidents.

Harrison and the Shawnee Indians

The first president to die in office (elected in a zero year) was William Henry Harrison. By the time Harrison became president, most of the Indians had been reduced to poverty, their hunting lands had already been carved up by the new farmers in their midst, and they were regularly victimized by traders. Harrison had added more than fifty million acres to the public lands" (Source: *The Presidents*, Bill Harris).

Harrison, born in Virginia, became the governor of Indiana. For years, he dealt with the Indians and purchased their lands on behalf of the government. Among Harrison's contacts were a highly respected Shawnee Indian named the Prophet and his brother Tecumseh. Harrison considered the Prophet to be cunning and unreliable, so he negotiated with Tecumseh on several occasions. Harrison was careful in his negotiations because he did not want the Indians to ever side with the British.

Tippecanoe served as the Shawnee capital much like Washington, D.C. served as America's capital. When tension rose between the Indians and the white men, Harrison had a stockade built and christened it Fort Harrison. Hostilities were brewing, but Tecumseh advised his brother not to attack until their Indian confederation was stronger. However, the Prophet ordered an attack just before daybreak. It took place on November 7, 1811, and it was a fatal battle for the Shawnees.

The presidential elections were held in November and, in some years, the election fell on the seventh of the month (including the election of 2000).

Harrison was known as the Indian fighter when he ran on the Whig party ticket in 1840. On May 29, 1840, over 30,000 Harrison supporters conducted a massive rally near Tippecanoe, drinking hard cider and eating roast beef. The event reminded everyone of Harrison's defeat of the hated Indians. The publicity helped his campaign and he eventually won the White House. Oddly, Harrison died a month after assuming the presidency, which some think was a result of a curse placed upon him by Tecumseh.

The white men commonly gave the Indians whiskey, causing them to get drunk. The Prophet denounced this action and told the Indians to refrain from drinking the whiskey. Even today, alcoholism is a problem among the Native American Indians. The Bible gives a specific warning to those who give their neighbors strong drink or alcohol:

"Woe unto him that giveth his neighbor drink, that puttest thy bottle to him, and makest him drunken also...the cup of the Lord's right hand shall be turned unto thee...violence shall cover thee..."
(Habakkuk 2:15-17)

Some historians have called the Indians wild savage scalp hunters. While this may have been true, in many cases, the Indians considered the white men to be enemies who intruded upon their land. Indians burned buildings and pillaged the white men's belongings because they wanted to run them off the land. Then the white men retaliated. In reality some, but certainly not all, of America's early leaders:

- shed the innocent blood of the Indians, including women and children;
- sold or traded whiskey and hard liquor, affecting Indian families to this day;
- expelled the Indians from land that had been theirs for centuries;
- marched Indians on foot across rough terrain, causing thousands of deaths.

On November 7, 1811, the Shawnees had been dealt a fatal blow. The next year The War of 1812 broke out. Many think that the Indians retaliated by joining the English. From 1840 forward, every twenty years in a year that ended in zero, an American president elected in that year died while in office (with the exception of President Reagan).

The Indian Connection

Another coincidence relates to the "zero cycle" and the Indians. From the early 1600s to Lincoln's day, Indians were killed and driven off their land. Two cultures clashed and the Indians lost much in the process. Many of the slain presidents were from states that were once highly populated with Indians and the sites of fierce Indian battles. The list includes Ohio, Illinois, Kentucky, Indiana, New York, and Massachusetts. Following is a list of presidents elected in a zero year who were from these states:

- 1860 - Lincoln was born in Kentucky but lived in Illinois
- 1880 - James Garfield was from Ohio

- · 1900 - William McKinley was from Ohio
- · 1920 - Warren G. Harding was from Ohio
- · 1940 - Franklin Roosevelt was from New York
- · 1960 - John F. Kennedy was from Massachusetts

Although Reagan survived the "zero curse," it is interesting that he was born in Tampico, Illinois, the same state where Lincoln lived when elected president. These six presidents were born in areas where some of the most severe bloodshed occurred.

In 1830, a law was passed that required the Indians to relocate. Ten years later in 1840, over 60,000 Indians walked the trail of tears on their journey westward. In 1840, William Harrison, the "Indian fighter," was elected president. He became deathly ill and died a few days after his inauguration, thus becoming the first president to fall under the "zero cycle."

First the Indians — Then the Slaves

It was not just the conflict with the Indians that impacted America. The scourge of slavery also plagued the nation. Abraham Lincoln, elected in 1860, was determined to set the slaves free. Some slave owners terribly mistreated the slaves, at times to the point of death. The soil of the young nation was again stained with innocent blood. By 1860, the nation was divided with brother turning against brother in the Civil War. Thousands died, cities were burned, homes were destroyed, and families were shattered. The Civil War brought an end to slavery, but the nation then witnessed the untimely death of its president.

I do not believe that America has ever repented or made atonement for the shedding of innocent blood within our borders. The frontiersmen fought natives, annexed land, and conquered through wars. The trail of tears is a sad example of how our government moved the Indian tribes from their original lands to make room for the white settlers. It is possible that both cultures could have eventually lived together in peace, but whenever the Indians resisted, it meant war. One Indian said, "I am a good man. Why am I treated this way?" The reply from an American soldier was, "The only good Indians are dead ones!"

If the "zero curse" originated because innocent blood was shed and it was sealed by the curse of a powerful Indian leader, can we look to the Bible to understand how the shedding of innocent blood can bring a curse? We know that "God hates the hands of those that shed innocent blood" (Proverbs 6:16-17). The Lord warned Noah, "Whoso sheddeth man's blood, by man shall his blood be shed: for in the image of God made he man" (Genesis 9:6). Scripture is not just a book of ancient opinions. It is filled with warnings from the Almighty, who also said, "Heaven and earth shall pass away, but my words shall not pass away" (Matthew 24:35). Because the Almighty is the same yesterday, today, and forever these warnings apply today.

The Commander in Chief

The President of the United States is the Commander in Chief of America's armed forces. God scolded Israel as He announced, "I gave thee a king in mine anger, and took him away in my wrath" (Hosea 13:11).

At age twenty, a male was old enough to become a soldier in Israel (Numbers 1:3). Interestingly, the "zero curse" has manifested with leaders elected at twenty-year intervals.

Cursed for Up to Four Generations

Scripture does refer to the "curse of shedding innocent blood." Christ rebuked His generation for its unbelief. He said that God would allow the sacred Temple and the city of Jerusalem to be destroyed because the Hebrews shed the blood of righteous men of God. Christ said, "That upon you may come all the righteous blood shed upon the earth, from the blood of righteous Abel unto the blood of Zacharias whom ye slew between the Temple and the altar." Jesus said that severe judgment would fall upon His generation (Matthew 23:35,36). About forty years later in the year 70 A.D., Rome's tenth legion destroyed Jerusalem and the Temple and killed men, women, and children.

God warned that He would "visit the iniquity of the fathers upon the third and fourth generation" (Exodus 20:5; 34:7; Numbers 14:18). An average generation is forty years long (Psalms 95:10). Since William Harrison, the first president to die in office was elected in 1840, four generations of 40 years each would bring us exactly to the year 2000. This brings us to a serious question. Was the "zero curse" permanently broken with Ronald Reagan, or will the president elected in the year 2000 have to break it again? Scripture says that the iniquity of the fathers continues to the third and fourth generation. Therefore, the president elected in 2000 would prophetically conclude the fourth generation.

The President Elected on the Year 2000

The 2000 election was unlike any other in our recent history. No one could predict the winner. The Northeast and West Coast states chose the Democratic candidate and the Southern and Midwestern states chose the Republican. Contrasting opinions from each side reflected America's moral and cultural divide.

During the Civil War, America was also severely divided. The issues of constitutional rights and secession were argued, but at the core of the conflict, it was the definition of life that divided the country. African-American slaves were denied the dignity of human life in the name of economic convenience, much as unborn children today are denied the right to live in the name of personal right to convenience. Then and now, we see controversy and divisiveness over the issue of who has rights over someone else's life.

Regarding the deaths of our presidents, some people believe that whatever will be, will be. Others believe that there is a specific time appointed for one to die. One Scripture disproves this view. It asks, "Why shouldest thou die before thy time" (Ecclesiastes 7:17)? Solomon implied that it was possible to die prematurely. In the book of Job, Satan invaded Job's life and brought calamity. Satan wanted to kill Job, but the Lord said, "You can attack his body, but you cannot take his life" (Job 2:4-7). It was Job's covenant relationship with God that caused a protective wall to stand between the enemy and Job's life!

In light of this, we can go to Scripture to understand how the "zero curse" can be broken. First, personal and national repentance is needed. We must denounce the innocent blood that has been shed and ask for forgiveness. Second, we must make right any wrong. Our instruction comes from the story of King David. When he was king, the nation of Israel was under a curse. David realized this and knew that it had to be broken, so he followed God's instruction and broke the curse.

David Broke the Curse in Gibeon

Second Samuel 21 tells a heartening story. There was a famine in Israel when David was king, and he sought the Lord to understand what had caused the curse. The Lord answered him and said, "It is for Saul, and for his bloody house, because he slew the Gibeonites" (2 Samuel 21:1). Before David, King Saul was responsible for killing a group of innocent people from the area of Gibeon. The famine that David witnessed resulted from the Gibeonite's bloodshed.

Few people understand God's teachings concerning blood. Scripture says, "The life of the flesh is in the blood" (Leviticus 17:11). The Hebrew word life comes from nephesh, which means *soul*. We could say, "The life-giving force of the body is found in the blood." When an innocent person's blood is shed, Scripture teaches that it literally has a voice that cries out to the Lord. When Cain murdered his brother Abel, the Lord asked Cain, "Where is your brother Abel?" Cain replied, "Am I my brother's keeper?" Then God replied, "The voice of your brother's blood cries to me from the ground" (Genesis 4:9-10). In Hebrew, the word blood in this text is plural and not singular. It reads, the "voice of thy brothers blood(s)." Rabbis teach that Cain killed not only Abel, but all of Abel's future children.

This is why shedding innocent blood, whether it belongs to an infant or to a mature adult, is so terrible. The very legacy of an entire family is erased from earth! Descendants from that lineage who will never be born could have impacted the very course of history. Since the blood type of a child comes from its father, God literally heard the secret voice hidden within Abel's DNA as it cried out from the earth. Apparently, in David's time, the blood of the Gibeonites also cried out from the earth. The Gibeonites were Amorite descendants. Israel had sworn an oath not to harm the Amorites, yet Saul broke that oath and murdered many of them.

When a person shed innocent blood under the old covenant, the murderer, if proven guilty without a doubt, was sentenced to death. Since Saul was already dead, his sons received the death sentence in order to remove the curse from the land. This seems radical, but blood was offered on the altar under the old covenant to make atonement for sins (Leviticus 17:11).

Breaking the Curse under the New Covenant

We are now living under a new covenant that was ratified through the death and resurrection of Jesus Christ. Scripture says, "Christ has redeemed us from the curse of the law being made a curse for us" (Galatians 3:13). It is as though we were held in prison, guilty as charged, and faced execution. Then suddenly, the jailor unlocked the door and said, "You are free if you want to be, because a man named Jesus has been executed in your place!"

The two main elements of redemption are repentance and forgiveness. To repent means to be sorry for one's actions. It also means to turn away from those sinful choices and to head in a new direction, or choose new behavior. To be forgiven means that you are released from the eternal consequences of your sin. For example, if I lie about you, I should ask you to forgive me; then, I should tell you that I regret having spoken the lies and ask you to release me from the offense it caused in your heart.

Regarding America's "zero curse," I want to sort out how to apply the New Testament model of forgiveness to what happened between the early settlers and the Native American Indians. The President and Congress, who symbolically represent the early settlers, should formally ask the Native American Indians for forgiveness. The government should change unacceptable laws regarding the Indians and make appropriate atonement.

Some people point out that some Indian lands were purchased with money, but this is not the point. There needs to be public repentance by asking for forgiveness on behalf of the "sins of the fathers." Remember, the unchanging Word of the Lord says, "The iniquity of the fathers will be visited upon the third and fourth generation" (Exodus 20:5).

Daniel understood this spiritual principle as he witnessed the Hebrews being carried away into Babylonian exile over 2,600 years ago. As the predicted seventy years of captivity came near its end, Daniel prayed to ask God to forgive Israel for the sins of the fathers (Daniel 9:4-19). Afterward, the Hebrews were permitted to return to Israel and to rebuild their nation and the Holy City of Jerusalem.

Often throughout history leaders have, in times of national emergency, war, or distress, called people to prayer. But how many, with the possible exception of Abraham Lincoln, have called an entire nation to repent for its sins? Today's society is so spiritually ignorant that many would ask, "What does the word repent mean?" or "What have we done wrong?" The fact remains that God honors His Word and those who will obey it will certainly have God's favor. With the possibility of this curse extending to the fourth generation and perhaps beyond 2000, what can our leaders do to break this cycle?

Four Spiritual Guidelines for Future American Leaders

1. Repent and make atonement to those who have been wronged.

Asking for forgiveness is not a weakness; to the contrary, it is a sign of moral character. Only the proud cannot ask for forgiveness and pride will eventually bring destruction (Proverbs 16:18). Asking people for forgiveness and making amends is the true Christ-like way to behave. This will ensure peace and God's favor, something man cannot give. There are other important guidelines.

If I were the president and believed that the "zero curse" resulted from mistreatment of the Native American Indians, I would call together the Indian leaders, truly apologize for the sins of the fathers, and pronounce spiritual reconciliation between the past and the future to the nation. I would not do this just to break a cycle; I would do it because it is the right thing to do.

2. Do not walk in fear.

Dake's Annotated Bible Concordance states that the words "fear not" and "be not afraid" are mentioned in some form 365 times in Scripture. So the Almighty has given us a "fear not" for every day of the year. People cannot be effective if they live in fear. Each of us must cherish the promises in Psalms 91 — when we abide in the secret place of the Almighty, we can be assured of His favor and His protection.

3. Don't ignore warnings.

The apostle Paul was a Jew who received Christ as Messiah. Afterward, many of his Jewish companions felt betrayed, so they persecuted Paul. Some made attempts on his life. On one occasion, the Holy Spirit warned Paul not to travel to Jerusalem because trouble awaited him (Acts 21:4).

Paul was warned of danger a second time, but he was stubborn and ignored the warnings and went anyway. He was arrested and imprisoned. Had he avoided Jerusalem at that time, his life's journey could have been different.

Abraham Lincoln also received warnings. His secretary urged him not to go to Ford's Theater the night of his assassination. Some claim that John Kennedy's secretary warned him not to go to Dallas. I have learned to listen to God's still, small voice concerning travel plans. I have also discovered that my wife has a type of inner radar that helps her discern impending danger. (A woman is seldom wrong when she judges a situation by her senses.)

4. Claim the promises in Scripture and pray.

One of the most beautiful promises in the Bible is in Psalms 91. It pronounces God's plan of protection from every form of danger. Scripture states, "No weapon that is formed against thee shall prosper" (Isaiah 54:17). An entire security team cannot defend a leader as well as one angel of the Lord! Let this be the promise of those who fear the Lord: "The angel of the Lord encampeth round about them that fear him and delivereth them" (Psalms 34:7).

5. Form a prayer covering.

Our ministry has a prayer group of over 700 intercessors that pray daily for our ministry and our protection. Christian leaders need a personal group of individuals who will stand with them in prayer. These prayers will form a prayer covering.

A president also needs a group of true believers to intercede for wisdom and protection. Good advice for any president would be to select a group of true men and women of God who come to the White House for periods of time simply to pray. This practice is also advisable for members of Congress.

All Christians are Biblically responsible to pray for those in leadership. Paul wrote:

"I exhort therefore, that, first of all, supplications, prayers, intercessions, and giving of thanks be made for all men; For kings, and for all that are in authority, that we may lead a quiet and peaceable life in godliness and honesty. For this is good and acceptable behavior in the sight of God our Savior" (1 Timothy 2:1-3).

May our national leaders repent for the sins of the fathers, and may American Christians pray for their wisdom, knowledge, and protection. With this support, our leaders can faithfully execute the responsibilities of their offices.

Chapter 10

PROPHECIES INVOLVING AMERICA'S PRESIDENTS

Stories of their Prophetic Destinies

"He changeth the times and the seasons: he removeth kings, and setteth up kings: he giveth wisdom unto the wise, and knowledge to them that know understanding. He revealeth the deep and secret things: he knoweth what is the darkness, and the light dwelleth with him." (Daniel 2:21,22)

Prophecy is becoming a household word in America. Novelists use brilliant word pictures to describe coming apocalyptic events. Hollywood producers have made millions by releasing apocalyptic blockbusters. The Christian community has released its own Biblically-based videos about end-time events.

The gift of prophecy is described in 1 Corinthians 12:10. Prophecy foretells future events. Throughout history, believers have been given dreams and visions regarding future events. Others have delivered verbal warnings, specific instructions, or details about the future. The key is that prophecy is inspired by the Holy Spirit and will never contradict Scripture.

I believe that the Holy Spirit actively speaks today, just as in the past, through believers who pray and fast often. The following accounts illustrate how specific prophetic utterances, dreams, and visions have impacted the destinies of American presidents.

Stories of American Presidents

Revisionists, those who attempt to rewrite history from their perspective, often intentionally omit events relative to God and the Bible. Generally, one should read the most original source of historical information in order to get the most accurate understanding of history.

Louis Bauman wrote a generally unknown version of Lincoln's assassination. Here is the account:

"On the evening of April 14, 1865, a bullet was fired into the brain of America's most beloved President, Abraham Lincoln. The nation was tremendously shocked and aroused to a frenzy. A great mob took possession of the streets of New York. The New York World, as a newspaper, had been unfriendly and critical of Lincoln. Suddenly a shout went up from the mob: 'To the World!' Instantly, the maddened people became an uncontrollable horde, surging toward The World building. Just then a strong man mounted some elevation and waved a small flag in an endeavor to still the people. Seeing him, several voices shouted, 'Another telegram from Washington!' Everybody stopped, of course, to listen to the telegram. Then that strong young man lifted his eyes reverently to heaven and in clear, deep, strong tones, said, 'Fellow citizens! Clouds and darkness are round about Him! In His pavilion are dark waters and thick clouds of the skies! Justice and judgment are the habitation of His throne! Mercy and truth shall go before His face! Fellow citizens! God reigns and the government at Washington still lives!' " (Source: *Russian Events in Bible Prophecy*, Louis Bauman, 1942)

Someone present at the scene wrote, "The crowd stood rigidly on the ground with awe, gazing at the motionless orator and thinking of God and the security of the government in that hour. The tumult subsided. A mighty voice, speaking a message from the Word of God, stilled a mighty passion. James A. Garfield was the young man who at that moment of danger, lifted his voice above the storm."

It was the same James Garfield who became the twentieth President of the United States. His words from Scripture that day calmed the angry mob. They were printed and people read them across the nation. Without realizing it, Garfield had planted seeds for his destiny by quoting Scripture. Stories like this about many American Presidents could fill a book. One such story that once appeared in our history books before being censored by revisionists concerns George Washington.

The Bulletproof George Washington

This is an excerpt from my book, *Anointed With Favor*. It tells how God's protection was upon Washington's life.

"He was a man of destiny. A strange, historical account reveals that even bullets could not kill him. In a letter to his mother, he acknowledged God's providence and protection. This man was George Washington, the first President of the United States. In April of 1755, British General Braddock invited Washington to assist in the French and Indian War. When Washington accepted the invitation, his mother was concerned for his safety. Washington wrote her: 'The God to whom you commend me, Madam, when I set out upon a more perilous errand, defended me from all harm and I trust He will do so now. Do not you?' Soon thereafter, on July 9, 1755, Washington served as an aid to British General Braddock. A terrible battle ensued near the Monongahela River. In the heat of the battle, hundreds of American and British soldiers were slain. Washington rode through gunfire and gave orders to soldiers. When the battle ended, sixty-three of the eighty-six British and American officers lay dead. Washington was the only officer on horseback who was not wounded. In a letter to his brother, Washington told a remarkable story proving Washington's destiny had been sealed by the Hand of God. 'By the all-powerful dispensations of Providence, I have been protected beyond all human probability or expectation; for I had four bullets through my coat and two horses shot out from under me. Yet, I escaped unhurt, although death was leveling my companions on every side of me' " (Source: George Washington's letter to his brother, July 18, 1755).

According to an early historical account, an Indian who was present at the time was reported as saying, "Washington was born never to be killed by a bullet. I had seventeen flairs fired at him with my rifle and, after all, could not bring him to the ground" (Source: *Pictorial Encyclopedia of American History*, Volume 2, page 96).

In the biography of Mary Draper, while being held by the Indians, she recorded that she overheard a conversation between French soldiers and her captors. They said that an Indian chief named Red Hawk personally told them that he shot Washington eleven times without killing him. Finally he ceased firing, and was convinced that the Great Spirit was protecting him.

David Barton wrote, "Eighty years after the battle, Washington's gold seal with his initials on it was found on the battleground. It was a belt buckle that had been shot off him in the battle. The relic is in the possession of the family. True to the Indian's prophecy, Washington was never wounded in any battle" (Source: *The Bulletproof George Washington*, David Barton). Considering the battles and the number of bullets fired at Washington, only the protective hand of God could have kept him alive.

Leaders Are Divinely Sent at the Right Time

One example of a leader being raised up at the right time is Harry Truman. Years ago, Truman's daughter told this story to a Jewish group in Tulsa, Oklahoma. When her father served in the war, he became close friends with a Jewish man. He and his Jewish friend spent much time in the field together. One day he asked the friend, "What are you planning to do when the war is over?" The man replied, "I will go to New York and get involved in the garment industry." He then questioned Truman, "What are your plans when the war is over?" Truman replied, "I want to get into politics and maybe someday I'll be the president!" When the war ended, the Jewish friend moved to New York and Truman eventually became involved in politics.

In 1944, Truman was elected to be Vice President during Franklin Roosevelt's fourth term. Eighty-two days after taking the oath of office,

President Roosevelt died suddenly in April of 1945, and Truman was sworn in as president. According to the book, *The Presidents*, " ...when the Trumans moved into the White House, the Democrats weren't too sure they had made such a smart move. They spent the next three years plotting to dump Harry before the 1948 election." Truman predicted, "There's going to be a Democrat in the White House in 1949 - and you are looking at him." Truman was right. He was re-elected in 1948, and an embarrassed news media that had already called the election for Dewey reported his success!

On November 29, 1947, the United Nations voted to divide Palestine, enabling Jews to return to their homeland and once again become a nation. Many people did not want Truman to support the resolution.

Meanwhile, in New York, the old Jewish friend was encouraged to contact Truman. His friends said, "You know Truman. Ask him to please vote in favor of the U.N. decision." He contacted Truman and, soon thereafter, America voted in favor of the U.N. partition. America had officially recognized the Jewish right to its homeland. God had the right man in authority at the right time when the Jews needed the U.N. resolution to pass. This one event among many is significant in terms of Harry Truman's destiny. Another man was destined to be president. His name was Ronald Reagan.

Ronald Reagan's Pre-Presidential Prophecy

Few Americans are aware of the personal prophecy given to Ronald Reagan while he was governor of California. It revealed that he would become President. The story begins in California in October, 1970. Herbert E. Ellingwood, Reagan's Secretary of Legal Affairs, brought several guests to visit the Governor, including singer Pat Boone, Mr. Bredsen, and a minister named George Otis. Pat Boone was a long time friend of Reagan.

The Governor would be facing re-election soon. That day the conversation included a discussion on Bible prophecy and how the Holy Spirit is moving in the last days. When it was time to go, Ellingwood led the group toward the front door so the final goodbyes could be said. One of the ministers spoke up and asked, "Governor, do you mind if we take a moment and pray for you and Mrs. Reagan?" "We would appreciate that," Reagan replied as his countenance turned rather serious. Then the group formed a circle and joined hands, and Reagan bowed his head rather sharply.

Prayer was offered asking for God's blessings. Suddenly, in the middle of the prayer, the unexpected occurred. George Otis recalled what transpired:

"The Holy Spirit came upon me and I knew it. In fact, I was embarrassed. There was this pulsing in my arm, and my hand, the one holding Governor Reagan's hand, was shaking. I didn't know what to do. I just didn't want this to be happening. I can remember even as I was speaking, tensing my muscles trying to get the shaking to stop."

As this transpired, Otis' prayer changed completely. The prayer changed from a basic prayer of blessing into a more steady declaration. The words coming from Otis' mouth were spoken directly to Reagan. He was addressed as "My Son" and his role as leader in a state that was the size of many nations on earth was recognized. His labor was described as pleasing. Then followed the words that will long be remembered by everyone present: "If you walk uprightly before me, you will reside at 1600 Pennsylvania Avenue" (Source: *Reagan, Inside Out*).

This was a personal prophecy under the inspiration of the Holy Spirit. Sixteen hundred Pennsylvania Avenue is the address of the White House. Ten years later in 1980, Reagan, against all odds, ran for president. He trailed behind ten other Republican candidates who sought the nomination. A major factor was his age; he was nearly 70. Political analysts criticized him and said that he was too old to make correct decisions and that he might even die while in office. Others said that he was incompetent and a mere actor. Despite the objections, Reagan won the presidency in 1980 and was re-elected for a second term in 1984.

Pat Boone, upon hearing that his friend had been elected, telephoned the Reagans at their Pacific Palisades home to offer congratulations. During the conversation, Boone asked if Reagan remembered the prayer in Sacramento ten years earlier. Reagan said, "Of course I do." Ten years earlier, God had revealed His will for Ronald Reagan. God appointed a man who was familiar with Bible prophecy to lead America during a profound era. Reagan was at the helm when the Iron Curtain fell and when the Union of Soviet Socialist Republics collapsed.

Time for the Iron Curtain to Melt

Sixty-two years before the rise of Communism, a man named Dr. Hudson Taylor was a missionary to China. Taylor loved China. It was written about him, "For forty years the sun never rose on China, but Hudson Taylor was on his knees for the salvation of the Chinese" (Source: *Hudson Taylor's Spiritual Secret*, Moody Press).

During one of his furloughs to England in 1855, Taylor was preaching when he suddenly stopped. He stood speechless for a time with his eyes closed. When he began to speak, he explained:

"I have just seen a vision. I saw in this vision a great war that will encompass the whole world. I saw this war recess and then start again, actually being two wars. After this, I saw much unrest and revolts that will affect many nations. I saw in some places spiritual awakenings. In Russia, I saw there will come a general all-encompassing spiritual awakening so great that there could never be another like it. From Russia, I saw the awakening spread to many European countries. Then I saw an all out awakening followed by the coming of Christ" (Source: From an original article by Hudson Taylor, titled Spiritual Revival, published in Finland in 1945).

In 1917, sixty-two years after Hudson's vision, the Russian Revolution birthed Communism. The anti-God system grew like a poisonous vine that choked individual faith in God. For almost seventy years, the sword of godless Communism dripped with the blood of Christian martyrs. No one in the west ever believed that the Iron Curtain would fall and allow a period of religious freedom.

Since a true Communist must be an atheist, western Christians reasoned that it was impossible for the Soviet Christians to ever be freed from the chains of oppression. Yet, a few underground believers were aware of a prophecy given in the 1930s, which revealed that one day religious freedom would come! A bishop in an unregistered Pentecostal church silently cherished that prophecy for more than fifty years. Several years ago while visiting Russia, the prophecy was told directly to Rev. Lovell Carey, former World Missions director for the Church of God.

1930 Prophecy Concerning Mikhail Gorbachev

Lovell was in Russia shortly after the fall of Communism. He met with one of the Bishops of the unregistered Pentecostal church. According to the Bishop, in 1930 a Christian delivered an unusual prophecy. It said that, in the future, a man would arise in the Soviet Union whose name would be Mikhail, and he would have a mark in his forehead. She continued to say that, during his time, there would once again be freedom to preach, and revival would come. However, this freedom would only be for a short time, then repression would return.

It would be over 50 years before this prophecy would be fulfilled. Mikhail Gorbachev (who had a large birthmark on his forehead), became the leader of the Soviet Union. "Glasnost" became a global word. A lesser-known part of the story concerning Mr. Gorbachev reveals the timing of the Almighty in the affairs of men.

Christian Mother Influences Gorbachev

Lavon Riley is a tour operator from Texas. In the late 1980s, Mr. Riley planned a trip to Russia and took many Christians with him. The Christians boarded a huge plane for their journey and stashed thousands of Bibles within their belongings. When they arrived, it was difficult to get permission to bring the Bibles into the country. Miraculously, Mr. Riley acquired a permit to do so and the army came with trucks and delivered the Bibles directly to the churches. Lavon Riley personally told me how, during this trip, the KGB called him into their offices. Great fear of being arrested came upon him. The KGB proceeded to tell him that they were aware of his every step. In fact, the head KGB agent said, "Let me show you your file." He proceeded to pull out a file that was about four inches thick that gave details of every time Lavon had traveled to Russia. It included the places where he had spoken, the hotels where he had stayed, and the restaurants where he had eaten. It turned out that the meeting was not to arrest or interrogate him, but to demonstrate to him that a new Russia existed and that the new Russia would permit religious freedom. Lavon was given a permit from Gorbachev's number three man to bring as many Bibles into Russia as Lavon desired!

It was at this time that Lavon learned that the mother of Mikhail Gorbachev was an Orthodox Christian. She had prayed for him for many years that he would become a leader in Russia. He also learned that, during Mikhail's birthday, his mother would make a special cake and place certain Scriptures on it. This was confirmed when Gorbachev appeared on the Hour of Power with Robert Schuller on October 22, 2000 and spoke about his mother's prayers and the fact that practically all of his family were Christians. During the interview, Mikhail said, "There can be no freedom without spiritual freedom, without human beings being able to choose."

Mikhail kept close ties with the Russian Orthodox Church. Perestroika created an atmosphere of co-existence and opened the door to freedom of religious expression for at least seven years. Apparently, the predestined purpose of Gorbachev was twofold: to bring religious freedom to the Soviet Union (Russia), and to release the Soviet Jews by allowing them to immigrate back to Israel. This action was also in direct fulfillment of ancient Biblical prophecies.

The Jewish Return From the North Country

During a tour to Israel in the late 1980s, my group was shopping in Bethlehem. Suddenly we got a report that a plane had been hijacked from Russia to Israel. My tour guide Gideon, my camera man Dwayne Kilpatrick, and I immediately raced to the Ben Guerin airport in Tel Aviv. We were forbidden to tape certain areas because we didn't have a pass. Then Gideon took us to a special side entrance where the hostages were being released. We later heard a rumor that several Soviet Jews were aboard the hijacked plane. There was speculation that they hijacked the plane in order to get to Israel, although the report was denied (perhaps for political purposes).

That night as I stood watching vehicles on the airport runway, I heard an inward voice say, "The north will let my people go!" I returned and told several friends that the Soviet Union will be releasing Jews shortly. They looked at me in disbelief, but Scripture had already decreed the event:

> "Therefore, behold, the days come, saith the Lord, that it shall no more be said, the Lord liveth, that brought up the children of Israel out of the land of Egypt; But the Lord liveth, that brought up the children of Israel from the land of the north, and from all the lands whither he had driven them: and I will bring them again into their land that I gave unto their fathers." (Jeremiah 16:14-16)

In ancient times, Israel was in Babylonian captivity for exactly 70 years (Jeremiah 25:11). God gave Israel Ten Commandments and He warned them that, if they disobeyed Him, the punishment would be seven times (Leviticus 26:18). Ten multiplied by seven equals seventy. In 1917, Communism imprisoned Russia for seventy years. In 1987, seventy years after the revolution, the breakdown of the Iron Curtain began. As Reagan spoke about tearing down the Berlin Wall in Germany, Mr. Gorbachev helped to unfasten the mighty iron curtain over Russia and Eastern Europe. Both men were Divinely sent for a specific season in history. The prophet Daniel wrote, "God changes times and seasons; He removes kings and sets up kings" (Daniel 2:21). The seventy years completed another prophetic cycle. The hand of God moved world leaders into position on His chessboard. One more move was needed to place Communism into checkmate!

The Prophetic Role of Karol Wojtyla

On May 18, 1920, Karol Joseph Wojtyla was born in Wadowice, Poland. While the Nazis occupied Poland, Karol pursued his studies and worked as a stonecutter to maintain his work permit that kept him from being deported or imprisoned. He joined the UNIA, a Christian democratic underground group. Jewish organizations like B'nai B'rith testified that he helped Jews find refuge from the Nazis. In 1942, he began studying for the priesthood and was ordained a priest on November 1, 1946. By 1967, he became a Cardinal and in 1978 at the age of 58, Karol Wojtyla became Pope John Paul II.

Near Assassination of Reagan and the Pope

Both Ronald Reagan and the Pope survived assassination attempts on their lives. The Pope was shot at Saint Peter's Square at the Vatican in Rome, Italy in 1981. Reagan was shot on March 30, 1981 in Washington, D.C. Both men credit Divine Providence for their protection. The Pope gave credit to Mary, and Reagan gave credit to God for his recovery.

Former Secret Service agent Louis Mason served four American presidents — Nixon, Ford, Carter, and Reagan. Louis directs security for Voice of Evangelism in our larger meetings. As Louis drove from the Hilton Hotel in Washington on the afternoon Reagan was shot, he heard on his scanner, "The president has been shot!" He immediately rushed to the hospital. He later learned that six shots were fired within ten feet of the president. A bullet ricocheted off of the bulletproof limousine door and entered Reagan's chest about one inch from his heart. Agent Jerry Parr's quick reaction may have helped save Reagan's life as he thrust the president head first into the protective limousine. Under such circumstances, the agent is to hit the president in the stomach to buckle his body and push him downward into the vehicle. When inside the car, Reagan commented to the agent, "I think you broke my rib." Upon seeing blood the agent said, "Sir, you have been shot!"

In his biography *An American Life*, Reagan said, "I remember looking up from the gurney trying to focus my eyes on the ceiling tiles and praying." Reagan was a praying man and was visited on several occasions by Billy Graham. In the emergency room, the President realized someone was holding his hand. The hand touched his hand and then held it tight. He remembers a comforting, reassuring feeling. He asked several times who was holding his hand but received no response. He later tried to find out who held his hand, assuming it was a nurse. He was never able to locate the person. Reagan said, "Someone was looking out for us on that day." He told several agents that he gave credit to God for protecting his life.

Pope John Paul II was shot on May 13, 1981, the anniversary of the alleged appearance of the Virgin Mary to three children in Fatima, Portugal. On May 13, 1917, the alleged apparition spoke messages about the future, including a series of prophecies involving Russia. According to the prediction, Russia would one day be converted if the Catholic people would dedicate Russia to the immaculate heart of Mary. The apparition predicted that one day, Russia would be converted and that the Virgin Mary would play a role in the process.

After being shot on the anniversary of this 64-year-old vision, the Pope felt that it was Mary who saved his life. He pledged himself to her and to her message. Pope John Paul II has a personal motto: totus tuus sum Maria, meaning *Mary I'm all yours*. One year later on May 13, 1982, the Pope prayed before the statue of our Lady of Fatima and consecrated the world to her as she had requested. On May 13th, 1984, he consecrated the world to her again based upon the promise of 1917, "If my wishes are fulfilled, my Immaculate Heart will triumph, Russia will be converted, and there will be peace!" It appears that, from that moment on, the Pope set in his heart to do all in his power to help fulfill the Fatima prophecy and "convert Russia to the message of Christianity and Mary." It was shortly thereafter that the Pope began to visit a number of Communist countries.

Three Men at the Right Place at the Right Time

With Reagan in America, Gorbachev in the Soviet Union, and the Pope as the spiritual leader of over 1 billion Catholics, including many in Communist countries, the stage was set to begin dismantling the Iron Curtain. Within ten years between 1980 and 1990, the changes in Communist Eastern Europe and Russia were so dramatic that outsiders stood in disbelief. The Berlin Wall crumbled as people chipped away at the concrete with picks and hammers. Jews once held against their will in the Soviet Union crowded into planes as they were set free from seventy years of captivity. Suddenly, western missionaries were overwhelmed by invitations to minister to overflow crowds in the Soviet block nations.

I personally ministered in Romania and Bulgaria shortly after the doors were opened to the Gospel. In several places, there were undercover secret police that followed our movement but, generally, we preached in open air crusades, small buildings, and former Communist halls without fear or opposition. Journalists were free to come, listen, and report our messages in the paper. I must confess I never dreamed in my lifetime that this type of freedom would ever transpire. Hudson Taylor's prophecy from 1855 concerning an all-encompassing spiritual awakening is coming to pass.

Ronald Reagan and Mikhail Gorbachev's destinies were both prophesied before their rise to power (1930 and 1970). Reagan and the Pope both understood the importance of Bible prophecy. An internationally known prophetic minister once shared with me that he spoke with Reagan on several occasions about Bible prophecy and how events during Reagan's administration would impact Scripture.

Some skeptics would claim that these men were trying to make Bible prophecy come to pass. I would reply that it is impossible to make something happen unless it is the prophetic time for the event to transpire. When Charlemagne attempted to reform the Roman Empire, he failed. So did Napoleon and Hitler. But the present day Common Market completes a picture of a unified Europe in the area of the old Roman Empire that was described in prophecy.

God simply places the right men in the right places at the right season. This only reinforces the verse that says, "God changes the times and the seasons: He removes kings and sets up kings" (Daniel 2:21). When the moment came for Israel to be restored as a nation, the right people were in place. A man named David Ben Gurion made the announcement from Tel Aviv. Ben Gurion was a believer in the Bible. The nation was called Israel, not Palestine, because the Bible prophets used the name Israel. Scholars turned to Isaiah 66:8 and read, "Shall a nation be born at once? For as soon as Zion travailed, she brought forth her children."

God can even use men who are unbelievers to fulfill His purpose. Consider the fact that two dreams in the Bible that foretold future events were given to two men — Pharaoh and King Nebuchadnezzar. Neither professed faith in the Hebrew God. Pharaoh dreamed a troubling dream that Joseph interpreted (Genesis 41), while Daniel interpreted the dream of the King of Babylon (Daniel 2).

The Presidency of Bill Clinton

When exploring the background of Bill Clinton to learn how he gained prestige in politics, the average person is left wondering, "How did he get to the top?" In the early 1950s, he accepted Christ at a Billy Graham crusade. He walked alone to church carrying a Bible under his arm. Clinton recalls at age 12 sending his tithe of ten cents to Billy Graham's evangelistic organization. He was water baptized and joined the church choir. A former pastor, Dexter Blevins, recalled, "He was in church every time the doors were opened." When learning about the difficulties in Bill's family, many Americans have asked, "How could a young man with such a difficult family background rise so high on the political ladder, unless he had some inside help?"

While staying with friends in the southeastern United States, I learned some interesting information about Bill Clinton. During my stay, I learned that my friend's mother was a friend to some elderly members of Arkansas' inner circle. According to her, when Bill was young, his mother became acquainted with a well-known Washington politician. Soon, a close relationship developed with the Washington insider. His visits to Arkansas included meetings with Bill's mother, Virginia. As a special favor to her, the politician was asked to help make a politician out of her son William. It was this man who assisted young Clinton in achieving his political ambition.

Clinton has been a real paradox. On the one hand, his trail of moral failures and spiritual weaknesses appears to have extended from the governor's mansion to the White House. Yet, when Lamar Vest, General Overseer of the Church of God, visited Clinton several years ago to discuss persecution of Chinese Christians, Clinton pulled a well worn, marked Bible out of his desk in the Oval Office. He stated to those present that he read the Bible and prayed for wisdom every day. After his indiscretion with a White House intern became known, he confessed that he had sinned.

Then there were situations such as the time he had the American flag removed from a public school near Camp David, Maryland. He did this before one of his peace negotiations between Israeli Prime Minister Barak and Palestinian leader Arafat because he didn't want to offend those attending the meeting. As one pastor near Camp David pointed out to me, "Clinton didn't mind flying the Israeli flag or the Palestinian flag, but God forbid he fly the American flag. It could offend someone." This is indeed an offense, but it is an offense to Americans and to the thousands of veterans who fought for the flag. One must ask, "How could the Commander in Chief of our armed forces keep the American flag from flying near Camp David?"

Few people are aware of a rather unusual event that happened to Clinton after he lost his election as governor. Clinton told the story while on a trip to Israel to members of the Israeli Knesset. An Israeli in Jerusalem related it to me in November of 1998.

Clinton addressed the Knesset in Jerusalem, Israel on October 27, 1994. He said, "The truth is that the only time my wife and I ever came to Israel was 13 years ago with my pastor on a religious mission. I was then out of office. I was the youngest former governor in the history of the United States. We visited the holy sites. I relived the history of the Bible, of your Scriptures and mine, and I formed a bond with my pastor. Later, when he became desperately ill, he said he thought I might one day become president. And he said, more bluntly than the Prime Minister did, 'If you abandon Israel, God will never forgive you.' He said, 'It is God's will that Israel, the Biblical home of the people of Israel, continue forever and ever'" (Source: transcript from the Knesset in Jerusalem, October 27, 1994).

After becoming president, an agreement had been signed on the White House lawn forging a peace between Israel and Palestine. From that moment onward, it seemed that Clinton worked to establish his legacy as a peacemaker between Israel and Palestine. Years later, when the secret negotiations were happening in Oslo, it seemed that the United States had been left out and that the Vatican had become the strong mediator. Clinton became involved once again in negotiating peace. After the assassination of Yitzhak Rabin, Benjamin Netanyahu became the new Prime Minister.

Insiders have told me that Clinton and Netanyahu did not get along well. It seems that Clinton felt Netanyahu would slow down, if not stop, the peace process because he was a hardliner. A personal friend of mine who works in Washington, D.C. and had access to the president informed me (in 1996) that every world leader is supposed to keep an advisor to the President informed of their whereabouts. In the event of a national emergency, terrorist threat, or the outbreak of war, the United States president would then be able to contact the leaders of each nation. As such, daily contact with key White House personnel is normal protocol. My source indicated that Mr. Netanyahu went for quite some time without speaking to Mr. Clinton.

On one occasion, when Netanyahu came to the states, he met with Baptist minister Jerry Falwell. Allegedly, during this time, some inside information was leaked and someone informed Falwell about Clinton's affair with a White House intern. Some think that Mr. Netanyahu revealed this to Falwell. When the news broke about the affair, Hillary gave a harsh reply on television when asked about the rumor of her husband's affair with a White House intern. Then on a national morning talk show, she declared the attack as a "vast right wing conspiracy." She was no doubt referring to Falwell. While she claims she was unaware of her husband's infidelity, she seemed to have knowledge that certain "right wing" persons were conspiring against him.

Clinton's legacy is unclear. Most Americans accept Clinton as a leader who was plagued by moral weaknesses. To Clinton's credit, several important meetings that the former President was involved in have supported religious freedom. First, when the Russian leaders were going to enforce a ban against western missionaries and limit Christian organizations, it was Clinton who interceded, telling Yeltsin not to pass the harsh legislation. This one action may have kept the door open for evangelism in certain parts of Russia a little longer.

Secondly, Clinton favored China perhaps more than any other president. While much has been reported about his China deals, especially those related to trade, nuclear secrets, and illegal campaign contributions, China has over 1.2 billion people who need to hear the Gospel. Let us hope that Clinton's liberal dealings with China may have opened a dialogue that could eventually help to send the Gospel into that land. Some areas in China are slowly permitting Christian programs and limited evangelistic crusades to take place, both of which were formerly forbidden by law.

According to Clinton, he was told that, if he turned his back on Israel, God would turn His back on him. It is interesting to note a turn of events. As Clinton began to pressure Israel to give up land for peace and bring Jerusalem to the table, a young Jewish intern named Monica Lewinsky ended up marring Clinton's legacy.

Clinton is still young. Barring accidents or ill health, it is possible that he will play a role in the United Nations, or become involved in New York politics in the future. I am uncertain how much he understands Biblical prophecy, but he may certainly be placed in an international affairs position in the future. Few are aware that Clinton has many Baptist and Pentecostal friends. At times, they have influenced Clinton and hopefully, they planted important seeds for the future.

George Washington, Ronald Reagan, and Bill Clinton are only three of America's forty-three presidents. If we could interview deceased presidents regarding their spiritual experiences in office, I am certain that many books could be filled with inspirational testimonies. There are many interesting stories that are seldom shared about America's leaders. One such story involved a woman named Mary D. Rouse.

Mary Rouse's Dream about the President's Secret Meetings

C.E. French, a former Associate Pastor of the North Cleveland Church of God, first told me this story. I was then able to personally contact Reverend E. Jack Matthews, a former pastor at the Wrens Church of God in Wrens, Georgia, to confirm it first hand.

E. Jack Matthews pastored in Wrens, Georgia from 1960 to 1965. One of his parishioners was a 98-year-old woman named Mary D. Rouse. Mary was the wife of a Methodist minister, a schoolteacher, and a music teacher. In her early years, she would be found on the convention floor of the Methodist conferences, praying in the prayer language of the Holy Spirit. Her husband would ask her not to go, but she would reply that she did so because the Lord wanted her to attend. According to Pastor

Matthews, Mary spent hours every day before the Lord in Bible reading and prayer. Often people mocked her for being overly religious. However, those who knew her personally told many amazing stories about how God used this humble woman.

Pastor Matthews saw Mary's obedience to the Lord in his personal life. After receiving his salary on Sunday night, he went to the bank the next day to deposit the check. On Tuesday, the bank called to tell him that he was overdrawn by $58.00. Neither he nor his wife could account for the mistake, and he was embarrassed to tell the church clerk. The next morning, he looked out the window and saw Mary D. sitting on the steps, so he invited her inside. Mary told Matthews and his wife, "The Lord wouldn't let me sleep last night. He said you had a particular need." She asked, "Would it be all right if I advanced my tithe to the church for six months?" The six months tithe was $64.00 and covered the overdrawn account at the bank. This was a faith-building incident for the Matthews family. It was later discovered that the banker was having an affair and had been juggling the accounts. The bank went out of business and the banker went to jail, while the church continued to be blessed!

Mary also lived in the same town as the writer Erskine Caldwell. He is noted for writing *God's Little Acre* and *Tobacco Road*. Caldwell's father was a Presbyterian minister in Wrens, Georgia. Erskine attended the Saint Matthews Church of God to hear Mary preach and, after hearing her, he would write articles about her sermons and print them in the Augusta Chronicle. Mary evidently crossed Caldwell in some way and he began writing negative things about her. Mary would refute his writings with Scripture in the Macon Telegraph, which had a larger circulation. When he felt that he had lost the battle with Mary, he wrote the novel *Tobacco Road*. The main character, Betsy, was based upon Mary's life.

Revelations Concerning the Presidents

Years before John Kennedy announced he would run for president, Mary began preaching that the president following Eisenhower would be a Catholic. She based this on a dream that she had in which the dome roof of the White House was covered with black crows and each one had a padlock on its beak. She asked God what this meant and the Holy Spirit revealed the interpretation: "This is a padlock to put on every Protestant church door in America." Afterward, she felt a Catholic president would rule from the White House. Years later, John Kennedy became the first Catholic President of the United States. Because Kennedy never finished his presidency, it is uncertain how this would have played out. Yet today, we know that the Catholic Church is the head of the National Council of Churches and Catholic leaders consider the church to be the one true church of Christ on earth.

Perhaps the most unusual event regarding Mary's life concerns President Dwight D. Eisenhower. One night while in prayer, Mary received a dream that she knew was from the Lord. There had been some disturbances in Turkey and the Middle East. Mary wrote the details of her dream that warned the president not to act on some decisions that he was secretly making. Her information was so accurate that President Eisenhower sent a group of government men from Washington to Wrens, Georgia, to investigate whether Mary was a spy or if she had escaped from that part of the world. According to Matthews, the area papers published articles about the men coming from Washington to visit Mary. When the men returned to Washington and informed the president that Mary was simply a praying woman, Mamie Eisenhower, the President's wife, sent her a bouquet of flowers and a letter complimenting her on her keen insight.

Dr. and Mrs. C.E. French ministered at the church that Mary attended. It was Dr. French who personally met Mary and related some of the marvelous incidents of this woman's life. Dr. French was shown the card from Mamie Eisenhower and a number of news articles regarding Mary's stories.

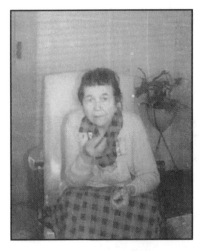

This is an old photograph of Mary D. Rouse, the woman whose prayers and a subsequent dream stopped President Dwight Eisenhower from making a terrible mistake.

When we hear marvelous stories like this, we should ask ourselves, "Where are the praying Americans who can truly hear from God? Where are the leaders who will allow praying believers to speak into their lives?" Have men become so fearful of opinion polls, intimidated by liberal lawyers, and skeptical of Christians that they build walls to prevent criticism? I would rather have ten saints of God praying for me every day, than a hundred Einsteins offering me counsel and rational reasoning.

God can prophetically reveal events concerning our nation to believers who will turn their ears and hearts toward heaven. This is the only way to counteract spiritual wickedness in high places.

Chapter 11

SPIRITUAL WICKEDNESS IN HIGH PLACES

The Media's Attack on Christianity

"For we wrestle not against flesh and blood, but against principalities, against powers, against the rulers of the darkness of this world, against spiritual wickedness in high places."
(Ephesians 6:12)

The March 1990 *Christian Information Bulletin* included an interesting article by David Hunt about a missionary in the 1930s who had worked among Tibetan Buddhist monks. One morning he observed mass confusion among the monks. When he inquired about the chaos, one of them explained that all of their big gods had gone to Germany that morning! The missionary recalled later that it was the day Adolph Hitler came to power in Germany.

As a student in Austria, Hitler frequented a museum that exhibited a collection of relics from the Holy Roman Empire. One display captivated him. It contained what was said to be the Roman centurion's spear that pierced Christ's side. Allegedly, since the third century, whoever possessed the spear ruled the world. Hitler stared at the spear for hours and meditated on its power. According to Hitler's diary, while staring at the spear he went into a trance. He wrote this about the experience:

"The air became stifling so I could barely breath. The noisy scene of the treasure house seemed to melt away before my eyes. I stood alone and trembling before the hovering form of a superhuman — a spirit sublime and fearful — a countenance intrepid and cruel. In holy awe I offered my soul as a vessel of his will..."

From that moment, Hitler became obsessed with the spear. In March of 1938, when the Nazis invaded Austria, Hitler promptly had the spear shipped to Berlin and ordered the excavation of a 900-foot-deep bunker to house it. While it was in his possession, Hitler marched on Europe and orchestrated the annihilation of six million Jews. When the Allies took Berlin in 1945, they confiscated Hilter's possessions. A month later, Hitler killed himself. Apparently he believed that the Allies had seized the spear, and he must have taken its alleged historic significance very seriously. History recorded that upon losing possession of the spear, one's power immediately collapsed (Source: *Guardians of the Grail*, J.R. Church).

I believe that Hitler was demonically possessed and that it probably happened when he witnessed the manifestation of the spirit described in his diary. A concept that I have preached about which emphatically applies to Hitler is "principalities rule through personalities." Ephesians 6:12 teaches that supernatural forces can motivate people. It states, "For we wrestle not against flesh and blood, but against principalities, against powers, against the rulers of the darkness of this world, against spiritual wickedness in high places."

Prince Spirits in High Places

Ephesians refers to warfare against principalities (Ephesians 6:12). In the Greek New Testament, the word principalities means *governments*. This implies that wicked spirits can influence governments and strive either for or against nations. When Satan tempted Christ, he offered the Son of God all the kingdoms of the world if only He would submit to him. Satan said these kingdoms had been "delivered unto him and he could give them to whomever he chose" (Matthew 4:8,9). If citizens of world democracies neglect to prayerfully vote for their leaders, they could end up with rulers who are influenced by dark spirits!

Daniel 10 indicates that wicked spirits can actually wage war in the heavens to affect events taking place in the nations. Daniel's account gives an example of how it works. He entered a season of prayer and fasting that lasted for three weeks (Daniel 10:2). God answered his prayer, but its fulfillment was actually detained by unseen forces. The wicked spirit that hindered Daniel's answer to prayer had a name, the prince of Persia (Daniel 10:13). The spiritual warfare was very intense because Daniel's prayer concerned Israel's deliverance from seventy years of Babylonian captivity. When the Medes and the Persians overthrew Babylon, Israel would be freed (Daniel 5:30-31). Since God loves the Jews and Satan hates them, the spirits of darkness targeted this battle and attempted to prevent Israel's liberation. It took persistent prayer and fasting to bring forth Michael the archangel and his angelic forces to thwart the prince of Persia's opposition!

Daniel 10 indicates that nations actually have specific ruling wicked spirits that influence their leaders. At high levels of government, the enemy can inflict great damage upon a nation. Men like Marx, Stalin, and Hitler effectively tapped into spiritual powers of darkness for their empowerment. The death, destruction, and hatred that resulted from their regimes points to the source of their powers.

I have written this to explain how spiritual forces can influence America in high places. The true enemy of our souls is unseen. One example of how unseen forces impact America negatively is the abuse of our national airwaves. Programs delivered into our homes suggest that sex out of marriage is okay, yet Hollywood producers neglect to show the devastation of broken homes, sexually transmitted diseases, and physical abuse caused by immorality. Shows mock Christians and their values, suggesting that wholesomeness and character is out of date. Shows promote alternative lifestyles but fail to mention what God has to say about them. This battle being raged over the airwaves is being empowered in high places, because it has eternal consequences.

The Battle for the Air

Scripture addressed the power of the air thousands of years before humans knew that airwaves existed. It teaches that Satan is the "prince of the power of the air" (Ephesians 2:2). Notice the phrase "the prince of the *power* of the air." In this text, the Greek word for power is exousia, meaning *authority*. The air actually has certain authority! Powerful, air-based communication tools like television and radio deliver millions of signals that are converted into messages. These messages can be either for God, or against Him. Satan wants to control these messages with his "power of the air."

This battle for the air began in the 1950s as television became popular. Evangelical Christians quickly learned just how much intolerance existed regarding the Bible. Oral Roberts broke the ice with his television ministry of preaching and prayer for the sick in the early 1950s. Roberts taped portions of his crusades to be aired on his weekly TV show. He truly pioneered the work of television evangelism in America. He also received widespread criticism from newspapers, magazines, and television programs for praying for sick people and airing it on national television. Outspoken skeptics felt that Roberts was a shyster who preyed on the weak. But visibly answered prayer before thousands of witnesses was not a sham. I have personally met hundreds of believers who were healed or greatly touched in the early days of Roberts' meetings.

Most ministers in the early 1950s used radio to reach larger numbers while Roberts' most effective evangelistic tool was television. Others attempted to imitate Roberts' style, but often failed, ending up in bankruptcy. Roberts experienced severe persecution from the onset of his television ministry and the mainstream media never supported his efforts. As his crowds swelled to as high as twenty thousand people per night, some liberal media personnel saw his popularity as dangerous, thinking such men could become too influential with the general public. The testimonies of healings were ridiculed and Roberts' methods were viciously criticized in print and on television. Some insinuated that Roberts lived extravagantly through large offerings that he received; yet, Roberts was on a salary and the offerings went into the ministry. Instead of attempting to defend himself, Roberts ministered in the 1950s using every tool to reach the lost.

The only way to stop Roberts' momentum was by using negative, biased media reports. This was done in 1956 in Australia during a cru-sade. Communist agitators and skeptical religious groups hounded Rob-erts until he had to close the meeting prematurely and flee the country for fear of violence. Roberts said that the press was ten times worse than he had ever seen in America. Whether or not one agreed with Roberts' theol-ogy or his methods, the biased, negative media was intended to harm the influence of Christian television in this nation. In 1988, the media jumped on a statement allegedly made by Roberts. There were probably few in America who had not heard the report that Roberts said that God would kill him if he didn't raise money for a medical facility. These reports were distorted and, in some instances, they were outright lies. Despite over fifty years of criticism from the liberal press, Roberts maintained his spiri-tual and moral integrity.

The Attack Against Rex Humbard

As television became affordable and grew in popularity, Christian ministries saw it as the best medium for reaching the masses. In Akron, Ohio, a minister named Rex Humard pastored a thriving congregation by the name of The Cathedral of Tomorrow. Humbard had a unique family-oriented ministry that impacted Akron and beyond. Humbard felt led to expand his ministry through television. He became one of the first people to establish a steady Christian television ministry.

During this time, a man named Demos Shakarian, founder and presi-dent of the Full Gospel Businessmen International, lived in California. One evening Demos received a troubling phone call from a politician from California who lived in Washington, D.C. at that time. He told Demos that he had seen a list of major television and radio ministers who were being targeted by the Justice Department. This took place during the Nixon ad-ministration.

On the list were Oral Roberts, Rex Humbard, Jimmy Swaggart (who at that time was on radio), Bill Bright, and others. Demos was troubled by the information but, at the time, had seen no direct government interfer-ence. During this time, the Full Gospel Businessmen International was a thriving organization. Demos was a close friend of Dr. Jerry Melilli, a physician from Baton Rouge, Louisiana, who was a frequent speaker at the Full Gospel Businessmen's conventions. Dr. Melilli shared with me some information that he had learned from Demos Shakarian.

Demos told Dr. Mellili that, when he arrived at the church, several men were leaving Humbard's office. Humbard followed with a pale look on his face. The men were from the Securities and Exchange Commission in Washington, D.C. Rex told Demos that they had shut the ministry down and would not allow the ministry to send any mail to a donor asking for support. Then Demos recalled the Washington insider's call.

Many churches during this time used bonds to raise funds. Rex had sold some bonds outside of Ohio, and the Securities and Exchange Commission used this to shut down the ministry. Demos and some other ministries pulled together and raised funds to pay off Humbard's bonds before the case went to court. Without their help, the ministry would have been seriously damaged, if not destroyed.

This episode was a visible example of how television ministries were being carefully monitored in high places. Other cases may not be as visible, but they are just as insidious.

The Threat of Major Television Ministries

As the media reports became more liberal and biased against Christianity, the need for more Bible-based programming increased. National television airtime costs were so high that average ministries could not afford airtime. Local stations weren't interested in airing television evangelists, so a series of Christian television networks began to be established.

One of the first was the Christian Broadcasting Network (CBN) founded by Pat Robertson. Starting out with one camera and God, Pat began broadcasting at three o'clock p.m. on October 1, 1961. His flagship program was The 700 Club, a very popular program with a talk show format. Soon other Christians began purchasing television stations to establish networks. Paul Crouch founded the Trinity Broadcast Network (TBN) in California, and a young man named Jim Bakker (a former Robertson employee) launched PTL Network in Charlotte, North Carolina.

As long as these Christian networks broadcasted Christian interviews, preaching, and gospel music, there was little conflict. But as the social trends in the nation leaned toward the left, the Christian networks began to use airtime to speak out against sin and spiritual wickedness in America. Immediately the media, including newspapers, rose up. Newspaper editorials blasted the networks and carried negative articles intended to cast doubt on the networks. Criticism became commonplace and, in some cases, hidden cameras were used to follow ministry workers to create exposés intended to cripple the networks' financial support. Others hunted for the occasional disgruntled former network employee to acquire negative information. The barrage persisted for many years and, between 1987 and 1988, the worst storm in the history of Christian television hit.

Three Major Ministries from 1987-1988

In the late 1980s, there were three prominent television ministers who reached into millions of American homes. Pat Robertson hosted the daily 700 Club from Virginia Beach, Virginia. Jim Bakker appeared daily, reaching over 15 million homes, and Jimmy Swaggart was considered to be America's most watched television evangelist.

In 1988, reports came out about Jim Bakker's one-time affair in 1980. Jim often spoke about his personal struggles and his and Tammy's marital problems from PTL's beginning. Information also surfaced in February 1988 about Jimmy Swaggart's moral failure. The news literally exploded on the media front, and all this happened about the same time that Pat Robertson made a bid for the presidency.

In 1988, beltway insiders never considered Robertson to be a serious contender until he organized a successful grass roots movement in Iowa. Pat's organization also showed strength in the straw polls, and some politicians worried that a television preacher might rally enough support to win the Republican nomination. Robertson's father had been a U.S. Senator and Robertson had attended Yale. His expertise in economics was appealing. Soon an arsenal of media assaults began flying like warheads as reporters hunted for dirt on Robertson. The personal attacks against Robertson failed, but the moral failures of the other two ministers helped to take the air out of the Robertson campaign.

Bakker's and Swaggart's failures fueled cynicism among the general public and discouraged Christians. The media enjoyed roasting ministries in general and television evangelists in particular. This turbulence impacted over one hundred Christian television stations that were unable to meet their financial obligations and eventually sold their stations over the next ten years.

Moral failure obviously led to the Bakker and Swaggart scandals. However, why did Bakker's seven-year-old, one-time affair come to light in 1988? While in Florida that year, I heard many suggest that the timing of the Bakker fiasco had political implications, intended to hurt Robertson's political possibilities. People on the left worried that liberal agendas would be neutralized if television ministers gained too many followers.

When Christians had their noses rubbed in the dirt with the scandalous reports from among their flock, the media had a heyday watching ministers sweat. As the so-called right wing faltered, the left wing soared high in the air.

The Secular Media is Now Controlled by the Ungodly

Fallen religious leaders not only open the door to scrutiny, they deliver its key to the media! I think that such scrutiny is reasonable to a point, but when detectives follow television ministers hoping to find dirt on them, this goes beyond journalistic investigation into the realm of witch hunting. Any human being is vulnerable to misrepresentation when a reporter's very assignment is to haul skeletons out of the closet. If one's social and moral beliefs conflict with today's liberal views, then that person will likely be singled out and made into an example of hypocrisy.

I have already said that this is a spiritual battle, but I have to remind myself of this when I get disenchanted with the media's condemnation of Christians. How many atheists and agnostics do you know who provide millions of tons of food to the poor like CBN's Operation Blessing? Do you know of any atheist who has ever built an orphanage for poor, abandoned children? Do the world's atheists donate money when national disasters hit? No, it is Christian organizations that help drug addicts, homeless people, the sick, disaster victims, the handicapped, and countless others in the name of Christ's love.

The fact that conservative Christians, who are forever labeled the religious right, are actually serving humanity is often hidden from the public. A conflict rages over who holds the power to speak to America and whose version of its story is broadcast over the airwaves. When revisionists rewrite history without including God, they imply that He had either little influence or a negative influence upon America. As the media casts doubt upon those who disagree with its political preferences, it implies that these Americans are unreasonable bigots. This struggle for power is alive and well, but God's plans for America will not be stopped. Persecution is nothing new to the Almighty or His people, but we must be wise as serpents yet gentle as doves.

One Rabbi's Opinion

Jewish Rabbi Daniel Lapin wrote the book *America's Real War.* Although not a Christian, Rabbi Lapin makes a strong case as to why Judeo-Christian values must be upheld if America is to survive. He tells how many American Jews have chosen unbiblical value systems to replace their Jewish faith and heritage. The American Civil Liberties Union (ACLU) is constantly seeking to unseat Christian values and symbols from America. According to Lapin, the ACLU has a disproportionate number of Jews among its membership. He says that Jews are often spokesmen for groups like Bisexual Veterans of America and The National Gay and Lesbian Task Force.

Without Christ's peace and joy, one's main motivation in life boils down to pleasure. Value systems that are not based on the Bible encourage people to justify their behavior and take the easiest way out. Christians, on the other hand, teach self-control and freedom from the bondage of sin. For example, Christians encourage deliverance from homosexuality with a new freedom in Christ. If this fact became widely accepted, the deception that homosexuals are born that way and cannot change would be exposed! The fact is that thousands of homosexual men and women have chosen to turn away from their lifestyles and walk into a new life with Christ.

Those who insist upon Biblical values become targets of those who oppose them; thus, the selective media attacks continued beyond 1988.

A Journalistic Setup

Ministries that have a track record of purity, purpose, and accountability can become a target of well-orchestrated plans to bring about their downfall.

Several years ago, a well-known minister was set up for scandal one night after conducting a large crusade. He returned to his hotel as usual and while stepping into the elevator, he noticed two scantily clothed women enter the elevator. The evangelist entered his security key and pressed the button for the top floor. He observed that the two women did not press a destination button, but rode the elevator to the top floor with him. When the door opened, a man with a camera was waiting and began to snap pictures as the women grabbed the minister by his arms. The minister began yelling and some of his staff ran from their rooms to investigate. The staffers grabbed the photographer, who confessed that he was attempting to get a compromising picture of the evangelist to sell to a tabloid magazine.

The plan was to ruin the minister's credibility in the public eye by printing the pictures in a national tabloid magazine. A seed of doubt would have been planted and he would have been pronounced in the wrong because of guilt by association. No amount of retractions would have restored the man's or the ministry's reputation. Would anyone have believed it was a setup? Had the photographer not been caught and confessed, a powerful ministry would have been destroyed by a calculated ploy. The following true story identifies yet another setup, this time on television.

Another Setup

Several years ago, a television tabloid show ran an exposé on three nationally known ministers. Its theme was exposing the lies and deceit of televangelists. While one of the ministers was correctly called to account due to dishonesty, the other two were attacked unethically.

In one case, the television show host contacted the minister and said they had heard that he would be the next Billy Graham. They wanted to interview him and do a special report on his ministry. Once they arrived and the cameras rolled, the interviewer said nothing about Billy Graham. The person began to accuse the minister of manipulation, improper fund raising, and other dishonest acts. The minister was grossly misrepresented, causing the decline of the ministry work. Those who knew the minister confirmed that the information presented by the media as fact was indeed a list of half-truths, contradictions, and lies.

Missionary and evangelist Jack Harris is a personal friend of mine. My family has stayed at his home when we ministered at the Life Christian Center in Fenton, Missouri. Jack attended a large church in Dallas, Texas and worked in the church's television ministry. Jack noticed from the outset of the television ministry that the minister spent a great deal of time in prayer and fasting. Jack said, "He was a very anointed man and we saw some outstanding spiritual results in the church and ministry."

As the television ministry grew, the minister hired a company in Tulsa to do ministry mailings and to receive prayer requests and donations. According to Jack, the organization had a reputation of integrity and was owned by a fine Christian businessman. Routinely, mail was opened, donations were removed, and prayer requests, which were written on envelopes, were sent directly to the minister. The minister placed the requests in a huge walk-in closet in his home and literally lay upon the pile of requests and prayed for the senders' needs.

As time passed, Jack Harris entered the mission field and conducted large crusades and pastor's conferences in India. The television minister contacted Jack and asked for help in organizing a series of crusades in India. Jack planned the crusades on three occasions and observed that this American minister spent $90,000, $150,000 and $350,000 dollars on advertising for these crusades.

Two Men and a Camera

Video taping of the India crusades was forbidden in order to avoid having visitors fraudulently use such tape. One evening Jack learned that a man in the crowd was taping the services. He looked like he was from Northern India and this particular crusade was in Southern India. The man ignored repeated warnings to stop taping, so a ministry team member confiscated the camera and his videotapes.

During dinner that night, Jack was interrupted by a team member who said, "Jack, there are two men at the hotel desk who want to see you." He went to the front desk and found two men who wanted their camera and tapes back. Jack got the camera and discovered that there was a piece of tape over the camera's on/off light to conceal when it was on. Another piece of black tape covered the owner's name. Apparently, the men were in some way connected with a major American television network office in northern India. He returned the camera but withheld the tapes. He didn't realize at the time that these men were paid to get the video footage for use in a television exposé that would be slanted against the American evangelist.

The Television Special

Months later, an American television network aired an exposé on three major ministers in America. What Jack Harris and others witnessed in the show was very different from what they knew to be true. The exposé included a portion of the video taken at the crusade in India. Apparently, the man in the crowd was able to keep some tape from being confiscated. The exposé implied that the evangelist spent more money on Dallas billboards than he did in India. Having observed the huge advertising campaigns and the money that was spent, Jack knew that was not true. A question was also raised concerning prayer requests being thrown into a dumpster outside of a bank after removing donations. According to Harris, while the report looked honest, it was filled with misinformation and untruths.

The evangelist sued the television network and Jack was called to give a deposition. The deposition confirmed that the evangelist did not carry any offering out of India. In fact, the evangelist did not personally raise one offering. Harris had raised $2,500 in one crusade and $3,500 in another. The money was used to feed poor Indian pastors and the evangelist took nothing home.

Regarding prayer requests and donations, the exposé implied that the minister took money from the prayer request envelopes and promptly threw them into a dumpster. Nothing was said about the requests being sent to the evangelist's home where he personally prayed over them. The exposé also implied that the evangelist raised funds for missions in Haiti that were never sent to the country. The deposition included a list of eight pages of missionary groups and organizations that received support from the evangelist. In fact, Jack Harris' ministry received financial support in excess of the ministry's Dallas billboard budget. Harris' first hand information disproved many of the deceptions in the exposé.

The minister has yet to receive an apology from the network. The videotape was legally retrieved from the network and Harris said, "One would be shocked to hear the comments of those editing the tapes. Comments like, 'We've got him now' or 'We've nailed him' revealed an absolute animosity toward the minister. The show seriously damaged the minister's reputation to the point that he was unable to eat in public restaurants without being cursed at or ridiculed by people."

While journalists have the right to report the facts concerning public situations, journalists who distort the facts in order to harm people are clearly unethical. Freedom of speech does not mean freedom to deceive! Too often, networks show little concern over biased reports as long as, in their eyes, those targeted deserve it.

Not all secular journalists are two-faced and deceptive. There are thousands of honest, objective journalists who report the news accurately and without bias. In Cleveland, Tennessee and in other areas of the country, local reporters are honest, family-oriented people who are after the facts.

I have been interviewed by the Los Angeles Times, the Tampa Tribune, The Charlotte Observer, The Orlando Sentinel, and papers in smaller cities like Augusta, Georgia. Those conducting the interviews were generally fair, although sometimes a biased slant was apparent.

It is Time for Discernment

No one should believe everything that is reported by the liberal media. Information is not always true, and in many instances, facts are twisted into half-truths. An investigative journalist employed by America's largest cable news network followed another prominent television evangelist for two years. The journalist attempted to find scandalous information in the minister's past and even interviewed former girlfriends from before he was married. In one case, the media reported that a minister had his first child out of wedlock. The minister explained on national television that this took place before his conversion to Christ. He also married the mother and has been happily married to her for many years. Of course, this revelation by the liberal media was designed to hurt the minister's credibility.

Reporting the news is a very important service to all of us. However, staging events so that slanted news reports can boost ratings is unethical and can be destructive. Reports about Israel are a good example of this tactic. Conflict between Muslims and Jews is an interesting topic in America. Footage of protests, political upheavals, and bombings brings good network ratings, and ratings drive the price of television advertising. I have seen reporters arrange Palestinian protests in order to tape them and sell them to American networks. Typically, the frenzy escalates when the cameras roll and afterward, the protest dies down. In the process, Americans are given misleading information about the Israelis. In fact, in the disputed territories, radical Palestinian groups often contact the news centers in Jerusalem to inform them of the date, time, and location of their protests. I was once in Bethlehem shopping and was told to wrap up our transactions in 30 minutes because a protest was planned. That night on CNN International, the violent rioting was aired for the world to see, implying that all of Bethlehem was under siege. Later that evening, I went back into Bethlehem and the stores and restaurants were open and everything was normal. In one area of about 200 square feet, the road was covered with stones thrown in the staged protest. Money exchanged hands and the protestors succeeded in sending a distorted political picture of Bethlehem around the globe.

Satan works so hard to control the airwaves because they can be used to deliver propaganda, or they can be used to deliver the truth of the Gospel of Jesus Christ. The secular, anti-God mindset that dominates the high places is often being manipulated by powerful unseen forces. The Scriptures tell us that it is the gods of this world that have blinded the minds of men who do not believe (2 Corinthians 4:4). People often become the voice of the adversary. Consider the ministry of Jesus, for example. Critics identified Him as the son of Joseph and not the Son of God (John 6:42). Others said His healing ability was of Satanic origin (Matthew 12:24). When Christ arose from the dead, the frightened Roman soldiers lied by saying, "While we slept, the disciples stole His body" (Matthew 28:13). The purpose of these verbal assaults was to destroy the reputation of Christ, thus hindering His influence.

The anti-Bible crowd will continue to print, publish, and promote anti-Christian values and assault those who accept the Bible as the Word of God. Believers must be aware of the subtle land mines being laid throughout the nation and be able to carefully discern the motive and content of news reports and media tactics designed to harm churches, ministers, and Christian organizations.

We must take advantage of the Christian television and Christian satellite programming that is available to us. We must support these efforts so the truth can be preached without distortion and distraction.

Prayer and truth can counter the spiritual wickedness in high places!

Chapter 12

HEALING THE BREACH BETWEEN THE JEWS AND GENTILES

The Prophetic Merging of the Vineyard

"After this I will return, and will build again the tabernacle of David, which is fallen down, and I will build again the ruins thereof, and I will set it up." (Acts 15:16)

In 1997, we lead a group on a tour of Israel. After a busy day, I thought we had settled in for the evening, but my son wanted to go swimming. While at the hotel pool I met a local Jewish man. He assumed that I was Jewish so he struck up an eye-opening conversation. He expressed his hatred for Germans for allowing the Holocaust, and continued by saying that Christians were also to blame because Hitler was a Christian!

We talked for over an hour and I shared with him that there is a difference between a self- proclaimed religious person and someone who actually follows Jesus' teachings. I informed him that many real Christians protected Jews during the Holocaust and that hundreds of thousands of true Christians died along with Jews during the war. I told him, "A true Christian loves everyone, including Jews, and would never harm anyone. There is a difference between those who call themselves Christians and those whose hearts have been changed by Christ."

For centuries, Romans persecuted Jews in the name of Christ. This persecution caused a division among the Jews. A spiritual rift exists between the religious Jews who adhere to the Law of Moses, and the secular Jews who experience their heritage as being more cultural than religious.

The First Century Church

An analogy that explains the relationship between Christianity and Judaism is a branch being grafted onto a tree. The Jews represent the tree with its roots going back to their father, Abraham. When many religious Jews rejected Christ as their Messiah, the Gentiles were given the opportunity to accept Him. Their act of faith in Jesus grafted them into the tree of promise, which symbolizes God's covenant with Abraham. The first century church consisted of Jewish believers. The Holy Spirit was poured out during the Jewish Feast of Pentecost upon 120 Jewish believers, officially pointing to the birth of the Christian Church (Acts 2:1-4). Peter and John went to the Temple to pray at the ninth hour, which was a customary Jewish time of prayer (Acts 3:1). Paul went to the Temple with a group of Jewish believers who broke their Nazarite vow by presenting offerings at the Temple (Acts 21:15-26). Paul was a religious Jew who adhered to the instruction of Moses; however, he was called by God to minister to the Gentiles.

It was the Apostle Paul, a former Jewish Pharisee, who gave insight into the spiritual relationship between the natural Jew and the Gentiles who converted to Christianity. Paul compared the covenant with an olive tree that had many Jewish branches. In Romans 11, Paul taught that, because of unbelief (rejection of Christ), some Jewish branches were broken off of the original olive tree and Gentile branches were grafted onto the tree (Romans 11:20). He said that many of his own people, the Jews, were spiritually blinded to God's plan to graft Gentiles into the Jewish covenant through Jesus Christ (Romans 11:7). He also stated that, when the "fullness of the Gentiles comes in," God would graft the natural

Jew back into the tree and "all Israel would be saved" (Romans 11:25-26). It may be a misunderstanding of this concept that caused the early Roman Church, as far back as the third century, to erroneously teach that God forsook the Jews and that they were a cursed people. The error spread during the third century when a symbolic method was introduced to interpret unfulfilled prophecy. Doctrine was espoused that said the Jews had forever forfeited their promised blessings under the covenant when they rejected Christ. This is called replacement theology and many groups today refuse to recognize the nation of Israel's Biblical right to exist. Those following replacement theology also teach that there are no legitimate Jews on earth, and that Israel means nothing in light of Bible prophecy. This fallacy is based upon a completely false interpretation of certain Scriptures.

Anti-Semitic attitudes were propagated throughout the centuries, and they climaxed in the Holocaust. Some argue that, at the crucifixion, religious Jews cried out, "His (Christ's) blood be upon us and upon our children," thereby pronouncing their own curse. According to the Law of Moses, the land in Israel became cursed when an innocent man was killed. An entire ritual was to be performed under the Law to remove a curse from a city when an innocent man was found dead (Deuteronomy 21). Part of the ritual involved washing the hands. This is why Pilate washed his hands before the Jews when declaring that Christ was an innocent man (Matthew 27:24). At the cross, it was Roman soldiers who actually hammered the nails and pierced the side of Christ. And Jesus prayed while dying, "Father, forgive them, for they know not what they do" (Luke 23:34). Christ forgave those who crucified Him, but the land of Israel fell under a curse of the law; thus, Jerusalem was ravaged 40 years later. Much misunderstanding has created a breach between traditional Christianity and the Jews.

American culture is based upon Judeo-Christian principles, which is to say that it is based upon teachings from both the Old and the New Testament. Paul wrote, "All Scripture is given by inspiration of God" (2 Timothy 3:16). God does not have two separate Bibles, one for Jews and one for Christians. His Bible unites both the old and the new in Christ. It contains 66 books that articulate a complete revelation for all of mankind! It is sad that most Jews reject the New Testament, and some Christians reject the Old Testament, because both testaments sanction one another.

Today many Jews are beginning to understand their spiritual ties to Christians, and many Christians are beginning to understand their Old Testament roots. Many Pentecostal and Charismatic congregations are beginning to have Hebraic worship. Christians are using Jewish tools of worship at specific times in services and during Jewish festival seasons. For example:

- Men blow the shofar and the ram's horn as a call to worship.
- Christians wear a tallit (prayer shawl) during times of prayer.
- During certain songs, tambourines are played.
- Beautiful banners with spiritual emblems and Hebrew names hang in churches.
- Hebraic worship teams and drama teams are being formed.
- There is a new emphasis on the Hebraic style of music and singing.

Some criticize the use of Hebrew tools of worship and say that ministers are attempting to bring ancient Jewish customs into the Christian church. Yet, in prophecy, it is clear that God plans to merge the Gentile branch of the church with Zion in the last days. The Gentile Christians and Messianic Jews will become one in Jerusalem during the one thousand year reign of Christ on earth (Revelation 20:4). During the one thousand year reign of Christ, known as the millennial reign, we will see and hear:

- shofars (trumpets) being blown as we worship in Jerusalem (Isaiah 27:13)
- people wearing Jewish skirts in Jerusalem   (Zechariah 8:23)
- the Feast of Tabernacles being celebrated   (Zechariah 14:16)
- sacrifices being offered in the new Temple in Jerusalem (Ezekiel 43 - 47)
- a new Priesthood in charge of the Temple in Jerusalem (Ezekiel 45)
- people keeping the Sabbath and the new moon   (Isaiah 66:23)

It is apparent to me that Jewish worship in Christian churches around the world is visible evidence that God is preparing to unite His people for the future reign of Christ on earth. Christ will rule from Jerusalem — not Washington, D.C. The center of the nations will be Jerusalem, and the nations will come to Jerusalem to worship the King (Zechariah 14:16).

God is preparing a people for the Lord (Malachi 3:1).

Yet, in North America, there are still many conflicts between Bible-believing Christians and secular, or cultural Jews. The conflict is most apparent when we look at lawsuits aimed at eliminating Christian influence from public places.

Secular (or Cultural) Jews and Christianity

Prayer before high school sporting events has been opposed, along with having the Ten Commandments and Christmas carols in public schools. Much of the legal action to remove Christian influence from public schools has been championed by the American Civil Liberties Union (ACLU), which has a large Jewish membership. According to the ACLU's Christian counterpart, the American Center for Law and Justice (ACLJ), such suits include Adams County, Ohio where the school board was sued for permitting a monument of the Ten Commandments in front of four district schools. In Elkhart, Indiana, the ACLU fought to remove a plaque of the Ten Commandments from city hall. The ACLU attacked displays of the Ten Commandments in Wilkes County, North Carolina; Scott County, Indiana; Rockville, Maryland; Morehouse Parish, Louisiana; Hagerstown, Maryland; and countless others.

Christians may wonder why some secular Jews would attempt to eliminate the Ten Commandments from public places. After all, the Ten Commandments came from Judaism and the Old Testament. Remember that a person with a Jewish heritage is not necessarily a practicing Jew. Likewise, a person with Christian heritage is not necessarily a Christian unless he or she personally embraces faith in Christ as Savior. Christians without a personal relationship with Christ and knowledge of the Bible can support social policies that are totally contrary to the Bible. Similarly, outspoken secular Jews with liberal views can be totally unaware of how these views are contrary to the Old Testament.

My Dear Jewish Friend

Gideon Shor, a tour guide from Israel, has been one of my closest Jewish friends since 1986. Throughout the years, he has conducted private tours for some of America's most well-known people, including Michael Dukakis, Hubert Humphry, famous athletes, movie stars, and very influential Jewish families.

In 1988, Gideon was a personal tour guide for a well-known Jewish man and his new wife (whom we will leave nameless). The man was a producer for a major American television sitcom. He and Gideon argued about religion in America. The producer, an avid unbeliever, told Gideon that religion was the problem in America. He felt that if America could rid itself of conservative Christians, the United States would become a more tolerant nation. Gideon said that he had been in America and that he believed it was the people who honor God that made America great, not the Hollywood crowd! He continued by saying, "I travel to America and stay in the homes of Christian people who pray before their meals and work hard every day. It is faith in God that has made America great." After the bickering, Gideon offered to be replaced by another tour guide. The man replied, "I disagree with you but respect you for standing up to me."

This conversation occurred around the time when Pat Robertson began his run for the presidency. In the conversation, the producer admitted that he was angered at Robertson's possibilities to influence the country. He said, "If I have to see to it myself, Robertson will never become President." This statement shocked Gideon. What the man implied was uncertain, but it was clear that he would use his influence in any way possible to stop Robertson because of his religious beliefs.

Why Such Animosity?

Why are many secular Jewish organizations so blatantly anti-Christian in their expression? Why does the ACLU focus on lawsuits that attack the Bible, prayer, or Christian teachings? Rabbi Daniel Lapin, in his book *America's Real War,* gave his opinion as to why Jews are fearful of the Christian right. He wrote, "Jews, for the most part, feel threatened by three specters: Christian efforts to convert Jews, a Christian takeover of America, anti-Semitism by Christians, and recollections of past anti-Semitism on the part of churches."

In addition, here are some of my personal conclusions as to why many Jews fear conservative Christians. These observations are based on personal encounters with Jews, especially those who live in Israel.

Many Christians feel strongly that they are to carry out the great commission that Christ bestowed upon the church before His ascension forty days after He rose from the dead. He said, "Go ye therefore, and teach all nations, baptizing them in the name of the Father, and of the Son, and of the Holy Ghost" (Mathew 28:19). Christians carry out the great commission by sharing the message of the Gospel to win souls to Christ. Over the past few years, an increasing number of Jews have accepted Jesus (Yeshua) as their Messiah. According to rabbinical Judaism, a Jew ceases to be a Jew upon converting to Christianity. If Jews become atheists, Hindus or Buddhists, they retain their Jewish identity. However, upon becoming a Christian, Rabbis teach that a Jew renounces his or her Hebrew identity. So Christianity is considered to be a threat to Jewish identity.

The act of converting from Judaism to Christianity is the highest insult to many religious and non-religious Jews. Throughout Roman Church history, Jews were persecuted, and the teachings of the Jewish Talmud and the teachings of the Christian church concerning Jesus' identity conflicted. Some Jews persecuted Christians in the first century, but many Roman Christians persecuted Jews for over 1,400 years. So, to many Jews, becoming a Christian is equivalent to becoming an enemy of the Hebrew people. In America, it would be comparable to a child who was raised in the Baptist denomination telling his or her parents, "I have become a Muslim."

The third reason concerns the Holocaust and the death of six million Jews at the hands of the Nazis. Holocaust survivors often tell of seeing Nazi soldiers brandishing crosses and telling the Jews that they were avenging them for the blood of Jesus. Oddly enough, it was a Jew from Nazareth named Yeshua (Jesus) who predicted that the Jews "would be hated above all nations for His name's sake" (Matthew 24:9). The Christian church in Germany did not take a strong enough stand against Hitler; therefore, Christians are often blamed for instigating, or at least not stopping, the Holocaust. The truth is that Hitler hated real Christians who loved Jews as much as he hated Jews themselves. Also, people such as Oskar Schindler and Corrie Ten Boom were noted Gentiles who cared more about the Jews than about their own personal security. Many Christians during that time protected Jews as much as possible.

The combination of distrust from the past and fear of conversion to Christianity causes many Jews to be apprehensive about associating with or trusting those who profess Christianity. If a Jew becomes a believer, some within the Jewish community consider this person to be a traitor. I have spoken to many Jewish friends and tried to empathize with them. It is easy to understand their feelings, considering all the blood that has been shed throughout the centuries in the name of Christ.

I have told my Jewish friends that the religion of the old Roman Empire does not represent all of Christianity. To compare all believers in Christ to the so-called Christians who murdered the Jews during the Holocaust is something like comparing all American Jews to all anti-Christian liberals in the country. Neither is an accurate comparison.

In terms of persecution, the Roman church has clearly victimized Jews throughout its history. However, many present-day groups such as the Pentecostals, Baptists, Methodists and others, do not follow the older Roman system that dominated the church between the fourth and seventeenth centuries. Jews in Israel and other parts of the world are leery of evangelical Christians because they feel that Christian love for them is based upon a desire to convert them. Actually, our love is based upon the understanding that Jews and Christians worship the same God, the God of Abraham, Isaac, and Jacob. Christians and Jews accept the Old Testament as true, and both groups believe in Israel's prophetic role in the end times. Evangelical Christians support Israel because the Bible teaches that the Jews will be the world's end-time evangelists, and Israel will be where the major prophetic activity will unfold in the last days.

In the United States, some Jews in the media and in prominent Jewish organizations lash out at Baptist, Pentecostal, and Charismatic groups who emphasize evangelism. But these three groups are some of the strongest supporters of Israel. Can the distrust and misunderstandings resulting from centuries of wrongful persecution be healed in these latter days?

Healing the Breach Between the Jews and Christians

Since Israel became a nation again in 1948, and since the reunification of Jerusalem in 1967, Evangelical Christians in America and Canada have supported Israel. In recent years, Christians have donated millions of dollars to assist Russian Jews returning to Israel. Despite this gesture of reconciliation, the spiritual rift between many Jews and traditional Christians still exists.

Prophetically, we believe that as the time of Christ's return nears, this chasm will close and there will be greater understanding, especially between Israeli Jews and American Christians. James predicted in the book of Acts that God would "return and raise up the tabernacle of David that is fallen and build up the ruins thereof" (Acts 15:16). In my twenty-one trips to Israel, I have observed the wall of distrust among many Jewish people begin to crumble. The first century church consisted of both Jews and Gentiles. This tells me that it is God's desire that His spiritual tree and its branches bear fruit together. A recent discovery in Israel indicates this.

Pottery On Mount Zion

An item called the "Messianic Seal of the Jerusalem Church" was discovered on several pieces of first century pottery in Jerusalem. Information about this seal can be found in the book, *The Messianic Seal of the Jerusalem Church*, printed by Olim Publications in Israel. The book relates the fascinating story of Ludwig Schneider.

In 1990, Mr. Schneider befriended a monk who lived alone in the Old City of Jerusalem. The monk was a Greek man named Tech Otheoos. Otheoos invited Ludwig into his tiny dwelling to show him something he found near Mount Zion in 1969. According to Greek tradition, the first church in Jerusalem resided near Mount Zion and was pastored by the Apostle James. To Ludwig's amazement, the monk showed him about forty pieces of pottery, including an oil lamp, clay jars, and other first century vessels that he had uncovered in an old grotto near King David's tomb.

It was not the pottery that registered with Ludwig, but an emblem that was either etched or painted on every piece. The emblem looked like a Jewish menorah drawn with a triangular base that had a triangular tail of a small fish overlapping the bottom of the menorah. The triangular base of the menorah and the triangular tail of the fish intersected to form a Star of David. This emblem is presently used on the national flag of Israel (*See Center Section Fig. 1*).

The monk gave Ludwig eight pieces of the pottery that carried the emblem. Many now believe this emblem was the Messianic seal of the first century church in Jerusalem. In fact, one large stone block that was excavated had etched upon it the words "for the oil of the spirit." Some suggest that the pottery jar in the collection may have held olive oil used for anointing early believers (S*ee Center Section Fig. 2*).

According to the Bible, James led the first church in Jerusalem. While Peter served the Jewish sect of the first church, Paul served Gentile believers. James wrote about the work of God in restoring the tabernacle of David and healing the breach (Acts 15:15-16). This early church emblem speaks of the Jews and Gentiles being one in Christ. James also mentioned the anointing of the sick with oil in the name of the Lord (James 5:14).

Some believe that this emblem is the seal of the Jerusalem church. Dr. Joe Van Koevering and I extended our stay after a tour of Israel in 1999 to tape programs for the January 2000 episodes of *God's News Behind the News*. During our stay, we asked our Israeli friend, Gideon Shor, to take us to the grotto where the pottery was discovered (*See Center Section Figs. 3-8*). On December 5, the three of us, along with our camera crews, found the actual grotto located about 75 yards from the tomb of King David. A concrete building and metal cage surrounds the underground chamber, which has chained double metal doors. After contacting a Greek Monk who teaches at the Greek school, we were permitted to enter the grotto and take still photographs.

Our Greek guide unlocked the metal doors and led us down a series of hewn steps that were chiseled by hand. He told us that the grotto was cut out of limestone and that it was an ancient cistern that may have once been a Jewish mikvot. The mikvot was an ancient baptismal pool where the Jews submerged themselves in water to become purified. At the bottom of the chiseled stairs and to the left were two small altars for prayer. To the right, we walked through a small opening into an adjoining room, again cut out of limestone. It was round and about 16 feet high. It wasn't very large and could have possibly held twenty people. We went through a small tunnel about twenty feet long that led into another room, which appeared to be another large cistern. The lighting was poor and the cistern was very dark. We were unable to see inside to determine its actual size. The chambers seemed to end at this point. The monk told us that the entire hill covered a series of tunnels that branch out and are similar to the catacombs under the city of Rome, Italy. Most tunnels have been sealed up or filled with debris and are no longer accessible, at least from the area of the ancient grotto.

The monk told us that Helena, the mother of Constantine, came to the Holy Land over 1,600 years ago and built a church on the same hill that is above these tunnels. The monk allowed us to visit the basement of the Greek school to view two sections of a small, mosaic floor that are the only remains of the church that Helena built above the tunnels where some believe the early Christians secretly met (Fig. 8 and 9).

The monk was not familiar with Teek Otheoos' story or the discovery of the pottery and the ancient seal. The 1969 discovery was made years before he came to the school to teach. He told us about others who might be willing to share information about the seal. Typically, without an inside contact, it is almost impossible to gather such research information.

According to Ludwig, Otheoos was in his nineties when he gave the eight pieces of pottery to him. Soon after, Otheoos passed away and the remaining pottery was removed from his home, along with his possessions. Some believe that the pottery is in the possession of a Greek monastery whose inhabitants refuse to discuss the subject. Fortunately, Ludwig has his visible evidence of the discovery under lock and key in Israel.

Gideon Shor saw a picture of a small stone block with the letters carved on the front. He confirmed that the letters were old Hebrew letters that were used during the first century. Reading right to left, the two words are Shemon Ruach, meaning *the oil of the Spirit*. The old Hebrew was used until about the fifth century, then the form of the letters changed. These Hebrew letters are physical evidence of the fact that believing Jews formed a sect of the early church in Jerusalem.

In 1996, Ludwig opened a gift shop in the old city and began selling souvenirs with the emblem he believed was the "Messianic Seal of the Jerusalem Church." Certain orthodox Jews learned of the souvenirs and became angry over the use of the seal. They stoned Ludwig's shop and he was forced to close it down. Apparently, the Jews were angered over the use of what appeared to be a Star of David on the souvenirs.

By placing the menorah (a Jewish emblem) and the fish (an early Christian emblem) together, few people would be upset. But on each piece of pottery, the menorah and the fish seemed to create a Star of David. Prophetically, the menorah signified the old covenant and the fish signified the new covenant. Tradition teaches that before Christians were martyred in Rome, one Christian was made to draw half of a fish in the sand, and the other Christian drew the other half, forming the fish emblem. The fish signified the martyrs' faithfulness to Christ. Others say that the fish represents the words of Jesus, "I will make you fishers of men" (Mark 1:17).

Imagine pottery from the early church containing an emblem that links to Christians who died 1,700 years before, and that the pottery was discovered shortly after Jerusalem was reunited as Israel's capital. Some in Israel want to discredit the emblem; however, Christians throughout the world are wearing it. The emblem symbolizes healing between Christians and Jews. It is very interesting that the menorah, symbolizing the old covenant, and the fish, symbolizing the new covenant, when placed together form a Star of David (Israel).

The emblem represents the unity between Jewish and Gentile believers in the first and second centuries. Despite some controversy over the authenticity of the pottery, the fact that this emblem has been made public, especially through Voice of Evangelism, is significant because God is using Christians to promote and support the reunification of Israel. Christians are meeting with Israeli leaders to show their solidarity, and Evangelical Christians are studying Hebrew and researching the New Testament from a Hebraic perspective.

The Restitution of All Things

The introduction of Jewish worship in some Christian churches and the discovery of the Jerusalem seal are two encouraging signs that there is new spiritual healing beginning on earth. Scripture states that the heavens will receive Christ "until the times of the restitution of all things spoken of by the mouth of all the holy prophets since the world began" (Acts 3:21). The word restitution means *a restoration*. Most prophetic scholars believe this restitution began in 1948, with the rebirth of Israel as a nation. No prophecy relating to the return of Christ could have been fulfilled unless Israel was restored as a nation, and the Jews returned to their homeland. When this restitution took place it produced a fivefold effect:

- In 1948, Israel was restored as a nation (Isaiah 66:7-8).
- In 1967, Jerusalem was reunited as the capital of Israel (Psalms 102:16).
- In 1988, Jews began returning to Israel from the North, or Russia (Jeremiah 16:14-16).
- In 1993, the latter rains began to return to the land of Israel (James 5:7).
- In 1994, the desert areas began to blossom and produce fruit (Isaiah 35:1-7).

In 1948, fulfillment of Bible prophecy began to unfold with the rebirth of Israel. That same year, the American Gentile church experienced its own restoration as great revivals spread throughout the land, many of which were held in large outdoor tents. Israel's first church was also held in a wilderness tent. It is exciting to note that, on some dates when prophetic events transpired in Israel, there were parallel spiritual events taking place in America! Here are some examples:

- In 1948, Israel was restored. Between 1948 and 1955, a spiritual restoration in America began to take place, in many cases, at huge tent meetings.
- In 1967, the city of Jerusalem was reunited as Israel's capital. The reunification physically took place as a giant concrete wall was broken down, uniting east and west Jerusalem. In 1967, the Charismatic renewal in America began breaking down denominational walls as the Holy Spirit visited many churches in North America.
- In the 1990s, the latter rains began returning to Israel and the barren places blossomed like a rose (Isaiah 35:1). In the 1990s, American churches blossomed spiritually as the Holy Spirit moved across the nation.

In the 1990s, Jews returned to Israel from the north (Russia). In Israel, they discovered their Jewish roots and began to study the Hebrew language and their Hebrew heritage. Likewise, in the 1990s, many American Christians began to discover their Jewish roots by studying the Hebrew language, feasts, customs, and culture.

I believe that America is God's end-time vineyard, a leading Gentile nation that is taking the message of Christ to the nations. Jesus said that when the Gospel of the Kingdom has been taken to every nation, then the end would come (Matthew 24:14). According to my understanding of eschatology, or end-time prophecy, when the work of the Gentile branch is complete, its spiritual assignment will be taken over by the Jewish branch. This analogy refers to Israel being represented by an olive tree that had a new branch grafted into it because the Jews temporarily rejected their Messiah. Another issue comes into play here, which has to do with the rapture, or the church being caught up to meet the Lord. Israel's spiritual role can come about only after the rapture of the Gentile church. This will happen at the beginning of the final seven years before Christ's return that is known as Daniel's last week (Daniel 9:27).

John Darby (1800-1882), who published many prophetic books wrote, "Once the time of the Church of Christ is over, the time of Israel will start again." The conclusion of the church age is called the dispensation of the grace of God in Ephesians 3:1-4. At this time, the spiritual decline among the Gentile nations will be so great that all spiritual attention, for seven years, will be placed on Israel and the Jewish people. At this time, God will graft the Jewish branch back into the olive tree and, "all Israel shall be saved."

The prophets warned, "Jerusalem will become a cup of trembling" to the nations of the world, and "all nations shall be gathered together against Jerusalem" (Zechariah 12:1-3). Many Israeli leaders are befriending American, Canadian and other Evangelical church leaders. They have found that Israel has few friends in the world and they understand the importance of cooperation between friends. One noted Jewish family obtained a 300-year-old Torah scroll that came from a Russian synagogue for our international ministry center. I was a good friend of Yehuda Getz, a chief rabbi in Israel who has since departed from this life. Two of my closest friends outside of America are Jews who live in Jerusalem.

I would advise Christians not to judge Jews by the few among them who seek to remove God and Christianity from American culture. I would advise the Jews not to judge all Christians by a handful of anti-Semitics who call themselves Christians. Look at those whose lives reflect the teachings of the Bible and, through love, seek to build bridges to their Jewish brothers and sisters. Christians believe that the Messiah is coming to restore all things, and that He was a Jew who was born of a Jewish mother. Is it any wonder that Christians love Hebrew people, Hebrew culture, and Hebrew Scriptures? Jesus died for Jews and Gentiles. A Jewish man allowed Christ to borrow his tomb, a Roman solder was converted while Christ was dying, and a black man named Simon the Cyrenian helped carry Jesus' cross. Jesus died for everyone (Matthew 27:60, Mark 15:39, Matthew 27:32).

I believe we are in the early stages of a restoration of the breach. Since Christ will rule from Jerusalem for 1,000 years, we must learn to understand our Hebrew roots!

Chapter 13

CURSED IN THE MIDST OF PROSPERITY

Seven Curses Affecting America

"But it shall come to pass, if thou wilt not hearken unto the voice of the Lord thy God, to observe to do all his commandments and his statutes which I command thee this day; that all these curses shall come upon thee, and overtake thee."   (Deuteronomy 28:15)

Power, position, and prestige can lead to pride. It is easy for national leaders (including ministers) to become legends in their own minds and claim responsibility for the nation's spiritual or financial blessings. Both political wings have laid claim to the idea that prosperity resulted from their leadership. Certainly good leadership can promote a stable economy and prosperity, but few men in leadership realize what tomorrow will bring. Is it possible to be cursed in the midst of prosperity?

The book of Deuteronomy, which is central to the Torah, was a revelation from God to Moses. The book contains detailed instructions for living, encompassing guidelines for practical living, methods of agriculture, rules of morality, and even dietary laws. Obedience to the commands in this book results in health and prosperity for those who will follow them. If the Hebrews disobeyed the instructions, severe consequences followed. Their blessings turned into curses and their successes were frustrated.

Some contemporary Christians believe the instructions in the Torah are only for the ancient Hebrews and have no bearing upon us today. Apparently, they are unfamiliar with many references in the New Testament that come from the Old Testament books.

Yet, during Christ's temptation in Matthew 4, He quoted three Scriptures from Deuteronomy. The Bible says, "All scripture is given by inspiration of God and is profitable" (2 Timothy 3:16). The basic laws that govern our nation are found in the book of Deuteronomy. America's early fathers used this book as a guideline for law and order in the nation. Our fundamental freedoms are based on Moses' revelation on Mount Sinai. The Declaration of Independence, the U.S. Constitution, and the Bill of Rights all contain phrases that originated in the Torah. Harry Truman said that these early documents of our nation are founded upon the Torah, the book of Isaiah, and the four Gospels.

Therefore, it should not be surprising that, if America has a unique Hebrew connection, God's commands to ancient Israel are also applicable for our nation. Americans can expect to receive the same blessings for obedience and the same curses for disobedience. Unfortunately, many of the curses pronounced against ancient Israel by the Lord are found throughout the United States today.

The Prosperity Syndrome

We have all heard of the American dream. It implies that every American, with proper educational opportunities and hard work, will have good wages and will own personal property, such as a home and a nice automobile. Few nations in the world have populations so richly blessed.

For several years, the word prosperity has become a political catchword. Yet, this concept often places an emphasis only upon material things. Even ministers have been caught up in guaranteeing their flocks abundance in exchange for giving money. Some have even based their ministries on the idea that material abundance will result from their contributions. The outcome of such an unbalanced message is presented in Revelation 3:17 when the Laodicean church declared, "I am rich and increased with goods and have need of nothing." This seventh church in Revelation boasted of having all of its needs met. Today, there is an emphasis on having one's needs met. In my personal life, having unmet needs makes me more dependent upon God. Saints without needs are usually also without prayer.

In this time of prosperity, many men gloat about their wealth and power. They announce to the media that, during their administration, blessings and prosperity manifested. They warn that, if their party loses power, American prosperity will come to a grinding halt. Yet, while Americans focus on Wall Street and an illusion of prosperity, behind the scenes things aren't going so well.

Just as God dealt with Israel, He is dealing with America. If we will seek His face, obey Him, and turn from our sins, we shall be "Blessed in the city and blessed in the field. Blessed when we come in and blessed when we go out. Our enemies that rise against us shall flee seven ways. The commanded blessing of God shall come upon us, bringing blessing to our livestock, our farms and our children" (Deuteronomy 28:1-14).

On the other hand, if our nation does not listen to the Lord and obey His commands, then Biblical curses will overtake us. Based on Deuteronomy 28, one can see that America is experiencing a curse in the midst of its prosperity. Notice the seven curses that overtake those who turn their backs on God and the Bible. These ancient warnings spring forth into our time and our nation.

The Seven Curses Coming Against America

1. The Curse of Mental Problems

"The Lord shall smite thee with madness, and blindness and astonishment of heart." (Deuteronomy 28:28)

Teens are murdering each other in public schools, and pre-teens are raping and killing in the inner cities. A recent news report told of a young 13-year-old girl who was raped by twenty young men from a public school. Our public schools are becoming increasingly unsafe.

More Americans than ever depend upon anti-depressants and drugs. Depression and mental conditions plague society. While we boast of our intellectualism, mental problems increase.

What causes a mother to throw a baby into a dumpster, or a father to beat his child to death? What makes a wife hire a hit man to kill her husband, or a mother hire a man to kill a young cheerleader so her daughter can take her place? It must be a curse of madness.

2. The Curse of Drought

"And thy heaven that is over thy head shall be brass, and the earth that is under thee shall be iron. And the Lord shall make the rain of thy land powder and dust: from heaven shall it come down upon thee, until thou be destroyed."
(Deuteronomy 28:23,24)

Drought, causing the devastation of millions of dollars worth of crops, has been in American headlines for the past few years. The words "worst drought in seventy years" should cause us to think. In Scripture, drought signified God's disfavor on the nation because of sin.

Because of Ahab's wickedness, God withheld rain for forty-two months, which caused a severe drought throughout Israel (1 Kings 17:1). Only the prayers of Elijah reversed the judgment (1 Kings 18:42-46).

3. The Curse of Disease

"The Lord shall make the pestilence cleave unto thee, until he have consumed thee from off the land, whither thou goest to possess it. The Lord shall smite thee with consumption, and with a fever, and with an inflammation, and with an extreme burning...The Lord shall smite thee with the botch of Egypt...Moreover he shall bring all the diseases of Egypt upon thee." (Deuteronomy 28:21-22; 27 and 60)

Jesus warned that pestilences would be a sign of His return to earth (Matthew 24:7). The word pestilence in Hebrew can mean *the plague that ends in death*. AIDS is certainly one disease that fits that description. While medical science has made remarkable strides toward curing disease, new viruses are being discovered faster than the ability of the medical community to respond. Recently I heard about a strange sickness called the West Nile Virus, which can result in death. The Bible warns that, if we keep sinning, the diseases of Egypt will come upon us. Interestingly, the Nile River runs through Egypt!

A medical doctor from Orange Country, California told me that, in the future, there will be so many flu epidemics and viruses that medical science will be unable to identify remedies fast enough. In other words, sicknesses will literally overtake us.

4. The Curse of Divorce

"Thou shalt betroth a wife, and another man shall lie with her: thou shalt build a house, and thou shalt not dwell therein: thou shalt plant a vineyard, and shalt not gather the grapes thereof.... Thy sons and daughters shall be given to another people, and thine eyes shall look, and fail with longing for them all the day long" (Deuteronomy 28:30-32).

It was Moses who permitted divorce under the law. Jesus said, "In the beginning it was not so", but God permitted divorce because "of the hardness of your hearts" (Matthew 19:7-9). Divorce is a curse that robs a father of his family and home, or a mother of her family and home. The divorce rate in America is about 50% and many children are its innocent victims. Since society accepts divorce and remarriage so readily, multiple marriages are common. God's best plan, however, is for a man and wife to remain faithful to one another, and to stay committed for a lifetime.

5. Children Will Become a Heartache

"Thou shalt begat sons and daughters, but thou shalt not enjoy them: for they shall go into captivity." (Deuteronomy 28:41)

Many youth are in a type of spiritual captivity, bound by drugs, pornography, and alcohol. Some face fines and jail sentences because of their violent acts and rebellion. Parents grieve as they reminisce about times when their young children embraced them with open expressions of love. The warm memories haunt them, as they pray that somehow their children will come to their senses and be restored to God. Wayward children bring much more sorrow than joy to their parents as they rebel and seek worldly pleasures. The warning of this curse has become a reality in America because we have broken God's principles.

6. The Curse of Strangers Owning the Businesses

"The stranger that is within thee shall get up above thee very high; and thou shalt come down very low." (Deuteronomy 28:43)

A group of ministers visited David Wilkerson, pastor of Times Square Church in New York City. While eating in a restaurant atop a skyscraper, Wilkerson asked the ministers to look out the window and tell him what they saw. One minister noticed the lights and the tall structures as any person would. Wilkerson said, "Look at the lighted signs on the buildings. Foreign nations own this city!"

As I have traveled around America, I have observed a large number of foreign-owned businesses. While our nation is a melting pot of many nationalities, foreigners own corporations that were at one time owned by Americans. Those Americans who work for foreign-owned businesses are working for the "stranger among us." While it may not be politically correct to point this out, the globalization of the world economy is a part of the end-time scenario.

7. The Curse of Abortion

"The tender and delicate women among you, which would not adventure to set the sole of her foot upon the ground for delicateness and tenderness, her eye shall be evil toward the husband of her bosom, and toward her son, and toward her daughter. And toward her young one that cometh out from between her feet, and toward her children which she shall bear: for she shall eat them for want of all things secretly in the siege." (Deuteronomy 28:56-57)

Scripture indicates that there were times of severe famine in Israel. Josephus, the Jewish historian, wrote about a famine in Jerusalem which was so terrible that one woman ate her own child. Some around her became angry because she did not share her meal with them. In Solomon's time, families sacrificed their children to Molech in a ceremony referred to as "passing their children through the fire" (Leviticus 18:21; 20:2-5; Amos 5:26).

This seventh curse of killing or sacrificing children is evidenced in America today, as women who have carried their children almost to term suddenly decide they don't want their babies. At abortion facilities, they don't sacrifice their children on altars; they simply "terminate their pregnancies." Then the bodies of these precious babies, whose hearts were beating within their mothers' wombs, and whose features were perfectly shaped down to the detail of their fingernails and eyelashes, are discarded. Some horrible reports tell of cases where babies' remains were found in dumpsters. God revealed that a time would come when a woman would turn against her husband, leave her children, and hate the children that she conceives and births. In part, this describes the curse of abortion.

A Cause of God's Disfavor

The act that greatly incites God's disfavor is articulated throughout the Bible. It began in Genesis when Cane killed Abel, and will continue through the end times when Mystery Babylon forces the slaughter of righteous believers. That act is murder, and its curse results from the shedding of innocent blood.

Many Americans have turned a deaf ear to abortion. Since Roe v. Wade was upheld in 1973, most citizens think nothing of the act or its consequences. God said, "Lo, children are a heritage of the Lord and the fruit of the womb is his reward" (Psalms 127:3). Children are a blessing and not a curse. Warnings were given to Israel throughout its history concerning the shedding of innocent blood. God literally hates the "hands that shed innocent blood" (Proverbs 6:16-17).

When Manasseh rose to power in Israel, he sacrificed his own children to idol gods. This was referred to as passing children through the fire of Molech (Leviticus 18:21). Molech was an idol made of iron, made to look like a man below the waist and a bull above the waist. The belly of the idol was hollow and contained fire. Worshipers passed their children between Molech's hot metal hands and threw them into the idol's belly as a human offering. God expressed His opinion about this idol worship in the Torah: "Thou shalt not let any of thy seed pass through the fire to Molech, neither shalt thou profane the name of thy God. I am the Lord. And the land is defiled: therefore I do visit the iniquity thereof upon it, and the land itself vomiteth out her inhabitants" (Leviticus 18:21,25). Some of Israel's kings fell into this ungodly sin.

Manesseh's decision to sacrifice his children filled Jerusalem with murderous violence. The Bible states, "Moreover Manasseh shed innocent blood very much, till he had filled Jerusalem from one end to another..." (2 Kings 21:16). The people followed their leader and began to sacrifice their children to idol gods. God sent the Babylonians to Jerusalem to destroy the city because its inhabitants shed the innocent blood of it children. The prophet Ezekiel lived at the time of the Babylonian attack and he proclaimed to Israel why God was allowing the enemy to destroy Jerusalem: "Wherefore I poured my fury upon them for the blood that they had shed upon the land" (Ezekiel 36:18). Ezekiel specifically wrote that infant sacrifices were the cause: "And I polluted them in their own gifts, in that they caused to pass through the fire all that openeth the womb, that I might make them desolate, to the end that they might know that I am the Lord" (Ezekiel 20:26).

In 1963, the stage was being set for America's spiritual decline, and in 1973 the decision to legalize abortion opened the curtain on America's moral decline. Since then, violence in the cities, sexually transmitted diseases, rape, and incest have ravaged America. The saddest part of all this is the spiritual ignorance among people who call themselves Christians! As Jeremiah warned, "My people know not the judgment of the Lord" (Jeremiah 8:7).

It is clear that America is at the crossroads. Either we will return to our spiritual roots and repair our moral foundations, or we will continue to allow the gradual disintegration of our Judeo-Christian values.

It is time for believers to speak up and denounce wickedness and declare the true source of America's blessing and prosperity. Amid much clamor and opposition from those who choose not to honor God, the eagle is still flying because of the following:

1. Giving to Feed the Poor

Proverbs 19:17 states, "He that hath pity upon the poor lendeth unto the Lord; and that which he hath given will he pay to him again." Jesus instructed us to clothe the naked, feed the poor, and care for the fatherless. Many Scriptures teach that there are special blessings for those who help the poor. America has been a compassionate and generous nation. Our compassion stems from God's love within us. God has blessed America because of our service to the poor, the homeless, and the stranger.

2. Giving to Help the Widows and Orphans

James wrote, "Pure religion and undefiled before God and the Father is this, to visit the fatherless and widows in their affliction, and to keep himself unspotted from the world" (James 1:27).

In many nations, the widows and orphans are homeless and hungry. In Romania, orphans starve to death each year. In Russia, thousands of widows survive all alone without any support. Thank God that America has been so giving to the needy, the widows, and the orphans.

3. Giving to Spread the Gospel to the Nations

The Gospel of Christ must be preached to all nations and then the end will come (Matthew 24:14). Scripture states, "How then shall they call on him whom they have not believed? And how shall they believe in him of whom they have not heard? And how shall they hear without a preacher? And how shall they preach, except they be sent?" (Romans 10:14-15). Christians in America lead the world in support of missionaries who take the Gospel of Christ to unreached people. They also generously finance costly crusades, build churches, develop Bible schools, and establish orphanages. Because of this, all of America has been favored by God.

4. Supporting Israel and Jerusalem

In Genesis 12:3, God promised Abraham, "I will bless them that bless you and curse them that curse you." Believers in Christ are to "pray for the peace of Jerusalem; they shall prosper that love thee" (Psalms 122:6). America has been a safe haven for Jews from its beginning, and we also supported the Hebrews as they restored the nation of Israel in 1948.

Other nations, such as Egypt, Assyria, Babylon, Greece, and Germany, fought the Jews throughout history and are today either nonexistent or weaker nations than before. America has been blessed because, since 1948, American policy has supported Israel and Jerusalem as its undisputed capital. Scripture declares a special blessing for those who support Israel.

5. Praying and Honoring God's Word

America's blessings result from the same covenant relationship with God that Israel possesses. When the Israelites honored God with obedience, they received Divine favor. If America continues to obey God, it will also enjoy Divine favor. In contrast, disobedience inevitably brings curses. The following Scripture perfectly sums up the concept of God's covenant promises:

> "For thou art an holy people unto the Lord thy God; the Lord thy God hath chosen thee to be a special people unto himself, above all people that are upon the earth. The Lord did not set his love upon you, nor choose you, because ye were more in number than any people; for ye were the fewest of all people. But because the Lord loved you, and because he would keep the oath which he had sworn unto your fathers, hath the Lord brought you out with a mighty hand, and redeemed you out of the house of bondmen, from the hand of Pharoah king of Egypt. Know therefore that the Lord thy God, he is God, the faithful God, which keepeth covenant and mercy with them that love him and keep his commandments to a thousand generations. And repayeth them that hate him to their face, to destroy them. He will not be slack to him that hateth him, he will repay him to his face." (Dueteronomy 7: 6-11)

In times of prosperity, Americans have seen low inflation and unemployment, plus an abundance of jobs. In such times, people seem to spend more money and indulge in their blessings. Simultaneously, they fail to seek God, and they ignore warnings that their sins and disobedience will result in calamity. The Bible is full of stories about disobedient people who first enjoy their blessings, then ignore warnings regarding sin, until finally they experience God's judgment.

Could This Happen in America?

In prosperous times, non-believers mock the idea that America will decline because of its sin. A strong stock market and a thriving economy seem to contradict the possibility of our future economic failure. Israel again can be used as an example to explain that there is no contradiction.

Two hundred years before the terrible Babylonian captivity, Isaiah warned the king of Israel that Babylon would overtake Jerusalem (2 Kings 20:17). During the 200 years following the prophecy, few in Israel believed it would happen. They believed the prophets were prophesying about a future generation, not theirs. The vines were fruitful, the cattle and sheep grazed in green fields, and gold and silver coins filled investors' pockets. Years later, news that the Babylonian army was coming didn't frighten the overconfident Hebrews. They assumed that God would protect them as He did when He destroyed 185,000 Assyrian soldiers in just one night. Surely they thought that God would protect Israel again, but not so on this occasion. When King Nebuchadnezzar concluded his assault in 606 B.C., Jerusalem and the Temple lay in rubble.

The prophecy given by Christ 636 years later regarding Jerusalem's destruction by the Romans was received in a similar way. Few Jews believed that God would allow His holy city to be devastated again. The Jews revolted against Rome in an attempt to defeat its legions and liberate the Promised Land. They were certain about Roman defeat and ignored warning signs of immanent destruction.

The False Prophets Came and Prophesied

False prophets led the Jews in an attempt to overpower the Romans. A false prophet named Theudas arose. He influenced many to follow him into the wilderness by promising that he would divide the Jordan River to make a way of escape. A Roman procurator pursued the group and killed Theudas, along with many of his followers. In the year 55 B.C., another impostor, an Egyptian named Felix, convinced about thirty thousand Jews that they would see the walls of Jerusalem fall and the Roman garrison captured. However, it was they who were attacked by the Roman governor, and four hundred of them were slain. The rest were scattered.

The year 50 B.C. brought another false promise of deliverance. Another leader told the people that they should follow him into the wilderness and he would save them. He and his followers soon met their deaths at the hands of Roman soldiers. Until the final moments of Jerusalem's destruction, false prophets proclaimed victory for the Jews. Some did not believe that God would allow His city to be destroyed. Just prior to the burning of the Temple, another imposter stepped out and proclaimed that, if the people would follow him, they would see signs, wonders, and deliverance. About six thousand Jews, mostly women and children, followed him into the Temple. While waiting for deliverance, it was set on fire and not one person escaped (Source: *Josephus Antiquities of the Jews* - War of the Jews-Destruction of the Temple).

Remember The Connection between Israel and America

Before Americans claim to be exempt from Old Testament judgments, we must remember that our nation is spiritually connected to Israel. Just like the ancient Hebrews, few Americans believe that America could ever fall. Yet, we have been given so much knowledge of the truth and, where much is known, much is required. We are a nation that is sinning against knowledge and we know better. When God destroyed Sodom and Gomorrah, these cities had no Bibles, churches, Christian television, or Christian literature to proclaim the truth, yet Jesus said that, if the people in Sodom had witnessed His miracles, they would have repented (Luke 10:12-13).

America has twenty-four hour a day access to Christian radio and television. We have churches on many corners, Christian bookstores, and Christian schools and activities. Yet regularly, we seem to witness another anti-God court case over such things as public prayer or Christian landmarks. How long will a righteous God allow His name to be trampled upon in His own vineyard that He established? Spiritually discerning people must already hear the thunder before the coming storm in America.

Water, Wind, and Fire

The three basic elements of God's judgments have been water, wind, and fire. Along the east coast of America, violent hurricanes beat against the shores and cause millions of dollars worth of damage. In the central area of America, thousands of acres burn as fires scorch the land and leave devastation. On the west coast, the ground convulses with earthquakes. Floods often devastate thousands of acres. From east to west, God's elements are at work. Just as a woman experiences pain when she goes into labor, Jesus warned that certain events were the beginning of sorrows. The Greek word for sorrows is *birth pains* (Matthew 24:8).

Many previous empires have fallen from corruption and immorality. Will this be America's plight? Or will an enemy from a foreign land hold America hostage with nuclear and biological weapons? Perhaps a vision given to George Washington at Valley Forge will give us a preview of the final warning to America.

Washington's Vision at Valley Forge

During the dark, winter days at Valley Forge in 1777, George Washington had a vision concerning the future of America. Anthony Sherman, who was with Washington at Valley Forge, related it to Professor Totten, who later published the account. The vision concerns wars fought only on American soil.

"While preparing a dispatch in Valley Forge, all alone at the table, Washington fell into a trance, seeing what appeared to be a female standing beside him whom he did not know. He began to feel a sudden sensation as though one were dying. He addressed the person, but there was no response. A voice suddenly spoke and said, 'Son of the Republic, look and learn.' The visitor extended her arm eastward and a white vapor began to unfold. Before Washington lay Europe, Asia, Africa, and America. There was a rolling and tossing between Europe and America. At that moment he saw a shadowy being, like an angel floating in mid air between Europe and America.

The being took water from the ocean and sprinkled some upon America with his right hand, while with his left hand he cast some on Europe. Immediately, a dark cloud raised from these two countries and joined over the mid ocean. It soon enveloped America. Washington said, 'I heard the groans and cries of American people.' Soon the angel sprinkled water a second time. The dark clouds were soon drawn back and the billows ceased in the waters. The voice said, 'Son of the Republic, look and learn.' As Washington looked upon America, villages and towns were springing up until the whole land from the Atlantic to the Pacific was dotted with them. The voice said, 'Son of the Republic, the end of the century cometh, look and learn.'

'After this, the dark shadowy angel turned his face southward, and from Africa I saw an ill-omened specter approach our land. It fitted slowly and heavily over every town and city of the latter. The inhabitants presently set themselves in battle array against each other. As I continued looking, I saw another angel on whose brow rested the word union, bearing the American flag, which he placed between the divided nation and said, 'Remember ye are brethren.' Instantly, the inhabitants casting from them their weapons, became friends once more, and united around the national standard (flag).

Again I heard the mysterious voice say, 'Son of the Republic, look and learn.' At this the dark, shadowy angel placed a trumpet to his mouth and blew three blasts; and taking water from the ocean, he sprinkled it upon Europe, Asia, and Africa. Then my eyes beheld a fearful scene; from each of these countries arose thick black clouds that were joined as one. Throughout this mass there gleamed a dark red light by which I saw hordes of armed men move with the cloud, marching by land and sailing by sea to America, which was the country enveloped in the volume of the cloud. I saw these vast armies devastate the whole country and burn the villages, towns, and cities that I saw springing up. As my ears listened to the thundering of cannons and the clashing of swords and shouts of millions in mortal combat, I heard again the mysterious voice saying, 'Son of the Republic, look and learn.' When the voice ceased, the shadowy angel placed his trumpet to his mouth and blew three long dreadful blasts.

'Instantly a light of a thousand suns shone down from above and pierced through the dark clouds which enveloped America. The same angel bore the name Union, carrying the flag and a sword, descended from heaven attended by legions of the bright and spirited.' Washington continued, 'They were immediately joined by the inhabitants of America, who were well nigh overcome, but who immediately closed their ranks and renewed the battle. Amid the fearful conflict the shadowy angel, for the last time, dipped water from the ocean and sprinkled it upon America. Instantly the dark clouds rolled back together with the armies that it had brought, leaving the inhabitants of the land victorious. Then once more I beheld towns and villages and cities springing up where they had been before, while the bright angel who had brought the flag cried with a loud voice, 'While the stars remain and the heavens send dew upon the earth, so long shall this republic last,' and taking from his brow the crown on which was emblazed the word Union he placed it upon the flag while the people kneeling down said, 'Amen.'

The scene instantly began to fade and dissolve as I at last saw nothing but the rising, curling vapor I at first beheld. This also disappearing I found myself staring again at the mysterious visitor, who in the same voice I heard say before, 'Son of the Republic, what you have seen is thus interpreted. Three great perils shall come upon the Republic. The most fearful is the third, passing which the whole world united against her shall not prevail against her. Let every child of the Republic learn to live for God, his land, and his Union.' With these words the vision vanished, and I stared from my seat and felt I had seen a vision wherein was shown me the birth, progress, and the destiny of the United States'" (Source: *True Visions of the Unseen World*, Gordon Lindsey).

The first part of the vision may have dealt with the War of 1812 that came 35 years after Washington's vision at Valley Forge. The second warning seems to refer to the Civil War and expresses how America would be divided and again reunited. The third part of the vision, pertaining to the dark red light, may suggest a future invasion by a Communist nation.

In 1973, a former CIA agent who was a member of my father's church in Arlington, Virginia warned that, in the future, a major terrorist group could obtain nuclear weapons and America may be attacked from within. Today, nuclear weapons, which can now be carried in a suitcase, are only one threat to us. Biological attacks are easier and more likely. Whatever Washington saw, the third revelation has not transpired. Some military experts foresee a time when China will move against the United States. Only time will tell.

There is Time to Repent and Turn Away from Sin

During the dark days of the Civil War, on July 2, 1864, Congress adopted a resolution that sounded like an Old Testament prophet's lamentation. The resolution requested citizens to "confess and repent of their manifold sins, implore the compassion and forgiveness of the Almighty, and beseech him as Supreme Ruler of the world not to destroy us as a people" (Source: *Lincoln the Unknown*, Dale Carnegie).

Prior to his death, Lincoln met a Catholic priest named Charles Chiniquy. The Priest started a Canadian movement to outlaw liquor. Finally, after a severe battle that he won in June of 1850, liquor was outlawed in Canada. He became known as the "Apostle of Temperance" in Canada. Chiniquy knew Abraham Lincoln when he was a lawyer. Lincoln had tried a case that began on May 19, 1856 in which the priest had been accused of misconduct. It is alleged that Chiniquy heard of a plot to kill Lincoln from Mr. Morse, the inventor of the Morse telegraph. Morse had been in Rome and learned of the plot there. Chiniquy went to see Lincoln and recounted his conversation with Mr. Morse. They discussed how Lincoln was similar to Moses of the Old Testament.

Mr. Lincoln read to him out of the Bible about Moses in Deuteronomy 3:22-28. Then he said, "The more I read those verses, the more it seems to me that God has written them to me as well as to Moses. Had he not taken me from my poor log cabin by the hand, as He did of Moses in the reeds of the Nile, to put me at the head of the greatest and most blessed nation of ancient times? Has not God granted me a privilege that was not granted to any living man when I broke the chains of four million men and set them free? Now I see the end of the terrible conflict with the same joy as Moses."

"And I pray my God to grant me to see the days of peace and untold prosperity which will follow this cruel war, as Moses asked God to see the other side of Jordan and enter the Promised Land. But, do you know what I hear in my soul as the voice of God giving me rebuke that was given Moses? A solemn voice which tells me that I will see these things only from a distance and that I will be among the dead." It should be noted that the last act of Congress signed by Abraham Lincoln was to require that the motto "In God We Trust" be inscribed on American coins.

In short, no nation outside of Israel has such roots and connections to the Hebrew Scriptures and to the God of Abraham, as does America. The patterns of the land, the federal buildings, the documents of the Founding Fathers, and the patterns of the presidents give evidence to America's divine design and prophetic purpose.

Because we know the truth, our responsibility to it is greater than that of other nations. If we sin against truth, we deserve the punishment meted out upon the scales of justice in heaven's Temple. As the times of the Gentiles begins to climax, it is not too late to turn the corner and bring the nation back to its spiritual foundation, at least for a season.

One Old Testament Biblical command is as valid today as when it was written. Christ said, "Heaven and earth shall pass away but my words shall not pass away" (Matthew 24:35). One of the greatest promises for our nation is found in 2 Chronicles:

"If my people, which are called by my name, shall humble themselves and pray, seek my face, and turn from their wicked ways, then will I hear from heaven and will forgive their sin and heal their land."

(2 Chronicles 7:14)

Turning from your wicked ways requires repentance. Repenting in Biblical terms means more than apologizing. It requires a turning away from wrong and a turning toward that which is good. Criminals can say that they are sorry for their crimes, when in reality they are sorry they were caught. True repentance happens when you say, "I am sorry and will not do it again. I will do what is right." When America is in trouble, we know how to pray. The Gulf War was a prime example of that, but America has forgotten how to repent.

The clock is ticking and time is passing by. This American vineyard has a predetermined amount of time in which to bring in the harvest and finish its task. That time may be coming to a climax, as the patterns of the American presidents may indicate.

Chapter 14

ISRAEL'S KINGS AND AMERICA'S PRESIDENTS

Israel's 42nd King and America's 42nd President

"The thing that hath been, it is that which shall be; and that which is done is that which shall be done; and there is no new thing under the sun." **(Ecclesiastes 1:9)**

As previously explained, history unfolds in strange, repetitive cycles. An example of this is seen in the parallels between the lives of Abraham Lincoln and John Kennedy. American history is filled with Hebraic patterns and cycles. We see another interesting pattern when we compare ancient Israel's 42nd king and the 42nd president of the United States.

Israel began as a theocracy. A priest or a prophet received direction from the Holy Spirit, announced God's will to the people, and the people were to follow. Eventually, Israel rejected their theocracy. They rejected God as King and wanted a human king like the surrounding nations had. Israel's first king was Saul, and he was "a head taller than his brethren." The first American President was George Washington, and he was also a head taller than most other Americans were. In Saul's time, there were thirteen tribes and, in George Washington's time, there were thirteen colonies. Both Saul and Washington were hesitant to accept their offices.

Scripture records that, beginning with King Saul to the time of the destruction of Jerusalem and the Babylonian captivity, a total of forty-two kings ruled in Israel. A list of these forty-two kings follows:

The Three Monarch Kings

1. Saul, 40 years
2. David, 40 years
3. Solomon, 40 years

After the death of Solomon, the kingdom was divided between the north and the south. There were 19 northern and 20 southern kings, until the time that Babylon invaded Israel and destroyed Jerusalem along with the Temple. Here is a list of kings from the northern and southern kingdom of Israel:

The Northern Kingdom		The Southern Kingdom	
1. Jeroboam	22 years	1. Rehoboam	17 years
2. Nadab	2 years	2. Abijam	3 years
3. Baasha	24 years	3. Asa	41 years
4. Elah	2 years	4. Jehoshaphat	25 years
5. Zimri	7 days	5. Jehoram	8 years
6. Omri	12 years	6. Ahaziah	1 years
7. Ahab	22 years	7. Athaliah (queen)	6 years
8. Ahaziah	2 years	8. Joash	40 years
9. Jehoram	12 years	9. Amaziah	29 years
10. Jehu	28 years	10. Uzziah	52 years
11. Jehoahaz	17 years	11. Jotham	16 years
12. Joash	16 years	12. Ahaz	16 years
13. Jeroboam II	41 years	13. Hezekiah	28 years
14. Zechariah	6 months	14. Manesseh	55 years
15. Shullum	1 month	15. Amnon	2 years

16. Menahem	10 years	16. Josiah	31 years
17. Pekahiah	2 years	17. Jehoahaz	3 months
18. Pekah	8 years	18. Jehoiakim	11 years
19. Hoshea	9 years	19. Jehoiachin	3 months
		20. Zedekiah	11 years

The Number 42

In Scripture, the number forty-two means either division (rebellion) or completion. The seven-year tribulation is divided in two halves, each in periods of forty-two months. In Revelation 11:3, the two witnesses complete their testimonies at the conclusion of the first forty-two-month period. In this case, forty-two speaks of completion. During the second half of the tribulation, the Gentiles (the antichrist's armies) trample down the city of Jerusalem for forty-two months and divide the city once again (Revelation 11:2). In this example, the number forty-two pertains to division, or rebellion.

From King Saul to the Babylonian invasion, there were a total of forty-two kings. The 42nd king, King Zedekiah, saw the nation divided and Jerusalem destroyed. King Zedekiah marked the completion of fourteen generations from King David (Matthew 1:17).

The 42nd President and the King of Babylon

A Hebrew pattern again appears with the 42nd King of Israel, Zedekiah, and the 42nd President of The United States, William Jefferson Clinton. During the reign of Israel's 42nd king, trouble brewed in Babylon. Babylonian King Nebuchadnezzar invaded surrounding nations. In the eleventh year of King Zedekiah's reign, the King of Babylon invaded Israel, destroyed Jerusalem, and took many Hebrews into slavery (Jeremiah 52).

During Bill Clinton's term (America's 42nd president), Saddam Hussein of Iraq was a "thorn in the flesh." Iraq resides in the exact area of ancient Babylon. In fact, Bagdad is not far from the ruins of ancient Babylon, home of Nebuchadnezzar. The pattern becomes more bizarre when considering that before Iraq's war with Iran, Saddam spent hundreds of millions of dollars to rebuild the ancient ruins of Babylon. The bricks of rebuilt Babylon contain an imprint of Saddam and old King

Nebuchadnezzar. Saddam desired to build a new Islamic empire, with Babylon as its capital.

During his eight years in the White House, Bill Clinton dealt with Saddam Hussein, who was a pseudo-king of Babylon. Saddam was an enemy of America during that time as the spirit of Babylon again emerged. Biblical prophecy indicates that the time will come when the final world dictator (more than likely a radical Muslim) will arise from the same territory and rule for forty-two months.

In addition, King Hussein of Jordan died while Clinton was in office. According to Jordanian newspapers, Hussein was the 42nd descendant of Mohammad, the founder of Islam. This means that the Islamic religion is entering its 43rd generation of leaders in Jordan, while America inaugurates its 43rd president!

Since the number forty-two also refers to completion, it relates to the 42nd American presidency. Clinton's administration ended a millennium. Although the new millennium was celebrated at the start of 2000, the new millennium actually started in 2001. Therefore, the 42nd president concluded the old millennium, and the 43rd president began the new millennium at his inauguration on January 20, 2001.

In Summary:

- From Israel's first King Saul, "the man who was a head taller," to King Zedekiah, there were 42 kings. From America's first President, George Washington, "who was a head taller" to Bill Clinton, there were 42 presidents.

- During the rule of Israel's 42nd king, the Babylonians became the "thorn in the flesh" of Israel. During America's 42nd presidential term, Iraq's Saddam Hussein (from the area of ancient Babylon) was the nation's "thorn in the flesh."

- The number 42 means both *division (rebellion)* and *completion*. The end of the millennium coincided with the end of Clinton's term as the 42nd president. A new (43rd) presidential term coincided with the beginning of the new millennium.

Considering these facts, let's look at the prophetic patterns and implications for the 43rd president, George W. Bush.

The Prophetic Timing of the 43rd President

I have researched another possible prophetic pattern that relates to the 43rd President of the United States. In order to understand its prophetic significance, we must consider several important issues: the calendar, covenant time, and prophetic time.

The first point concerns the calendar. People often ask me what prophetic calendar I think God uses when He speaks to us. This is a complicated concept. For centuries, sincere believers have attempted to time the events regarding the return of Christ by using numbers in Scripture and relating them to certain years. For example, in the years 666 A.D., 1000 A.D., 1260 A.D., 1290 A.D., and as recently as 2000 A.D., some zealous Christians have predicted Christ's return. Because some of these numbers are found in certain prophecies relating to end times, anxious believers have attempted to apply them to the timing of Christ's return. This type of manipulation is futile and produces many skeptics. Part of the difficulty in determining the present prophetic calendar is that there is a problem in determining which calendar is correct.

There are Four Calendars

There are four types of calendars that have been used from Roman times to the present: the Jubilee, the Jewish, the Julian, and the Gregorian calendars. Let's look at each of these.

1. The Jubilee Calendar

The Jubilee calendar is mentioned in the book of Jubilees in the Dead Sea Scrolls. It is also mentioned in the book of Enoch. It uses 364 days as a solar calendar year. Divided into twelve months of thirty days each, it has four additional days added each year on March 31, June 31, September 31 and December 31. It uses 52 weeks a year divided into four quarters of 13 weeks each.

2. The Jewish Calendar

The Jewish calendar is a lunisolar calendar. The months are based on lunar orbits and the years are based on complete solar orbits. There are 354 days in a lunar cycle (the total number of lunar orbits in a year), which fall 11 days short of a solar year. Therefore, seven times every nineteen years, an extra month was added to ensure the seven feasts would fall on the proper months and seasons.

3. The Julian Calendar

By 45 B.C., there was much confusion over the calendar time. In the year 45 A.D., Julius Caesar choose the solar calendar to correct the confusion. It consisted of 365 days with a leap year falling every 4 years. Leap years contained 366 days. The problem was that it was 11 minutes and 14 seconds longer than the physical solar year, again throwing off the holidays.

4. The Gregorian Calendar

Another calendar was needed to correct the errors of the Julian calendar. It needed to make the vernal equinox fall on March 21. Pope Gregory XII issued a decree in 1582 that dropped 10 days from the year. Called the Gregorian calendar, it begins counting years with the year in which Christ was born. Britain adopted this calendar in 1752, and later it was adopted worldwide.

With the various calendars used over the past 2,200 years, it is impossible to perfectly pinpoint exact prophetic dates. For example, the Jews say there have been 5,761 years from Adam to the present (dating the creation of Adam from the year 2001). Yet, if we count time according to Christian scholars, about 6,000 years have passed from Adam to the present. So which time frame is correct? The Christian and Jewish time frames are different by 240 years!

I have often taught that when God is dealing with Gentiles, He recognizes Gentile time. According to the book of Revelation, when God turns His attention to Israel during the final tribulation, the calendar reverts to a 360-day year. This is clear when considering that forty-two months is a period of 1,260 days during the tribulation (or 360 days making one year). This confuses the matter even more when trying to determine God's prophetic timing. Perhaps a solution is to understand the concept of covenant time.

God Calculates Time Based on Time Between Covenants

To better understand prophetic time, we must understand that God counts time based on when covenants were made. Literally, He keeps count of covenant time. A covenant is an agreement between two people that was sealed in blood during ancient times. This is why religious Jews circumcise their sons on the eighth day, because they keep the covenant God gave to Abraham in Genesis 17:10-14. God also made a special covenant with Noah concerning the earth following the flood (Genesis 9:8-13). God later made a covenant with Abraham promising him that a great nation would come from his son. This covenant promise marked the birth of the nation of Israel. The evidence (token) of the covenant between God and Israel was circumcision (Genesis 17:11-13).

Matthew's Gospel lists the names in the linage of Jesus. Matthew wrote, "So all the generations from Abraham to David are fourteen generations and all the generations from David to Babylon are fourteen generations and all the generations from Babylon to Christ are fourteen generations" (Matthew 1:17). Matthew began his list with Abraham, not Adam. This is because Abraham was the first man to make a covenant with God symbolized by circumcision.

The reason Abraham, David, Babylon and Christ are listed is because each name signifies a major covenant event, or a promise. Abraham was the father of the covenant because he was the first man to covenant with God by faith; therefore, covenant time began with him. God promised Abraham the land that became Israel. Fourteen generations later, God made a covenant with David concerning the city of Jerusalem, which became the eternal capital of Israel. Fourteen generations later, Israel went into Babylonian captivity because they broke the commandments of God and judgment came upon the land. After repenting, the Jews were delivered from Babylon and returned to repossess Israel and rebuild Jerusalem. From Babylon to Christ was fourteen generations, because Jesus Christ established another covenant. Christ's covenant produced a new nation (the Christian church), with a new city (a heavenly Jerusalem), and a new people (the followers of Christ)!

There are three sets of fourteen generations mentioned in Matthew 1:17. When adding up the three sets of generations, there are forty-two in all. From Abraham to Christ, there are a total of forty-two generations. There are fourteen people between each major person or event. This is clearly a pattern. The first Biblical reference to the number fourteen is found in the story of Jacob, who later was named Israel. Jacob worked fourteen years before he received Rachel, the woman he desired to marry (Genesis 31:41). The second Biblical reference to the number fourteen concerns the number of children born to Rachel and her maids:

"These are the sons of Rachel, which were born to Jacob: all the souls were fourteen." (Genesis 46:22)

Rachel's last son was Benjamin, whose name means *son of my right hand*. Christ, the Son of God who is seated at the Father's right hand, ratified the new covenant (Hebrews 8:1 and 10:12). After fourteen years, Jacob married Rachel and she gave birth to two sons, Joseph and Benjamin. Strangely, America's fourteenth president, Franklin Pierce, had a son named Benjamin, who died at age twelve shortly after his father was inaugurated.

God counts time as it relates to His covenants. The prophet Daniel received a revelation that confirms how God's prophetic timekeeping is connected to His covenants.

Daniel's Prophecy Concerning Prophetic Time

In Daniel 9:24-27, the prophet Daniel received a revelation that concerned prophetic timing. This revelation, known as "Daniel's seventy weeks," is divided into three distinct, consecutive time periods. After Israel's Babylonian captivity, God's prophetic time clock began ticking with the decree to rebuild Jerusalem. The time period was to conclude with the onset of everlasting righteousness on earth. The prophecy delineates a period of 490 years from beginning to end. To simplify it, I will identify the blocks of time in actual years during which specific events would transpire.

- Daniel refers to seven periods of seven years. This total of 49 years begins with the decree to rebuild Jerusalem until its completion. Nehemiah and Ezra led the building program that took 49 years to finish. The 49 years represented Daniel's first prophetic time cycle (Daniel 9:25).
- Daniel's second block of time begins with the decree to rebuild the city until the time that the Messiah was cut off. This was a period of 483 years (Daniel 9:25). The Messiah being cut off referred to the crucifixion of Christ (Daniel 9:25-26).
- Daniel's third time period is 7 years. At the conclusion of the final 7-year period, everlasting righteousness would begin, as the Messiah returned to earth (Daniel 9:27).

When the Jewish leaders rejected Christ as Messiah, many scholars believe the prophetic clock stopped ticking with regard to Israel. At Pentecost, the Christian church was born and weeks later, the Gentiles were grafted into God's covenant with Abraham's descendents. At this point, God's covenant timekeeping shifted to the Gentiles and started at the time of the crucifixion of Christ, the Messiah who was cut off. Even some rabbis teach that God has stopped counting time with reference to the Jews because of their unbelief. Jesus continually rebuked the Jews for their unbelief. The crucifixion of Jesus is believed to have occurred in April of 32 A.D. Christ predicted the destruction of Jerusalem and the Holy Temple (Matthew 24:1-2). This came to pass in 70 A.D. From the time of Christ's death until this present generation, God has been keeping time based on the new covenant. When the time of the Gentile nations is completed, the Lord will once again base prophetic timing upon His beloved nation Israel. The final seven years before Christ's return, called Daniel's seventieth week, is also called the seven-year tribulation.

Let me emphasize that confusion over how to calculate the timing of prophetic events can be solved when we understand how God counts in covenant time. Jesus Christ formed a new covenant through His death and resurrection. According to Matthew 1:17, a total of forty-two generations existed from Abraham to Christ. These generations cannot be traced by a specific calendar, but each generation consists of forty to fifty years. Each generation represents one man who had a son, who then had a son and so forth. We could say that there are fourteen people from Abraham to David, fourteen people from David to Babylon, and fourteen people from Babylon to Christ, thus generating a total of forty-two people from Abraham to Christ.

The Covenants — Israel and the Church

Abraham is the natural father of the Jews. When God made a covenant with Abraham, He promised a multitude of children as large as the number represented by "the stars of the heavens and the sand of the sea" (Genesis 22:17). Abraham birthed a natural nation, but through Abraham's promised seed, Jesus Christ, God would birth a spiritual nation that is the church. Two nations came through Abraham — one natural and one spiritual.

Many people do not realize that the Old Testament predicted Israel's rejection of God's plan, and that the Almighty would raise up a new nation from a people that did not exist. Moses articulated this in the Torah:

"They have moved me to jealousy with that which is not God; they have provoked me to anger with their vanities: and I will move them to jealousy with those which are not a people; I will provoke them to anger with a foolish nation." (Deuteronomy 32:21)

Paul made reference to Deuteronomy 32:21 when he wrote to the Gentiles (in Romans 10:19) about the fulfillment of this prophecy. In Abraham's time, the Christian church was non-existent, and non-Jews were not part of the covenant. As Israel began turning away from God, the Lord began to speak through the Hebrew prophets about a new nation consisting of Gentiles who would be raised by the Lord. Isaiah wrote that Gentiles would seek after the root of Jesse (Isaiah 11:10). He continued, "I will...keep thee and give thee a covenant of the people a light of the Gentiles" (Isaiah 42:6). God spoke through Isaiah by saying, "I will lift up mine hand to the Gentiles..." (Isaiah 49:22), and "the Gentiles shall come to thy light..." (Isaiah 60:3).

The covenant blessing came upon the Gentiles in Acts 10, when Peter preached to a group of Italians (Gentiles), and the Holy Spirit fell upon them (Acts 10:45). At that moment, the Gentiles were grafted into the covenant, where they have remained ever since. Peter later wrote about the church, "You are a chosen generation, a royal priesthood, a holy nation..." (1 Peter 2:9). On the day of Pentecost, a group of Jews received the Holy Spirit. In Acts 10 a group of Gentiles received the Holy Spirit. Afterward, both Jew and Gentile believers formed the true church. A unique pattern is also connected to the redemption plan of God and the church.

The Church is the 43rd Generation

The Scripture predicted, "A seed shall serve him; it shall be accounted to the Lord for a generation" (Psalms 22:30). Matthew indicated that Jesus was the 42nd generation from Abraham. The Body of Christ, the church, is called a chosen generation (1 Peter 2:9). How many generations have there been in the church from the time of Christ to the present? Jesus represented the first generation, then Peter and Paul, followed by Timothy. After Timothy, we could count Polycarp and others. The true answer indicates that the church is one continuous generation. In Paul's final letter to his spiritual son Timothy, Paul wrote, "I have finished my course" (Acts 20:24; 2 Timothy 4:7). The word course in Greek is dromos meaning *a running of a race.* It comes from the root word edramon meaning *to run.* In his ministry, Paul ran his part of the race, then transferred his authority to Timothy.

This new nation, the church, is one unending race of faith. We pass the baton on to the next generation and they continue to run the race. Eventually, we will come to the finish line and God will catch away the church (the spiritual nation) signifying Israel's final restoration. At that time, God will fulfill the final prophecy in Daniel 9 concerning the seven-year tribulation period (Daniel 9:27). Through it Israel shall be saved.

From the birth of the church on Pentecost (Acts 2:1-4) until the present, the church has been one unending generation. Christ is the 42nd generation from Abraham and since the new nation, the church, was born out of Christ's death, the church is the 43rd generation. So the church is not a series of generations, but one complete generation! This number forty-three is also linked to the Day of Atonement.

The Number 43 and the Day of Atonement

Another pattern of forty-three appears in relation to the High Priest's ritual on the Day of Atonement. In ancient Israel, once each year the High Priest entered the Holy of Holies and sprinkled the blood of goats and bulls upon the Ark of the Covenant. Jewish author Alfred Eldersheim wrote that the sacrificial blood was sprinkled on the ark, before the veil, and upon the altar forty-three times (Source: *The Temple*, Alfred Eldersheim, page 316). Therefore, Israel's atonement was complete only after the 43rd time that the High Priest ceremonially sprinkled blood on the 10th day of the 7th month, known as Yom Ha Kippur. The remaining blood was poured out on the west side of the base of the altar of burnt offering.

Since America and Israel share many profound patterns, could there be a connection between our 43rd president and the fact that atonement was completed only after blood was ceremonially sprinkled forty-three times? Could the 43rd president serve this nation during a season when the fullness of the Gentiles nears its end? The word fullness used in Romans 11:12 refers to the completion of the number of Gentiles who receive the blessing through the Gospel (Source: *Vines Expository Dictionary of New Testament Words*). When this fullness of the Gentiles is complete, two things will happen. First, the Gospel of Christ will have reached all Gentile nations of the world, and second, the church will have completed her assignment and the "catching away" of the true church will happen.

The possible time frame for the United States and the fullness of the Gentiles may begin in the year 2001 and climax between 2007-2008. I have determined these approximate years based on the parallel between Christ's prophecies over Jerusalem and the miraculous reunification of Jerusalem that occurred in 1967. Therefore, we may be nearing the climax of the fullness of the Gentiles, especially in God's vineyard of America.

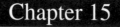

Chapter 15

2001 TO 2008 AND THE FULLNESS OF THE GENTILES

The Church's Final Assignment

"Having made known unto us the mystery of his will, according to his good pleasure which he hath purposed in himself. That in the dispensation of the fullness of times he might gather together in one all things in Christ, both which are in heaven, and which are in earth, even in him."
(Ephesians 1:9-10)

I am always skeptical of authors who predict dates in connection with prophetic events, unless those events have been fulfilled and can be seen clearly in Scripture. We know that Israel's restoration in 1948 was a fulfillment of Isaiah 66:8. We also realize that, according to Psalms 102:16, Jerusalem must be built up in order for the Lord to return. Before accepting the dates of 2001 to 2008, please examine the reason why I selected this time frame.

Again, I refer to two prophecies — one relating to the vineyard, and one relating to the olive tree. The vineyard is a literal nation; the olive tree is the Gentile church. Christ used the parable of the vineyard to explain how God would transfer His blessings from the nation of Israel to another nation that would bring forth fruit in its season (Matthew 21:43). I have shown how the British lion symbolically represents America being birthed by England, and how America has been the leading Gentile nation in terms of proclaiming the Gospel for over 225 years. Paul used the analogy of the olive tree to represent Israel, and the grafting of a new branch onto the olive tree to represent the Gentile church. When the fullness of the Gentiles is complete, the Gentile branch will be removed and replaced by the original, natural Jewish branch.

Israel and the Church

When God made a covenant with Abraham, He promised Abraham many children. In fact, Abraham's descendents would be a group so large in number that it would compare to the number of "the stars of heaven and the sand which is upon the sea shore" (Genesis 22:17). This promise revealed that through Abraham, God would produce a natural seed (Israel) through Isaac and a heavenly seed (the church) through Christ. The sand symbolizes Israel and the stars represent the church. There are five different factors that distinguish the earthly and the heavenly seed of Abraham:

- Israel was given earthly promises, and the Gentile church is given heavenly promises.
- Israel was promised an earthly kingdom, and the church was promised a spiritual kingdom.
- Israel will rule from an earthly Jerusalem, and the church will rule from a heavenly Jerusalem.
- Israel is the theme of the old covenant, and the church is the theme of the new covenant.
- Israel is promised the Second Coming of Christ, and the church is promised the Rapture.

Israel, God's original vineyard, was given the responsibility of following the Law, along with the institution of Divine service in the Tabernacle and the Temple. For centuries, Israel was a fruitful, spiritual nation. By the time of Christ, religion was formalized and powerless. Traditions of men had replaced the truth, and Temple services became boring, routine rituals without meaning (Mark 7:13; Mark 7:6). God, in His infinite knowledge, knew that the Hebrews would be dispersed for over 1,900 years. God selected the church to bring forth spiritual fruit in Israel's absence. Jesus said that God would let out His vineyard to other husbandmen who would bring forth fruit in their season (Matthew 21:41). In Greek, the words let out mean *go give forth to lease*. The church and the Gentiles have a lease on the vineyard, which will eventually expire.

The Circumcised and the Uncircumcised

Paul explained how God would raise up the Gentile church to minister to the world. In Romans 10 and 11, he explained in detail the mysterious relationship of Christ to natural Israel and to the spiritual Israel, the Christian church. Since natural Jews confirm their covenant relationship to God through circumcision, Paul used the term circumcised when speaking about natural Jews, and the phrase uncircumcised when speaking about the Gentiles (Romans 3:30). Paul was Jewish, yet he was called of God to "bear the Lord's name to the Gentiles" (Acts 9:15). Paul wrote, "I preached among the Gentiles..." (Galatians 2:2) and confessed that he "preached among the Gentiles the unsearchable riches of Christ..." (Ephesians 3:8). Peter was ordained by the Holy Spirit to minister to the Jewish branch of the Christian church, while Paul served the Gentiles. Paul confirms this when he wrote, "The Gospel of the uncircumcision (Gentiles) was committed unto me, as the Gospel of the circumcision was unto Peter" (Galatians 2:7). The first church was one unit consisting of two distinct branches, one being Jewish and the other Gentile. Both preached the same Gospel and received the same Holy Spirit. Due to religious and cultural differences between the two groups, contention often arose within the church that had to be settled by leaders on both sides.

In Romans, Paul used the imagery of two olive trees. He taught that there was a natural olive tree (the Jews) and a wild olive tree (the Gentiles) (Romans 11:17 and 11:24). I believe that Paul used imagery previously found in Isaiah 11:1, which reads:

"And there shall come forth a rod out of the stem of Jesse, and a branch shall grow out of his roots." (Isaiah 11:1)

David, whose father was Jesse, was given the promise of a future kingdom that would be ruled by a Messiah coming from David's decendents. The Messiah would be from the house of David and would rule all nations with a rod of iron (Revelation 2:27). In Isaiah 11:1, the Messiah is identified as a "rod from the stem (tree) of Jesse." The Hebrew word for rod is cheten, which means *a twig* or *tender shoot*. This correlates with another Messianic prophecy in Isaiah 53, which states that the Messiah would "grow up before him as a tender plant and as a root out of dry ground" (Isaiah 53:2). We know Jesus was born in Bethlehem, the city of David and He is from the tribe of Judah. This fulfills prophecy. Isaiah 11:1 states, "A branch will come forth out of his roots." The word for a single branch in Hebrew is netzer, and the plural form is netzrim. Netzrim is the Hebrew word for Nazareth, where Christ was raised. There is evidence that the first Christians were actually called Netzrim before they were called Christians in Antioch (Acts 11:26). I have learned from Jewish friends that Netzrim is also the contemporary Hebrew word for Christian. We could translate Isaiah 11:1 to read: "There will come forth a rod from the stem of Jesse and Christians shall grow out of his roots." When Paul used the analogy of the olive tree to illustrate the acceptance of the Gentiles into the covenant, he might have been referring to Isaiah's prophecy.

Paul taught that there are two olive trees — one is a natural olive tree representing Israel, and the other is a wild olive tree representing the Gentiles. According to Paul, the natural branches of the tree were broken off "because of their unbelief" (Romans 11:20). Christ came to His own people and was rejected by the priesthood and the religious leaders (John 1:11). Therefore, God grafted in branches from the wild Gentile olive tree (Romans 11:17). According to Paul, the root of the tree is Jewish in nature but the branches are now Gentile. Paul reveals to the Gentile believers that the natural branches were broken off so that we (Gentiles) might be grafted in (Romans 11:19).

In the beginning of Christ's ministry, He worked only with Jews and told His disciples to avoid the Gentiles (Matthew 10:5-6). Eventually, the religious Jews began rejecting Christ's ministry and accused Him of being of the devil (Mark 3:20-30). In the middle of Christ's ministry, He began reaching out to the Gentiles. Later, at Christ's public trial, many of the religious Jews told Pilate, "His (Christ's) blood be upon us and upon our children" (Matthew 27:25). This rejection of Christ was unbelief, and Paul said it caused Israel's natural branch to be severed.

The first church was a Jewish congregation, consisting of one hundred twenty believers in the upper room (Acts 1:14-16). Shortly thereafter, religious Jews began persecuting Jewish believers in Christ (Acts 13:45, 50; 14:2; 18:12). In Acts 9, Rabbi Paul received Christ as his Messiah, and shortly thereafter the Gentiles received Christ and the gift of the Holy Spirit (Acts 10:45). From that moment on, the Gospel was preached to the Gentiles throughout the Roman Empire.

The Fullness of the Gentiles and the Dispensation of Grace

This acceptance of the Gentiles into the new covenant began the season called the "times of the Gentiles" (Luke 21:24), and the "dispensation of the grace of God" (Ephesians 3:2). Since the first century, a Jewish remnant of believers worked alongside Gentiles to advance the Gospel. After the destruction of Jerusalem, the headquarters for Christianity was eventually moved to Rome, Italy. From that point, the number of Jewish believers began to decline as the Greek-Roman culture overpowered the smaller, Hebraic remnant in the church. The Gentile believers flourished for over 1,900 years. This dispensation of God's grace, commonly called the church age, will continue until the return of Christ for His church.

Paul warned the Gentiles that, if they fell into unbelief, God would remove their branch from the olive tree and replace it with the original branch. Paul wrote, "For if God spared not the natural branches, take heed lest he also spare not thee" (Romans 11:21). Paul also taught that Israel's spiritual blindness would be removed when God completed His mission among the Gentiles.

"For I would not, brethren, that ye should be ignorant of this mystery, lest ye should be wise in your own conceits; that blindness in part is happened to Israel until the fullness of the Gentiles be come in. And so all Israel shall be saved..." (Romans 11:25-26)

The end-time pattern is as follows: the Gentiles will preach the Gospel to every nation, "then shall the end come" (Matthew 24:14). The word end does not mean the end of the world, but the end of God's dispensation of grace upon the Gentiles. Matthew 24:15 refers to the "abomination that makes Jerusalem desolate." This abomination causes the Jews to flee to the wilderness. These events are recorded in Revelation 13 and 14, and they will happen in the middle of the seven-year tribulation period. This brings us to two issues; first, the time when the fullness of the Gentiles will be completed; and second, the time when Israel will be grafted back into the olive tree.

When the Gentile church completes its mission to witness to all nations, then its assignment will be complete. The two witnesses in Revelation will ascertain the time when Israel will be grafted back into the natural olive tree.

The Final Seven Years

The final seven years of time, prior to the one thousand year reign of Christ, is called the great tribulation (Matthew 24:21). Jeremiah calls it the "time of Jacob's trouble" (Jeremiah 30:7). This phrase points to the incident where Jacob worked seven years for a wife and received Rachel's sister instead. He then worked another seven years until he received Rachel as his wife (Genesis 29). During the seven year tribulation, God will lift His blessing from the Gentiles and bring worldwide judgment against Gentile nations that are corrupt, sinful, and filled with unbelief. The judgments in the book of Revelation will occur at this time. Just as first century Israel was judged for shedding innocent blood and God turned to the Gentiles, in the future, the Gentiles will be judged for shedding innocent blood and God will turn back to Israel.

According to the book of Revelation, there will also be a time when many Jews in Israel will become believers and accept Jesus as their Messiah. In fact, 144,000 men from the region of Israel's twelve tribes will be sealed and protected from the tribulation judgments (Revelation 7:4). Two mysterious men called two witnesses will lead these Jewish men.

The Two Witnesses

During the first forty-two months of the tribulation, two men known as the two witnesses will appear in Israel. John's apocalyptic vision tells of two men in Jerusalem who will have a following of 144,000 Jewish believers. Through supernatural power, they will shut up the heavens and cause a drought for forty-two months. They will call fire upon their enemies, and pronounce plagues upon unbelieving Gentile nations (Revelation 11:5-6).

John identified these two men as "two olive trees and two candlesticks standing before the Lord of the earth" (Revelation 11:4). The prophet Zechariah mentions these two for the first time 650 years prior. In Zechariah's prophetic vision, he saw two men standing before the throne of God. Zechariah saw a candlestick with seven pipes (a menorah) and two olive trees standing one on the right and one on the left side of the lamps (Zechariah 4:11-12). The significance of the two olive trees and the two olive branches is explained as being "the two anointed ones standing before the Lord of the whole earth" (Zechariah 4:14). The prophet describes what the two men represent by using the symbols of olive trees and olive branches.

Paul also spoke of two olive trees — the Jewish tree and the Gentile tree. He spoke of two olive branches, one Jewish branch and one Gentile. Paul may have had Zechariah's vision in mind when he compared his two trees to Zechariah's two olive trees. According to Revelation 11, the two men will lead a major revival among Jewish men in Israel. Who are these two witnesses?

Without a doubt, one of the two witnesses or "olive branches" is the prophet Elijah. According to 2 Kings 2:1-11, Elijah was transported into heaven alive, as he rode on an angelic chariot of fire. In the last book of the Old Testament, the prophet Malachi revealed that God would send Elijah "before the great and dreadful day of the Lord" (Malachi 4:5). Religious Jews throughout the world believe that Elijah will appear in the future and announce the coming of the Messiah.

Scholars debate the identity of the second witness, but evidence strongly suggests that it will be Enoch. Enoch was the seventh man from Adam and he was considered to be the first prophet in the Bible. "Enoch the seventh from Adam, prophesied of these saying, Behold the Lord cometh with ten thousand of his saints..." (Jude 14). Enoch lived for 365 years (Genesis 5:23), and was also translated alive into heaven (Hebrews 11:5). Enoch and Elijah are the only two humans who have never experienced death. Prophecy indicates that these two men will reappear on earth as two witnesses during the first half of the seven-year tribulation.

The Wild Olive Tree
GENTILES

The Natural Olive Tree
ISRAEL

Natural branches are broken

Gentile branches grafted in

Two Olive Trees and Two Branches

One point favoring Enoch and Elijah relates to Paul's reference concerning the natural and wild olive tree. Both Zechariah and John identify these two men as two olive trees. One is Jewish and one is Gentile. Enoch lived hundreds of years before Abraham; therefore, he is a Gentile. Elijah, on the other hand, was a Jew. So we have one witness representing the Gentile olive branch, and one representing the Jewish olive branch. Paul alludes to two olive trees, and the two witnesses are identified with the analogy of two olive trees.

The Final Re-grafting

The re-grafting process will begin when the Gentile branch is removed. Just how will God remove the Gentile branch? The Gentile church will complete its final work of harvesting souls around the world, and then the end will come. At the predestined time, the conclusion of the age of grace will climax and the fullness of the Gentiles will occur. Afterward, the catching away of the church will transpire.

> "For the Lord himself shall descend from heaven with a shout, with the voice of the Archangel, and with the trump of God; and the dead in Christ shall rise first. Then we which are alive and remain shall be caught up together with them in the clouds, to meet the Lord in the air and so shall we ever be with the Lord."
> (1 Thessalonians 4:16-17)

Immediately after this catching away, the two witnesses will appear in Israel. This season of prophetic history will combine two major events. First, the catching away of the church will conclude the fullness of the Gentiles and the dispensation of the grace of God. The Gentile olive branch will be plucked from the olive tree. Second, the natural branch, Israel, will begin to be re-grafted at the appearance of the two witnesses. The 144,000 Jews are called the first fruits of the Lord (Revelation 14:3-4).

The catching away of the church is known by many Christians as the Rapture. It is referred to in Ephesians 1:9-10 as the "gathering together unto him." At this glorious event, also called the "blessed hope"

(Titus 2:13), the dead in Christ will be raised and the living saints will be caught up to meet the Lord in the air. At that moment, God will remove the Gentile branch from the old olive tree, and He will send two Old Testament prophets, one a Jew and one a Gentile, to Israel. Enoch and Elijah will lead a Divine mission to the Jewish remnant in Israel in the same manner that Peter (a Jew) ministered to the Jews, and Paul ministered to the Gentiles in the first church.

Again, there is a remarkable correlation here. In the first century, two apostles were used to unite the church and, in the last days, two prophets will be used to unite Israel.

Spiritual unbelief caused Israel to be severed from the natural olive tree, and faith in Christ brought the Gentiles into the covenant. During the first forty-two months of the tribulation, severe judgments will strike Gentile nations throughout the world as the wrath of God visits those who will not repent of their wickedness (Revelation 9:20; 16:9; 16:11). As a minister, I have seen a preview of this tragedy in America as it becomes more difficult to reach people with the Gospel. In our nation, hearts are being hardened like stone and people scoff at the idea of sin. This is a sign that the fullness of the Gentiles is nearing. When Israel rejected Christ as Messiah, great trouble followed; likewise, as America rejects Christ the Messiah, trouble will surely follow.

America is Forgetting the Bible

Recent surveys show that about 92 percent of all Americans own at least one Bible. Yet, according to a Gallop Poll, Americans are Biblically ignorant. Only half of Americans can name the first book of the Bible (Genesis), and only one third know who delivered the Sermon on the Mount (many named Billy Graham instead of Jesus). Most did not know that the Christian reason for observing Easter was to celebrate Jesus' resurrection. In the 1980s, about 73 percent of Americans occasionally read the Bible. Today less than 59 percent read the Bible at all. George Gallop said, "We believe in the Bible, but we don't read it." May I add that many Americans believe in God and prayer, but they seldom repent. The world's leading Christian nation is entering a post-Christian era. America's greatest opportunities to reach the end-time harvest are before us, but the doors will not remain open forever.

The Vine and the Olive Tree

America was ordained by the Lord to be a spiritual vineyard. Its purpose was to be a lighthouse to the world, shining the light of the Kingdom of God into every dark corner. America is the only Gentile nation in history that can trace its origins and prophetic patterns to Israel. Just as Jesus predicted that the vineyard would be taken away, the Hebrew prophets also predicted that God would return to His vineyard (Israel) with blessings.

"Return, we beseech thee, O God of hosts: look down from heaven, and behold, and visit this vine. And the vineyard, which thy right hand hath planted, and the branch that thou hast made strong for thyself. It is burned with fire. It is cut down..."
(Psalms 80:14-16)

This is a picture of the destruction of Jerusalem by the Babylonians in 606 B.C., which was repeated by the Romans in 70 A.D. The Holy City was burned, yet Isaiah gave this encouraging word to Israel:

"In that day sing ye unto her a vineyard of red wine." (Isaiah 27:2)

"He shall cause them that come of Jacob to take root; Israel shall blossom and bud, and fill the face of the world with fruit." (Isaiah 27:6)

Paul wrote, "Has God forsaken his people which he foreknew? God forbid!" This prophetic picture continues when examining the oil and the wine in Scripture.

The Oil and the Wine — The Story of Noah

Olive trees produce oil and vineyard fruit produces wine. It is interesting that in the story of Noah's flood, a dove with an olive leaf and a vineyard are central features in the aftermath of the flood. Jesus said, "As it was in the days of Noah, so shall it be in the time of the coming of the son of man" (Matthew 24:37). The 4,000-year-old flood story contains hidden clues regarding future prophetic patterns.

The dove symbolically represents the Holy Spirit (Matthew 3:16).

A dove was sent from the ark on three occasions. The first time, the dove returned to Noah having found "no rest for the soles of its feet" (Genesis 8:9). Seven days later, Noah released the dove again and it returned with an olive leaf in its mouth (Genesis 8:11). Seven days later, the dove left the ark and never returned (Genesis 8:12). It was during the second journey that the dove plucked an olive leaf off an olive tree and brought it to the ark.

The Lord told Noah, "My spirit will not always strive with man" (Genesis 6:3). At the baptism of Christ, the Spirit descended upon Him like a dove (Matthew 3:16). Yet, the religious leaders in Israel rejected Christ. The dove had no place to rest His feet. Then the Gentiles were grafted into the olive tree! The dove plucked an olive leaf from an olive tree, carrying it into the ark, typifying a time when the Gentiles would be plucked from the wild tree and brought into the safety of God's provision. After seven days, the dove left the ark permanently. This suggests the time of the seven-year tribulation, when God will remove His Spirit and visit the Gentiles with judgment instead of mercy!

When the flood subsided, Noah and his family settled once again on the land. Noah planted a vineyard and made wine from its grapes. Noah even became drunk from the wine (Genesis 9:21). In this drunken condition, his son Ham saw his father naked and told his two brothers. As a result, Ham's son Canaan was placed under a curse (Genesis 9:25). This may point to the warnings given to Israel concerning the vineyard. It was to produce fruit, but instead it brought forth wild grapes (Isaiah 5:2). The overseers of the vineyard were cast out (cursed) and ownership of the vineyard was given to others. After Ham's son was cursed, Ham's promised blessings were passed to Shem.

Another story about oil and wine comes from a parable of Jesus called the Parable of the Good Samaritan (Luke 10:33-36). A man left Jerusalem and went to Jericho. While journeying, he was robbed and beaten. Both a Priest and a Levite avoided the wounded man on the side of the road, but it was a Samaritan, who was part Jew and part Gentile, that found the man and poured oil and wine into his wounds (Luke 10:34). This parable reveals a preview of prophetic events. Many of the religious Jews (Priests and Levites) rejected Jesus, but the outcast Samaritans experienced great revival (Acts 8). It was the Gentiles who received the oil (the Holy Spirit) and the wine (the vineyard) and ministered the Gospel. They loved the lost and bound up their wounds.

The Tribulation and the Oil and Wine

During the first half of the tribulation, famine strikes the earth. In his vision, John heard a voice saying, "Hurt not the oil and the wine" (Revelation 6:6). During the tribulation famine, a Jewish remnant of 144,000 will be protected from the judgments. At this time, God will begin to restore the olive branch (the oil) and the vineyard (the wine) to a remnant of natural Jews! God's will is that all Israel shall be saved (Romans 11:26). God will begin to pour out His wrath upon Gentile nations. This is called the "winepress of the wrath of God" (Revelation 14:19). The ancient winepress was used to crush grapes to produce wine. John saw an angel gathering a cluster of grapes and throwing them into the winepress of God's wrath.

"And the angel thrust in his sickle into the earth, and gathered the vine of the earth, and cast it into the great winepress of the wrath of God." (Revelation 14:19)

Notice that the vine is gathered up and thrown into a winepress that applies great weight to crush the grapes. This is a picture of God's judgment on the nations for their blasphemy, sin, and faithlessness. Two thousand years ago, the vine of Israel was destroyed and a new vine was planted. During the tribulation, the Gentile vine will be crushed, and God will establish His original vineyard, Israel, once again. This is the teaching of the Hebrew prophets and Paul.

The process of crushing olives and grapes to produce oil and wine is threefold:

1. The separating

The olives are shaken from the tree, and grapes are cut from the vine. In Revelation 14:19, an angel comes with a sickle and severs clusters of grapes from the vine. During the first process, there must be a separating of the olives from the tree and the grapes from the vine.

2. The crushing

The same process is used to crush both the olives and the grapes. The olives are placed under a large stone with heavy weights, and oil emerges when they are crushed. Grapes were crushed in a similar way.

3. The gathering together

The oil or grape juice is then collected and stored in a safe place. Leftover by-products are discarded.

This three-fold process of separating, crushing, and gathering illustrates God's Divine order in preparing the church and Israel for their prophetic future.

1. The separating

In Christ's parable of the wheat and tares, He explained that wheat and tares grow together until harvest time (Matthew 13:24-30). At the end of the age, there will be a separating of the wheat from the tares. A similar separation happens within the church, as is illustrated in the parable of the ten virgins. The five wise virgins make it into the wedding, yet the five foolish ones do not (Matthew 25:1-13).

2. The crushing

God will allow a crushing to occur in the church in order to remove compromise and sin from our lives. Sinners are destroyed during the tribulation (Isaiah 13:9). To crush olives or grapes, a large stone was used as a weight to create pressure. Jesus is the stone that will put pressure on the kingdoms of the world (Daniel 2:45).

3. The gathering together

The church will experience a gathering together in Christ at His coming (Ephesians 1:9-10). After the tribulation, the surviving Jewish remnant will be gathered together at the sound of a great trumpet, and return to Jerusalem to worship Messiah (Isaiah 27:13).

When God re-grafts the Jewish branch into the old olive tree, the Gentile nations that were most blessed by hearing the message of the Gospel will experience the greatest wrath. Some may wonder why the tribulation is called Jacob's trouble if, during this period, Israel (Jacob) is not at the forefront of suffering. The antichrist and the false prophet will bring great distress to Israel, but the trumpet and vial judgments of God will be poured out upon all nations, not just on Israel.

The year 2001 to 2007-2008

By now you may be wondering about the significance of the years 2001 to 2007-2008 regarding the fullness of the Gentiles. The answer relates to Israel, Jerusalem, and the Jews. There is a cycle from Christ's time that I believe will repeat itself.

In Matthew 24:1-3, Jesus predicted that the Jewish Temple in Jerusalem would be destroyed. This prediction was made around 30 A.D. Forty years later, in 70 A.D, Christ's words were literally fulfilled. Jesus also said that Jerusalem would be "trodden down of the Gentiles, until the times of the Gentiles be fulfilled" (Luke 21:24). Consider this:

- The fullness of the Gentiles refers to the completion of the church's mission to preach the Gospel to the world.
- The "times of the Gentiles" relates to Gentile nations controlling Jerusalem.

Since 70 A.D., every nation controlling Jerusalem was a Gentile power. A change came suddenly in 1967, during the Six-Day War, when the Israeli defense forces captured east Jerusalem and annexed the city, bringing east and west Jerusalem together.

From the time of Christ's public ministry to the destruction of the Temple, forty years transpired. Christ saw much unbelief among the people (Matthew 13:58), and predicted that God would judge Jerusalem with destruction. Forty years is the Biblical time frame that represents a generation of unbelief. Judgment came to Jerusalem and to the Temple within one generation.

Jerusalem was reunited in 1967, which was the beginning of the spiritual and natural growth of Israel. The 1960s were the beginning of spiritual decline in America. In 1967-68, the Charismatic renewal swept across North America, Canada, and Latin America. Another forty-year cycle will conclude in 2007-2008. This cycle may complete the generation of unbelief among the Gentile nations, especially America. If this happens, within the next few years we will experience the climax of America's greatness as a spiritual nation. Reports suggest that the EEC (European Economic Community) is expected to become an exceptionally strong economic force beginning in 2004. With the possibility of twenty to twenty eight nations in the EEC, it could become the strongest single superpower in the world; thus, America would be following instead of leading.

If my understanding of prophetic patterns proves to be correct, then between 2001 and 2008 we will see:

- the greatest initiative of Gospel preaching in the history of the world (Matthew 24:14);
- the greatest outpouring of the Holy Spirit in the history of the world (Acts 2:16-18);
- the formation of a major European superpower;
- the slow decline of America — morally, spiritually, and economically;
- a series of selective judgments, such as storms and earthquakes (Matthew 24:7).

Many Americans questioned why such a conflict ensued during the election of the 43rd president. The importance of the 43rd president may have been as prophetically important as the election of the first president of the United States. The first president greatly impacted the moral tone for America. The 43rd president will greatly impact the moral tone during the final stages of America's greatness or future decline.

Prophetically, I believe that one reason George W. Bush won instead of Al Gore had to do with Gore's emphasis on globalism. I do not believe it is time for the United States to be controlled by the United Nations, nor is it time to lose our sovereignty as a nation by joining a global union. Gore's writings indicate that he had some unusual ideas that few voters were aware of (Source: *Earth in the Balance*, Albert Gore). I believe his ideas were prophetically too premature for our nation at this time.

Those things will be fulfilled in God's timing. Only God knows what is coming to the nation and, when people pray, God can and will intervene to bring us the right leaders for the right season.

The possible prophetic importance of the 43rd presidency may be connected to these three interesting observations:

- The church is the 43rd unending generation.
- The high Priest completed the atonement after sprinkling the blood 43 times.
- The 43rd president could serve during the early phase of the climax of the Gentiles, or the peak of America's spiritual greatness.

Even if the 43rd president is elected for a second term from 2004 to 2008, I believe that America will more than likely have a 44th or even a 45th president. We can assume this based upon the fact that the tribulation will be seven years long and, if Christ tarries, America may have many more presidents. I emphasize the number forty-three because I see it as a prophetic signal pointing to the end of the fullness of the Gentiles and a completion of America's assignment and evangelism.

The final judgment upon Israel and Jerusalem came within a forty-year period, from the time of Christ's ministry to the invasion of the Romans in 70 A.D. Since 1967, Jerusalem has been united in the hands of Israel. The Lord has been building up Zion (Jerusalem) since 1967. A complete forty-year cycle will conclude between 2007 and 2008. Our 43rd president will serve during part and perhaps all of the final seven years of this cycle.

Evidence of the Climax of the Dispensation of the Church Age

Is the church fulfilling the great commission of Mark 16:15 to "Go ye into all the world and preach the Gospel to every creature"? The answer is yes. This is the greatest evidence that the church age could climax within a few years.

According to Terry Law Ministries, there were 140 million people living when Jesus was born. There are presently over 6 billion people on earth today. It took over nineteen centuries for the earth's population to increase from 140 million to one billion people. Yet, in just 100 years, the population grew from one to six billion. Because of the number of people alive today, more people accepted Christ as Savior between 1987 and 1997, than between 33 A.D. and 1987! What was not accomplished in 1,900 years was accomplished in just 10 years.

One of the greatest challenges of the church is to translate the Bible into every language on earth. According to missionary sources, there were about 13,000 language groups in 1995. Since many do not speak English and cannot receive Christian television or radio, how can they be reached? In 1995, there were 1,739 unreached language groups. Christian organizations and missionaries have been targeting these unreached groups, and five years later, only 526 major unreached language groups remain.

"And this Gospel of the kingdom shall be preached in all the world as a witness unto all nations, and then shall the end come."
(Matthew 24:14)

Notice that the Gospel does not reach every person, but every nation. The Greek word for nation is ethnos and it often refers to Gentiles. Today we would say ethnic group, or missionaries would say language group. The Gospel will be preached to every ethnic and language group. Voice of Evangelism supports men like Jack Harris, Kelvin McDaniel, and Russell Domingue who travel to remote regions of the earth and minister to the unreached groups. This represents the fulfillment of the words of Jesus, who taught that after this final thrust of global evangelism, the end would come.

The Greek word end is the word telos. According to the *W.E. Vines Dictionary of New Testament Words*, telos can mean *the limit which a person or thing ceases to be what it is.* The dispensation of the grace of God is given to the Gentiles (Ephesians 3:2). When this time frame is complete, Christ comes for the church. Paul said it this way:

"That in the dispensation of the fullness of times, he might gather together in one all things in Christ, both which are in heaven, and which are on earth; even in him." (Ephesians 1:10)

The fullness of times is connected to the fullness of the Gentiles (Romans 11:25). Both are linked to the Gentile Christian church and its mission to reach the Gentile nations with the Gospel of Christ.

During the next few years, I believe we will see the greatest efforts of global evangelism in world history. Many nations in Western Europe are hardened to the Gospel and blinded by religious tradition. In Africa, the threat of radical Islam is spreading. Doors will not always be open, and the time will come when evangelism will be restrained. The world will move toward a global Roman church system and make other Christian faiths obsolete. America must retain her Christian identity and enforce religious freedom. There must be one nation on earth where believers can take refuge and freely share the Gospel. It is up to our national leaders to set the example and to continue to support America's Biblical foundations. If, as a nation, we remain divided over Christian values, we will pluck the wings of the eagle and experience great decline. America must finish her assignment, and then the end will come.

Chapter 16

THE PROPHETIC IMPLICATION OF ELECTION 2000

The Post-Election Patterns of President George W. Bush

Six days after the 1992 presidential election, I was putting the final touches on a series of messages for our annual fall convention in Pigeon Forge, Tennessee. On Monday night at approximately 10:30 p.m., a strong inspiration from the Lord moved deeply in my spirit. I reached for a pen and wrote, "The same spirit that came upon Ahab and Jezebel in the Old Testament is coming to Washington, D.C." I was stunned by what I had written but was convinced that it was a word from the Holy Spirit. Eight years later, it was clear that the message was from the Lord because of the patterns that followed between 1992 and 2000.

For those who are unfamiliar with the Biblical story of Ahab and Jezebel, they were a husband and wife who ruled in ancient Israel when Elijah was Israel's prophet. Ahab seemed to have a heart that was sensitive to spiritual things, but his wife had a strong-willed, domineering personality, and she upstaged the king by manipulating circumstances for personal and political gain. Ahab respected true prophets of God, but he surrounded himself with false prophets, idol worshipers, and godless influences. Ahab is an example of a leader with potential who surrounded himself with the wrong type of people who influenced him and turned him away from righteousness.

By carefully examining 1 Kings 18 through 1 Kings 22, we see another interesting parallel. Ancient history once again mirrors modern day events. Ahab and Jezebel correlate in many ways to Bill Clinton and his wife Hillary. A list comparing historic events in ancient Israel to recent events in America follows:

King Ahab and his wife Jezebel	Bill and Hillary Clinton
* They lived in an ivory house.	* They lived in the White House.
* Ahab was the visible leader, but Jezebel made many decisions.	* Bill was the visible leader, but insiders say that Hillary directed many decisions.
* They became involved in a land deal.	* They were involved in a land deal (Whitewater).
* The land deal fell through.	* Whitewater fell through.
* An innocent man died (Naboth).	* An innocent man died (Vince Foster).
* She signed papers involving the deal.	* Hillary signed Rose Law Firm papers.
* Walking in sin was a light thing.	* Bill's sin was considered irrelevant.
* An enemy was raised up against them.	* Enemies were raised up against them.
* The true prophets were ridiculed.	* Conservatives were ridiculed.
* Severe drought hit the nation for 42 months.	* Drought has hit America.

Perhaps the most bizarre aspect of the story of Ahab and Jezebel involves the time that Ahab prepared for an upcoming war. A prophet of God named Micaiah revealed that God had sent a lying spirit to come forth from the mouths of Ahab's prophets in order to deceive the king (2 Chronicles 18:21). This is the only reference in the entire Scripture to a lying spirit. Therefore, Ahab experienced defeat because he followed a lying spirit. The parallel is that the impeachment charges leveled against Clinton stemmed from evidence that he lied under oath.

Many other parallels can be listed when comparing King Ahab and Clinton. In early 1992, I had no clue this pattern would play out in such detail. As an additional note, Jezebel continued to be in political power for some time after her husband's demise. In fact, when she reappeared in the narrative, she was in the ivory house surrounded by eunuchs in 2 Kings 9:30-32 (eunuchs are similar to security personnel). Years ago, I told my wife, "If this pattern follows through, Mrs. Clinton will be elected to a high office after her husband has left the White House." Today she is a Senator representing New York and, according to reports, she will likely run for president in the future.

Let me make it clear that I am not calling the Clintons "Ahab and Jezebel," but I am comparing historical patterns to show how "that which has been is that which shall be" (Ecclesiastes 1:9-10). It is clear that history did repeat itself.

What about the prophetic season America is in? Are there any Biblical or historical patterns relating to the 43rd president or beyond?

The Holy Spirit Always Knows the Will of God

I want to make it clear that I am not a politician, nor am I involved in politics. I am a minister who has never publicly endorsed a particular political party or candidate. However, I have at times received revelation from God regarding future events. With that being said, you will understand why I only shared the following information with a few close personal friends.

Scripture teaches that the Holy Spirit will "teach you all things and guide you into all truth" and "show you things to come" (John 16:13), and He will "reveal mysteries" (1 Corinthians 14:2). One work of the Holy Spirit is to inform the believer regarding future events. Information is given through prophetic Scriptures and through the inward leading of the Holy Spirit that results in spoken words of prophecy.

My Experience in the Spring of 1998

In April 1998, I had an unusual spiritual experience in the early hours of the morning. As I was coming out of a deep sleep, I was aware that I was lying in bed beside my wife. Suddenly I heard a voice say, "It is My will for the Governor of Texas to be the next President of the United States." I leaped out of the bed and awoke my wife saying, "You won't believe what just happened! I just heard a voice speaking to me." I repeated the words to her and she smiled, said a few words, and went back to sleep. I dressed and went into my office to tell my office manager about the incident. We checked the Internet to confirm that George W. Bush was the Governor of Texas. I told my office manager, "This is the man who is supposed to be the next president." I felt odd talking about the incident since no one, not even Governor Bush, had announced his run for the presidency. While I said nothing publicly, I confided only in a few close friends and family members. I experienced the same inner inspiration that I had when the word came to me in 1992 concerning the spirit that would come upon the nation. An unexpected event in Israel seven months later confirmed to me that the word from God was accurate.

In November of 1998, I hosted a group of Americans on a tour of the Holy Land. The group of 150 had just toured the Temple Mount in Jerusalem. My video crew, along with the *God's News Behind the News* crew, was leaving the Temple platform when my office manager noticed five men dressed in suits coming to the Western Wall for prayer. He said to me "That looks like George Bush, the Texas Governor!" It was indeed the Governor, along with four other men.

My office manager and I rushed toward the Western Wall where Bush had concluded a brief visit and was leaving. I walked up to him and introduced myself. He said, "You're the fellow who has the tour group." I replied that I had 150 Americans with me. The Governor asked, "Where are you from?" I said, "Tennessee." I mentioned again that I was leading the tour group and said to Mr. Bush, "They want you to run for president!" He laughed and said, "All right." I said, "I just want to encourage you. God bless you" (*See Center Section Photo of Perry meeting Bush*). Moments later, my group greeted him, shook his hand, and took pictures (*See Center Section Photo of Bush Meeting the Group*).

On that day, November 29, 1998, I knew that I had met the future 43rd President of the United States. Governor Bush had made no announcement that he was running. He had just been re-elected for a second term as Governor of Texas. On March 2, 1999, he appointed a committee to research the feasibility of a successful presidential bid.

On April 15, 1999, Governor Bush announced his plan to seek the Republican nomination. I was always curious as to when Bush actually decided to run. Prior to our meeting in Israel in November of 1998, I recall no one saying that he would run. During an interview in September of 2000, Oprah Winfrey asked Governor Bush when he decided to run. He said that it was in December of 1998, which would have been shortly after his three-day trip to Israel. I later read Bush's testimony on the Internet, and I also read his book. He mentioned his three-day tour to Israel in 1998 and how he was touched by his journey. He also mentioned being in Jerusalem, praying at the Western Wall, and the men who were with him. At the conclusion of his biography, he wrote about one of his friends telling him how the Jews and Gentiles are coming together. When I read this I thought that it was very unusual, since this is what the Holy Spirit had been showing me. According to his personal testimony, Bush recalled a message a pastor preached in December of 1999, after which his mother, Barbara Bush, said, "He is talking to you." This was a strong confirmation to him that he should run for the presidency.

I do not believe that our meeting had any bearing on his choice to run for president. But I do believe that the meeting was for my benefit in order to confirm that I had heard from the Lord.

Six Days Before the Election

As the time for the election drew near, I began considering the words I had heard. I never heard God say that the Governor *would* be the next president, but I heard that it was "God's will." This puzzled me, because whenever the Holy Spirit impresses my spirit, it is always with a very clear word. Six days before the election I understood why the Holy Spirit's word to me was, "It is My will" and not, "It is guaranteed to happen."

Six days before the 2000 election, I was preparing to speak at a banquet in Tampa, Florida, hosted by the prophetic ministry *God's News Behind the News*. Israel Arobaugh, a Jewish friend who was visiting from Jerusalem, called unexpectedly and said, "Perry, I am in Cleveland and I feel that I am supposed to come by and pray with you." Israel arrived, sat down in my office, and began to share with me an important update involving Israel. Afterward, we began to pray. We both prayed in English, but soon we started praying in our prayer languages (1 Corinthians 14:2-3). The prayer was very intense, and suddenly Israel said, "Perry, I can understand the language you are praying in!" I was praying in a form of Arabic, and Israel speaks both Hebrew and Arabic. As we continued, Israel grabbed my hand and began to switch them one over top of the other. It reminded me of Genesis 49, where Jacob blessed Ephriam and Manesseh while switching hands. Suddenly, through the Holy Spirit, Israel shouted,

"The Lord is saying the House of Ishmael is on the left." Then he cried out, "They are trying to switch the blessing! They are trying to switch the blessing!"

Israel was repeating what I actually said as I prayed in Arabic, a language that I cannot speak in the natural. When we concluded, I sat down and began to write these words: "The 2000 election will be about the will of God versus the will of the people."

When I arrived in Tampa, Florida on November 3 to speak at the *God's News Behind the News* partners meeting, there were over 400 Floridians present. The message that night was prophetic.

My opening statement was, "This upcoming election will be about the will of God versus the will of the people." The host, Dr. Joe VanKoevering, said, "I was in prayer and the Holy Spirit told me to watch Florida because it will determine the outcome of the election." Little did anyone know about the explosive battle that would follow in Florida!

On election night, Florida was first called for Al Gore, even before polls had closed in the Florida panhandle. I told my wife Pam, "Well, it's over. Bush can't win without Florida. I guess the will of the people has prevailed." Before the night ended, the state had been called for Bush, meaning he had won the election with one more electoral vote than he needed to win. Before morning, everything had changed to "too close to call."

The Battle over the Will of God Versus the Will of the People

Since there were two major presidential candidates, it was impossible for both men to be in God's perfect will for the nation. Only one man would represent the perfect will of God for the prophetic season that our nation would soon enter. The other would represent the "permissible will," meaning the Lord would permit it because of the will of the people. God permits us to choose other than His best and, when this happens, the decision is referred to as His "permissible will."

In the Bible, God sometimes allowed the will of the people to override His will. Because He gave mankind the freedom to choose, He allows people to choose their own course of action, however unwise or sinful. But in the end, if you do not follow the will of God, you may not be happy with the choices you have made.

An example of this is the story of Abraham and Sarah. God's perfect will was for Sarah to give birth to Isaac, who would become the father of one nation, Israel. However, as the years passed and the couple grew old, Sarah suggested that Abraham have a son by her handmaiden, Hagar. When Ishmael was born (Genesis 16:15), God expanded His perfect plan and blessed not only Isaac, but Ishmael as well. Sarah and Abraham doubted God and it caused them to take matters into their own hands, but God remained faithful to them. Yet, their choices caused a family feud that is still raging today between the Jews (Abraham's children through Sarah), and the Arabs (Abraham's children through Hagar)!

Another example is when the Holy Spirit warned Paul not to journey to Jerusalem because his life would be endangered (Acts 20:22-23 and Acts 21:11-13). Despite the warnings, Paul chose to make the journey (Acts 21:10-14). While at the Temple in Jerusalem, he was arrested and, from that moment forward, he spent much time in prison (Acts 21:27-40). Some scholars believe that Paul operated in his own will instead of God's perfect will.

The Bible tells us that there is the mind of the Holy Spirit and the mind of man. Paul wrote, "What man knoweth the things of a man, save the spirit of man which is in him? Even so the things of God knoweth no man, but the Spirit of God" (1 Corinthians 2:11). There is a vast difference between people speaking out of their own spirits, and speaking with the inspiration of the Holy Spirit. Psychics and false prophets, for example, speak from the spirits of men. However, Godly men and women speak from the counsel and wisdom of the Bible, and frequently by the inspiration of the Holy Spirit. A psychic might tell you what is on your mind, but a prophet of God will tell you what is on God's mind! Only the Holy Spirit can reveal future events with one hundred percent accuracy. Don't waste your time or money on counterfeit sources.

Missing God's Will Through Voting

Since Americans are blessed with the freedom to vote, our leaders are not necessarily ones that God would put into office. This happens because all professing Christians and observant Jews in America do not fast and pray to seek the will of God for our elections. If they would, then together they would vote with one voice for the best leaders for the nation, and we would see a landslide vote in favor of God's choice. Yet, because the political parties are so far apart in policy and ideology, typically each candidate will get about thirty percent of the more ideological voters on each side, leaving the remaining forty percent of the population to determine the final outcome.

The Bible makes it clear that people can miss God's will through voting, and the Lord will give the people what they demand even if it is not best for them.

The will of God was clear when Moses led the Israelites out of Egypt into the desert. They were on their way to the land that God promised them and it was to be theirs simply by entering and possessing it. Yet Moses, acting on his own, sent twelve spies ahead into the land to survey it. Upon their return, they were to vote on whether it was safe and desirable to enter. Only two men, Joshua and Caleb, believed that God would help Israel take the land, while ten men said, "There are walled cities and giants in the land. We cannot take it" (Numbers 13). Thus, ten men who voted out of fear hindered three million people from entering into God's best.

Another example is that of King Saul. From the time of Adam until the time of Saul, Israel was a theocracy. Judges were appointed by God and physically anointed with oil by the prophets. Yet, Israel observed that other nations had kings ruling over them. Under the prophet Samuel, the Hebrews demanded that they have a king to rule over Israel (1 Samuel 8:5). They rejected God as their King and sought to replace His authority with the authority of a man. The Lord warned Israel that this would bring them under the control of a man-made government, and that the people would cry out because of the king they selected. The Lord warned, "When you cry I will ignore you" (1 Samuel 8:18). The prophet Samuel selected Saul from the tribe of Benjamin to be Israel's first King (1 Samuel chapter 9). Saul's humble beginnings turned into pride, and pride became his downfall. Saul's arrogance and jealousy caused him to want to look good in the eyes of the people (1 Samuel 15:30). You might say that he was definitely concerned about the opinion polls.

Eventually, the entire nation suffered because the will of men overrode the will of God. I have said, "God will give people what they want, but they won't like what they get." This happened with King Saul as people began to turn against him.

Parallels Between Saul's Time and Contemporary America

When God allowed Israel's will to prevail, six problems arose within Saul's administration. They were:

- The people were heavily taxed to finance the government (1 Samuel 8:15-17).
- The morale of the military declined to an all time low (1 Samuel 17:19-24).
- The people were in debt, discontent, and discouraged (1 Samuel 22:1-2).
- There was arrogance and abuse of power (1 Samuel chapter 22).
- The righteous were persecuted (1 Samuel 18:9-12).
- The leaders practiced divination instead of seeking God (1 Samuel 28:7).

We have similar circumstances in America today. While Hebrews paid a ten percent tax on their wealth, Americans pay a much higher rate. The Biblical ten percent, or tithe, was initially established by God to support the Temple and the priests.

The morale of Saul's armies was at an all-time low as the Philistines captured the Ark of the Covenant, and Goliath taunted Israeli soldiers in the Valley of Elah for forty days. Not one soldier was willing to challenge Goliath and even King Saul refused to go to war. Yet, under Moses, the Hebrews conquered two giant kings, Og of Bashan and Sihon of Moab. Joshua and Caleb were each over eighty years old when they ran giants out of the land. Joshua led Israel as it conquered over thirty-one Canaanite cities. Even though America remains the greatest military power on earth, the morale of its armed forces has weakened. One military expert told me that it is very difficult to recruit young people, and terrorist attacks, like the one on the USS Cole, do not help matters.

The people in Saul's kingdom were in debt, discontented and discouraged. This resulted from Saul's unrighteous leadership. He ruled from a fleshly heart instead of by the leading of the Spirit of God, so God's favor was not upon him. Americans are in severe debt, many are discouraged, and most are discontented with their lives. They seek materialistic pleasures to fill the void in their spirits.

Saul's arrogance led to his abuse of power. King Saul and the prophet Samuel each had specific God-given realms of authority. One was never to infringe upon the other's Divine influence. For example, according to the Law, only Levite priests were to offer animal sacrifices. But more than once, Saul broke the Law and performed the sacred rite of offering burnt sacrifices (1 Samuel 13:9-14). In doing so, he performed righteous acts in an unrighteous manner. His abuse of power caused God to take the kingdom from him and place it into the hands of young David, son of Jesse.

Saul's disregard for the Law also manifested in a brutal personality change. This honorable king from the tribe of Benjamin became a ruthless tyrant. He had eighty Hebrew priests killed, and he attempted to murder David twenty-one times. Saul's jealousy raged over David's anointing from the Lord as he realized that his kingdom would crumble as the hand of God moved from him to David.

We can see a ruthless disregard for God's Law today in America as babies are killed and abortion is justified as a God-given freedom, and fighting to protect babies' lives is labeled radical activism. Those who stand for righteousness are called religious fanatics as their character is assassinated because they define good and evil in terms of God's will. Those in power (the Sauls) fear that those who stand for righteousness (the Davids) will rise to power and replace old policies with new policies, based on the word of God.

Because Saul could not hear from the Lord, he sought guidance from the witch of Endor, who had a familiar spirit. This angered God and caused Saul's demise. During a battle on Mount Gilboah, Saul and his sons were slain (2 Samuel 16:10-16). Thus the people's choice eventually failed miserably.

The Condition of the Average American

Some of Saul's leaders slowly began to defy Saul and shift their loyalties toward David. These discerning men knew that Saul was still the king, but that God's anointing upon him had lifted. Before David became king, more than six hundred chief men aligned with him. David respected Saul's position and never resisted his authority.

The condition of the Hebrews is similar to that of Americans today who trusted in the will of man and not the will of God. We read that the people were "in debt, discontent and discouraged" (1 Samuel 22:1-2). Debt is a financial condition, discontent is an emotional condition, and discouragement is a spiritual condition. Their lives were in turmoil, yet they knew something better was coming from God, if they could find God's man to lead the nation in the right direction.

Americans often look for a man to solve their problems in the same manner that the ancient Israelites did. We must find men of faith and moral character to lead, instead of ones who make promises and break vows. The comparison between Saul and David illustrates this practical advice: it is better to have a leader who is humble before God than a genius who leads with arrogance.

Election Confusion

The Florida election became a lawyer's dream as lawsuits and allegations flew. The confusion flourished with incorrectly marked ballots, pregnant chads, dimpled chads, uncounted military ballots, and charges of confusing ballots and denied opportunities to vote. To those who are spiritual, this was not a political conspiracy, but a true spiritual battle similar to the one fought in the heavenlies in Daniel 10.

When something of this nature happens, great insight comes by evaluating prophetic patterns to determine if the people involved have a particular pattern for that time. I do not believe there are patterns in every event, every election, or at every moment in history. However, I do believe that when events transpire during a prophetic season, the patterns they reflect can have prophetic implications.

As I began to research the four candidates names (George W. Bush, Albert Gore, Dick Cheney and Joe Lieberman), I began to see that Bush and Lieberman seemed to have various patterns connected to the prophetic season that we are in. But I found little or nothing relating to Vice President Gore or Mr. Cheney. I will not, under any conditions, give the details of the various patterns we researched. I have told my wife some details that I believe could happen over the next several years, but I will not share that publicly. However, I do wish to show you why I believe it was destined that Bush would win Florida. It is in the prophetic numbers.

It's All in the Numbers

Because much of my study of Scripture involves Hebraic research, I am aware of the importance of the Hebrew alphabet and the meaning of its coinciding numbers. Some people misunderstand this concept and consider it to be based on the occult. In reality, the Bible is filled with numbers and each number carries a specific meaning. The number three always means *unity,* the number six always means *man* or *mankind,* and the number seven always means *completion* or *perfection.* My research uses the numbers in the Bible to identify and explain patterns.

The Hebrew alphabet is unique because its letters are interchangeable with numbers. Each of the twenty-two letters of the Hebrew alphabet corresponds to a number. Because of this, letters can have dual meanings (*See Hebrew chart Page 243*).

Upon converting letters into numbers, we discover that they can point to prophetic dates. For example, the seven Feasts of Israel have both a literal and a prophetic fulfillment. Many of America's major historical events have fallen on dates that coincide with the Feasts of Israel. I call these prophetic parallels. They occur when recent events fall on the same dates, or cycle of years, on which previous events have fallen. For example, both Jewish temples were destroyed over 670 years apart but on the same day of the year — the 9th of Av. Though separated by many years, the fact that these two events occurred on the same calendar date is considered to be a prophetic parallel.

Because Arabic numerals (1, 2, 3, etc.) were not used in antiquity, many alphabet letters doubled as alpha and numeric characters. The Hebrew alphabet is one such set of letters. Because of this, the letters are often interchanged with numbers, and certain meanings can be derived from both the letters of the alphabet and their numeric equivalents (*See Hebrew chart*).

November 29 and the Israel Connection

While the 2000 election turmoil was brewing in Florida, I was in the Crown Plaza Hotel in Jerusalem, packing to return to America. I received a call from my friend, Israel Aurobach, who had been in my office praying weeks earlier. He was in the hotel lobby and immediately came to my room. We sat down and began to discuss the prayer session he and I

Hebrew Alphabet, Transliterations, and Numerical Values

Hebrew Character	Name	Transliteration	Numerical Value
א	Alef	omit	1
בּ, ב	Bet, Vet	b, v	2
ג	Gimel	g	3
ד	Dalet	d	4
ה	He	h	5
ו	Vav	v	6
ז	Zayin	z	7
ח	Het	ḥ	8
ט	Tet	t	9
י	Yod	y	10
כּ, כ	Kaf, Khaf	k, kh	20
ל	Lamed	l	30
מ	Mem	m	40
נ	Nun	n	50
ס	Samekh	s	60
ע	Ayin	omit	70
פּ, פ	Pe, Fe	p, f	80
צ	Zade	ẓ	90
ק	Kuf	k	100
ר	Resh	r	200
שׂ, שׁ	Sin, Shin	s, sh	300
ת	Tav	t	400

had at my office prior to the election, and how the Holy Spirit had revealed to us what would actually take place in Florida.

I reminded my friend that George W. Bush had been in Israel exactly two years before, to the day. Israel said, "You mean Bush was here on November 29, 1998?" I replied, "Yes, why?" He said, "You don't know what today is?" I laughed and said, "Yes, it is November 29th!" He replied, "This is not just November 29th. This is kuf tet. This is the day that the United Nations voted to partition Palestine in order to allow the Jews to come back to Palestine and establish a homeland!"

Then we then sat down and began to look at the names of the candidates when written in the Hebrew language. I wrote down each name with its Hebrew transliteration beneath it. Then I decided to look at the numbers in the Florida recount to see if there were any meaningful parallels. Israel said, "Oh, Perry, this election is prophetic. It is not the average election." After examining the names of Bush and Gore and the recount numbers, I was certain that a pattern pointed to Bush. I left Jerusalem believing that Bush would eventually win Florida and become the next president. I believed that the patterns were overwhelmingly in his favor.

The Name Bush in Hebrew

The name Bush consists of three Hebrew letters: beit, vav, and shin. As mentioned earlier, each Hebrew letter has a numerical value as well as a symbolic meaning. For example, the first letter alef has a number value of one, and its symbol is an ox. This is because the earliest form of this letter looked similar to the head of an ox. The second letter in the Hebrew alphabet is the letter beit. Its numerical value is two and its symbol is a house.

The three Hebrew letters comprising Bush's name are:
   B — beit — which is symbolized by a house
   U — vav — which is symbolized a hook
   SH — shin — which is symbolized by teeth, and is also the
      symbol of the name of God, Shaddai

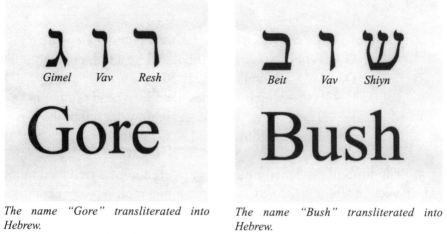

ר ו ג
Gimel Vav Resh

ש ו ב
Beit Vav Shiyn

Gore

Bush

The name "Gore" transliterated into Hebrew.

The name "Bush" transliterated into Hebrew.

The Hebrew letters have been reversed to read from left to right!

The third letter, shin, is the most interesting of the entire alphabet. Shin is the twenty-first letter and it represents the name of God (Shaddai). The letter shin appears on every mezuzah in the world. (A mezuzah is a small case containing a piece of parchment inscribed with the Shema, or verses from Deuteronomy, and placed on the doorpost of a Jewish home or business.) The value of shin is 300. George Bush was ahead by 300 votes in two of the numerous Florida recounts. So the last two letters of Bush's name in Hebrew are equivalent to two of the recount totals.

Considering the connotation of the Hebrew letters that spell the name Bush, its meaning could be tied to the idea of *connecting God and the house* or *connected to the house of God*. It is fascinating that during the campaign, the Bush team did not use the traditional "V" sign using two fingers to signify victory, but they used a "W" by holding up three fingers. The Hebrew letter equivalent to "W" in form is the letter shin. As far as sound, the equivalent is the letter vav, which is translated back into the English alphabet as the letter "V" or "W." Yet, the ancient form of the letter shin, in the time of Moses, was actually written like the English W is today. While these meanings are interesting, they should not be overly emphasized since many English names also contain the letters beit and shin. Also, it should be noted that this is not the Hebrew meaning of the name Bush, but the meaning of the symbols of the Hebrew letters.

The Name Gore

The name Gore consists of three Hebrew letters. They are:

G – Gimel – which is symbolized by a rich man in motion

O – Vav – which is symbolized by a hook

R – Resh – which is symbolized by a head or the top

E — There are no vowels in Hebrew, therefore the E is dropped from the end of the name

The form of the letter gimel is considered to be a rich man in motion. In ancient Hebrew (Moses' time), the gimel represented a camel, and carried the meaning of *pride or arrogance*. The vav is symbolized by a hook and means to *connect to something*. The letter resh is symbolized by a head bent over. Resh means *head*, or *the top*. The Hebrew word for head is rosh. This may seem strange, but the name Gore could indicate *a rich man with his head leaning over*, or *a proud look or proud leader.*

Again, I do not wish to place too much emphasis on this method of interpreting names. I am simply pointing this out as an interesting fact. In addition, resh is the twentieth letter of the Hebrew alphabet. The ordinal value of resh is twenty (or twenty of twenty-two) and it can be interpreted as meaning *the beginning of the end*. Should Gore run for the Presidency in 2004 and win, the Hebrew meaning points to the possibility that it could introduce *the beginning of the end,* or the possible last four years of the fullness of the Gentiles. It is an interesting thought.

The Florida Count of 930

When the overseas ballots were counted, the Bush advantage rose to 930. This is another unique number in the Bible which relates to Adam's age at the time of his death. The Bible records this in Genesis:

"And all the days that Adam lived were nine hundred and thirty years: and he died." (Genesis 5:5)

The word for man in Hebrew is Adam. The death of Adam signified the close of one dispensation of time and the beginning of another. Adam was alive at the same time as Lamech, Noah's father. According to the Jewish historian Josephus, Adam predicted that God would destroy the earth twice, once by the violence of fire, and once by a quantity of water. According to Josephus, this warning was passed on to Adam's son, Seth, whose sons inscribed their discoveries on two pillars of stone and brick in the land of Siriad (Source: *Josephus Antiquities of the Jews*, book I, chapter 2, section 3).

Enoch, the seventh descendant from Adam, was warned in a dream that the flood was coming and he named his son Methuselah, meaning *his death will bring or initiate.* Research indicates that Methuselah died the year of Noah's flood, possibly seven days before the flood actually engulfed the earth (Genesis 6 and 7).

Since Adam lived for 930 years, and upon his death an old chapter closed, it is interesting to see how the number 930 correlates to the 43rd president, who was elected during the final year of the old millennial chapter. He was sworn into office twenty days into the new millennium. The new millennium actually began in 2001, even though much emphasis was placed on the year 2000; therefore, the number 930 suggests a major transition in time and history.

American History Reveals More Patterns

Let's look at another presidential pattern in American history. Historically speaking, 1824 was the last year in which the son of a former President was elected. John Adams was America's second President and his son, John Quincy Adams, was the sixth President. The elected son of each president had the first name of his father. President Bush, the father, was born just a few miles from where the second president, John Adams, was born. When John Quincy Adams was elected, the electoral votes were split three ways. John Quincy won the election, but Andrew Jackson, who was from Nashville, Tennessee, contested its results. George W. Bush, won the election, but Albert Gore, who was from Nashville, Tennessee, contested its results.

Before Adams could take his oath of office, friends of Jackson predicted that he would successfully run against Adams in four years. Four years later, Jackson returned and became the seventh President of the United States. Before Bush ever took the oath of office, friends of Gore said they believed that he would run again in four years. Only time will tell.

The Election of 1876 and the Election of 2000

News commentators compared the 2000 election to the election of 1876, but they did not explain why they were similar. The 1876 election candidates were Rutherford Hayes and Samuel Tilden. Following is a list of remarkable comparisons between the two elections:

— There were three candidates in 1876:	—There were three major candidates in 2000:
Rutherford Hayes-Republican Samuel Tilden-Democrat Peter Cooper-Greenback	George Bush-Republican Albert Gore- Democrat Ralph Nader-Green Party
—The Democrat won the Popular Vote	—The Democrat won the Popular Vote
—The Republican won the Electoral Vote by 1 (185 for Hayes and 184 for Tilden)	—The Republican won the Electoral Vote by 1 (271 for Bush; he needed 270 to be elected)
—The election in Florida was disputed	—The election in Florida was disputed
—The nation was in a partisan split	—The nation was in a partisan split

The Parallels Between Lucy Hayes and Laura Bush

Before comparing the presidents, I want to look at some parallels between Mrs. Lucy Hayes and Mrs. Laura Bush. Lucy Hayes disapproved of alcohol and she and her husband did not drink it. She did not allow alcohol to be served in the White House, and she and her husband both agreed on this policy. George Bush stopped drinking alcohol after his 40th birthday in 1986 at the insistence of his wife, Laura. Lucy Hayes spear-headed literacy efforts and Laura Bush, who is a former librarian, also champions literacy. In fact, in Texas she helped to raise $600,000 to support state libraries. As did Lucy Hayes, Laura Bush will promote literacy as the first lady. Lucy Hayes was a devout Christian who belonged to the Disciples of Christ, a Methodist church. Laura Bush is a devout Christian, and she and her husband attended a Methodist church in Texas. Laura is a voracious reader, as was Lucy, and both ladies encouraged their families to read. It is said of Mrs. Hayes that she much preferred a literary circle or informal party to a state reception. An article in *USA Today* on December 14, 2000 stated that the Bushes have little for the ceremonial trappings of office — the formal dinners, the speeches, and the press conferences.

The Parallels Between Rutherford Hayes and George W. Bush

Not only are the elections of 1876 and 2000 similar, the candidates are also similar. Hayes dealt with the effects of Andrew Johnson's impeachment, along with the scandals of the previous President, Ulysses Grant. Bush's election followed the impeachment of the 42nd President and a series of numerous scandals. Hayes' administration focused largely on the economics of the middle class. Bush's proposed plans emphasize tax cuts to help the middle class and not just the wealthy. Hayes stressed the need of all Americans to be educated, and historians report that education was Hayes' strong point. Likewise, Bush's top priority is education, and he emphasizes that every child must learn to read. Hayes served two terms as Governor of Ohio and Bush was serving his second term as Governor of Texas at the time of his election. Hayes came out of retirement to serve a third term. He was noted for uniting rival factions even within his own party. Those close to Bush have praised his ability to unite factions. Hayes was a Washington outsider compared to his opponents. Compared to Gore, Bush was considered an outsider. Hayes did not campaign for the presidency, but made two appearances at the Philadelphia Centennial Exhibition. The Republicans nominated George W. Bush in Philadelphia.

In 1876, it appeared that the Democrats had won, but Republicans disputed ballot tabulations in four states, including Florida. In 1876, a large number of Democrat ballots were disqualified. The Democrats cried foul, but the Republicans produced evidence to show that thousands of blacks who wanted to vote for Hayes had been kept from the polls. Much criticism has come from black Americans concerning the 2000 election. In 1876, Congress appointed an electoral commission to validate the electoral votes. The commission included five Supreme Court justices. The 2000 election was contested in court and eventually, five out of nine Supreme Court justices ruled that the Florida recount method was unconstitutional. In 1887, an eight to seven commission majority gave the election to Hayes, generating a one-vote win. In the 2000 election, the Supreme Court voted to stop the Florida recount, thus giving Bush a one-vote electoral win.

The Democrats in 1876 attempted to delay the inauguration and create a Constitutional crisis. This was considered during election 2000. Hayes only served one term, perhaps because of the controversy. He and Lucy were so loved by the public that, when they left the White House, people across America cried (Source: *The Readers Companion to the American Presidency*).

While the comparisons are remarkable, I do not wish to imply that Bush could not, or will not, be elected to a second term. Hayes simply chose not to run again. Some Americans believe that Bush is an invalid president because he did not carry the popular vote. From a faith-based view, it is clear that George W. Bush was ordained of God to enter the White House during this prophetic season. The pattern between Hayes and Bush gives credence to the Scripture, "That which has been is that which shall be," and the verse, "That which hath been is now; and that which is to be hath already been" (Ecclesiastes 1:9; 3:15).

There are other patterns or cycles regarding Election 2000; however, they are not as dramatic as those above.

Two Hundred Years Ago in 1800

During the election in 1800, each state elector cast two votes for president. The candidate with the most votes became president, and the candidate with the second most votes became vice president. In 1800, each candidate got 73 votes, or 52.9% for Thomas Jefferson and 52.9% for Aaron Burr. It took 36 votes in the House of Representatives to break the tie and give the election to Thomas Jefferson. Two hundred years later, the Presidential election was split, and after 36 days the electoral majority was certified to George W. Bush.

The 2000 election in November fell on the same month as the 200th anniversary of the opening of the White House. It was built under the leadership of George Washington, but it was the president elected in 1800 who was first to live in the new "people's house."

The Contested Election in 1960

The most recently contested American presidential election was forty years ago in 1960. Richard Nixon contested ballot tabulations in his election with John Kennedy. In the Bible, the number forty represents testing. Goliath taunted Israel for forty days and Christ was tempted in the wilderness for forty days (1 Samuel 17:16 and Matthew 4:2). Forty years after the Nixon-Kennedy dispute, the 2000 challenge literally tested the patience of the nation. One of the biggest controversies in 1960 involved

Texas and Illinois votes. One expert calculated that there were 100,000 votes for Kennedy and Johnson that were simply non-existent.

At one polling station there were 4,895 registered voters and 6,138 votes were actually certified. Nixon carried 93 of Illinois' 102 counties, yet he lost the state by 8,858 votes. The huge turnout in Chicago under Mayor Richard Daley gave Kennedy its 450,000 votes. Some suggested that, if illegal votes, including votes of dead people, were removed from the tally, Nixon probably would have won by about 250,000 votes. Nixon, a Republican, was advised to file legal charges, but he refused. In six of the disputed states, there were different rules for recounting.

In election 2000, forty years later, the Democrats demanded a Florida recount even though recount rules varied between counties. Heading the charge was Bill Daley, son of Richard Daley, whose father was accused of padding the ballot boxes forty years earlier in Chicago. In 1960, Kennedy won Illinois with Daley's help. In 2000, Daley's son protested, but Gore eventually conceded the election.

During election 2000, some people pointed out that a third party candidate, Ralph Nader, took votes away from Gore's 2,842,567 votes, which could have cost Gore the election. Interestingly, when President George Bush ran for re-election in 1992, third party candidate Ross Perot got over 19 million votes, many of which would have gone to Bush. This could have cost Bush that election. When Clinton ran for re-election, some allege that Clinton talked Perot into running again as a third party candidate. In 1996, Perot got another 8 million votes, thus weakening Bob Dole's position. In election 2000, the third party candidate took votes from Clinton's vice president, thus giving former President Bush's son the election. Again, we see history repeating itself.

That Which Has Been and That Which Shall Be

In Scripture we often see events conclude in a manner similar to their inception. For example, the last two chapters of the Bible appear to parallel the first two chapters. In Genesis 1 and 2, there is no sin, sorrow, death, or pain and in the final chapters, Revelation 21 and 22, again we see no sin, sorrow, death, or pain. Another example that illustrates this principle is the ministry of Christ. In the beginning of His ministry, there was Mary, Joseph, and Herod, and at the conclusion of His ministry we see Mary, Joseph, and Herod. At the beginning of Christ's ministry, He fasted for 40 days, and at the end He was seen alive for 40 days. Christ ascended from the Mount of Olives and will return to the Mount of Olives.

After declaring independence from Britain and England, George Washington became the first President of the United States. The founding documents that would govern the nation and guarantee freedom to its people were drafted. The Bible and Judeo-Christian beliefs profoundly influenced the foundation of the Republic. Beginning in 1776, the story of the world's greatest Gentile nation unfolded. As with ancient Israel's first king, both King Saul and George Washington were taller than their contemporaries. Both hesitated in becoming the leaders of their respected nations, and both were noted for their successful battles.

America has come full circle and today another "George W." is President. Our first President, George Washington, was a Methodist and George W. Bush is Methodist. Our first President was nominated in Philadelphia, and so was George W. Bush. Both Washington and Bush announced their candidacies in the month of April — Washington on April 14, 1789 and Bush on April 15, 1999. Washington and his wife Martha enjoyed getting away and spending time on their plantation in Mount Vernon. Bush and his wife Laura enjoy getting away and spending time on their ranch in Texas.

I believe it is clear, even to the casual reader, that these parallels are not mere human coincidence. Such patterns are seldom found in American history, unless the events point to a strong prophetic season of purpose.

The Conclusion of the Election Saga

Many sincere persons wonder if is it possible that Gore actually won the election. Scripture states, "God...changeth the times and the seasons: he removeth kings, and setteth up kings" (Daniel 2:21). God's foreknowledge of global events may provide part of the explanation. God sets up times and seasons, and He sets up or removes kings. Perhaps Mr. Gore's approach would not have been in God's perfect plan for this prophetic season. For example, Gore has been known to lean toward a New Age type of philosophy and toward the United Nations' vision of globalism.

My prophetic studies indicate that there will be a future seventh empire that will grip the nations of the old Roman Empire into its hands. This new superpower is scheduled to arise between 2004 to 2008, if all continues as planned. Mr. Gore's global ideology would better fit a pattern between 2004 and 2008, or beyond 2008.

The importance of the number forty-three and the 43rd President cannot be underestimated. From 2001 to 2004, the greatest harvest of souls in history will be reaped for the Kingdom of God. Nations that are now open to the Gospel will one day be closed to non-traditional, non-Roman Church groups. When the church has finished her final world harvest and her mission is accomplished, the times of the Gentiles will be fulfilled.

If we are in a major prophetic cycle, similar to the time frame of the time of Christ to the destruction of the Temple (40 years), then from 2001 to 2007 – 2008, America, the vineyard, will bring forth its greatest harvest. Europe will rise and attention will be drawn to Israel and the Jews. The leaders during the next few years will set the pace in America for its final prophetic destiny. One thing is clear - these are the last days and we must keep the eagle strong!

Chapter 17

RESTORING THE STRENGTH OF THE EAGLE

Restoring America One More Time

"They that wait upon the Lord shall renew their strength, they shall mount up with wings as eagles; they shall run and not be weary, and they shall walk and not faint."   (Isaiah 40:31)

As mentioned before, the eagle is a symbol of liberty. Powerful wings enable eagles to soar freely and unrestrained at heights of 2,400 feet. Their strong wings even make it possible to carry other eagles to safety. And these majestic birds excel in strong winds because the turbulence facilitates higher flight. Incredible eyesight permits them to spot prey from a great distance. They mate for life as they return to the same nest on the same rugged ledge year after year. Eagles teach their young how to fly.

No greater emblem could have been chosen to represent America than the eagle. America is the greatest nation on earth. Yet, in the natural, even the strongest eagle experiences a time late in its life when it must experience renewal. During this period of renewal, the eagle physically experiences the process called molting. Five things happen simultaneously during the time period and the physical process:

- The feathers of the eagle begin to fall out.
- Calcium builds up on the eagle's beak, making it difficult to eat.
- The eagle can lose its appetite.
- Instead of flying, the eagle walks on the ground and becomes too weak to fly.
- The eagle's eyes become dry and they no longer cry.

Perhaps America is going through its own molting period. Just as an eagle's feathers helped to guide them, we were once being guided into the path of truth and righteousness, but we are now being misguided into unrighteous paths based on ungodly ideas. Hard working, tax-paying Christians face intimidation as they carry their Bibles to work and witness to fellow workers, or place religious symbols on their desks. While the local church still exercises its religious freedom, public work places and schools are sometimes inaccessible to Christians who want to share Christ. This represents our mouths being restrained, just as the calcium deposits weigh down the eagle's beak. The appetite for spiritual truth is dull in many areas. Traditional churches are forced to close their doors for lack of interest. There is a love for the wilderness, or the wild things, instead of taking the higher road where the atmosphere is clear and clean. There is hardness in the hearts of many, as we no longer weep over death, carnage, suicide, murder, and crime.

Voices From the Edge of Eternity

Has history taught us anything? The empires of Bible prophecy have vanished. The names of the nations are the same — Egypt, Syria, and Greece — yet their dominion over the world has all but ceased. The Babylonian Empire lies in ruins on the banks of the Euphrates. The cities of the Roman Empire are now tourist attractions and the delight of archaeologists.

Among the voices crying from eternity, the Babylonians are saying, "Our wealth could not save us." The Medes and Persians are crying,

"All the laws inscribed on stone tablets could not deliver us." The Greeks are crying, "Don't depend upon your pride and your human wisdom. Our empire finally fell and the wise men could not stop it." I can hear the trudging feet of Roman soldiers beating down the walls of Jerusalem, setting fire to the Holy Temple, capturing Jews, chaining them together like sheep marching to their slaughter. I hear Nero as he declares himself to be God. He conducts orgies and plans the persecution of Christians. Listen as he cries across the chasm of time and eternity to a proud America, "Your immorality will bring you down and carry you to where I now am." Since people pay little attention to history, perhaps an object lesson from nature will make the point and identify the way to overcome.

The Molting Period

America is in its molting period. Just as eagles experience change during their mid lives, the American eagle is experiencing change. As the eagle experiences this season, it will either renew itself or die in the wilderness.

Years ago, I heard a Baptist minister named Bobby Thompson speak on the subject of eagles and their periods of molting. An Indian took Bobby into the heart of the mountains to observe eagles. There, the minister saw five giant eagles that stood on the rocks of a wilderness valley. Their heads hung over to the side because calcium deposits had built up on their beaks and weighed down their heads too much to fly. He noticed that their claws were covered with dried blood. The Indian told him that, as long as eagles fly high, the friction of the wind keeps their beaks smooth, but when they come down to the forest floor and begin to walk around, the deposits build up on their beaks. No one is certain why eagles come down from the high places into the wilderness. Perhaps it is curiosity, or maybe they tire of flying. Soon the eagles lose their appetite and their strength to fly high to hunt for food.

Bobby and the Indian watched as eight eagles flew in a circle around the five weakened birds. They began to descend lower, hovering over the five. These birds began dropping pieces of fresh rabbit and squirrel meat to their companions. It was up to the five birds to reach down and feed themselves. The Indian told Bobby, "If they feed themselves, they will gain strength and live. If not, they will die in a short time."

Bobby returned several days later to discover that three eagles had died. They did not eat and became so weak that they accepted death over life. Two eagles fed themselves, and gained enough strength to fly back to the cleft of the rock. They hit their beaks against the rocks and removed the calcium. The combination of eating properly, going back to its rock, and removing the calcium deposits enabled the eagles to renew themselves and fly high again.

Two eagles renewed themselves. The three that did not renew themselves died. Let us compare this process to empires that have come and gone. At the apex of their power, they chose the attitude of those on the Titanic: "Nothing can take us down. We are unsinkable." So how does the American eagle renew itself in these final days?

1. The nation must be fed the proper diet.

Just as the eagles in the wilderness had to eat to receive strength to fly again, the people of this nation must be fed the truth in order to gain spiritual strength. Have you observed the difference between a true Christian and an unbeliever? A true Christian has joy, assists others in need, and is fulfilled through his or her relationship with the Lord and by helping others. The word of God is more than information — it is revelation. As this revelation is received into your spirit, it brings illumination and produces inspiration! Your outlook on life changes and your lifestyle blossoms accordingly. After all, how many atheists do you know that have built orphanages and hospitals, or established inner city programs to help the poor? I know of none. I do know of many churches that are involved in helping others.

While unbelievers want to restrain Christian evangelism, they often overlook the Christian work that helps the poor and needy. We do this because we have been fed the true bread of life, the word of God. In a sense, we must drop the nurturing word of God into the lives of eagles that are in the dry places to encourage them so that they, too, can come out of the wilderness and fly in the high places.

2. The nation must set its eyes on the rock.

When an eagle walks in the wilderness, it forgets the rock on which it was born. Eagles were not created to walk on the ground like turkeys and chickens; instead, they were created to soar above the storms of life and perch in peace on high cliffs. In fact, the eagle never completely abandons the rock on which it was born, except when it is in the molting period.

The Bible teaches, "God is our rock" (Psalms 62:1-2). David wrote, "When my heart is overwhelmed, lead me to the rock that is higher than I" (Psalms 61:2). America has lost its spiritual direction as secular Humanism, New Age spiritualism, evolution, and materialism have replaced faith in God. Today, as a nation, we are divided and walking around in circles in the wilderness. Only when we set our eyes back on the rock of our salvation will we be infused with the strength to remove the "weights and sins that so easily beset us" (Hebrews 12:1).

3. We must learn to weep again.

When the eagle goes through the molting period, its eyes become dry and it is unable to cry. When an eagle flies, there is a covering over its eyes to keep them moist. Bobby Thompson observed that once the eagle settled upon the rocks, the water flowed from its eyes and down across its beak.

The eyes of many American hearts have become dry and unable to see the critical needs of those around them. Movies are filled with cursing, crime, rape, and immorality. When a person is murdered, raped, or wounded in the community, many no longer weep over these crimes against humanity. Their hearts are hardened and their spirits are cold. The media, whether intentionally or not, has fostered a cynical, skeptical society with calloused hearts. We must learn to bear one another's burdens and weep with them that weep. This will again occur when we return to the rock of our salvation. Weeping is not difficult when our hearts are filled with compassion.

Political renewal is merely a temporary bandage placed over a mortal wound. The eagle must experience spiritual renewal and reverse wrong thinking and attitudes of self-destruction. Spiritual renewal begins with the heart and works its way throughout the body. We must pray for leaders in the pulpit, in the White House, and on the local level who will stand for righteousness and for these principles:

- There is one eternal God who created all men equal.
- The Holy Bible is the foundation of our nation and it should be taught to our children.

- Prayer is communication with God. Students should be allowed to pray either before or after school as long as they do not force their will upon others.
- There should never be any restraint on freedom to preach the Gospel. After all, our nation was birthed upon the Bible and the preaching of the Word of God.
- Our Christian heritage should be taught in public schools, lest a generation forget the God whose sovereignty established this nation.
- Freedom of religion does not mean freedom from religion.
- The Bible is the only correct foundation for a value system based on right and wrong.

If the nation continues to be divided over these seven points, then beware of Jesus' words, "A house divided against itself cannot stand" (Matthew 12:25). We are a nation "built upon the rock" and we will not endure future storms if we begin to "build upon the sand" (Matthew 7:26).

Conclusion

After years of research, I have concluded that only two nations on earth are connected through the same prophetic history, cycles, patterns, and symbols. Those nations are Israel and America. Those in the Arab world often believe this is a social link driven by a political agenda. Many sincere Arabs and Palestinians fail to recognize that America's spiritual roots are founded deep in the bedrock of Hebraic concepts revealed to the Hebrew prophets of the Bible. Without this understanding, few will recognize America's prophetic significance or appreciate America's God-given assignment. I believe it is clear that the sovereign Almighty raised up America to complete an assignment that ancient Israel failed to complete. Israel's prophets were given the revelation of the Bible; yet, Scripture indicates they often failed to keep God's commandments. America was given the special assignment to preach and proclaim the God of the Bible; yet, as we enter the third millennium from Christ's birth, the ship is beginning to falter in the storms of unbelief and sin. America may believe in the God of the Bible but, as a nation, we are failing to follow his commandments.

Israel was given the assignment to birth the Messiah and proclaim His kingdom to the Gentile nations. This assignment was incomplete when Jerusalem was destroyed in 70 A.D. For the past 100 years, Christians in America have led the way in financing the Gospel of Christ to the Gentile nations of the world, supporting missionaries and evangelistic crusades to the remote parts of the earth. Yet, once the nations have heard the message, that assignment is complete (Matthew 24:14).

The symbolism of the vineyard and the olive tree unlocks clues to America's prophetic importance as a nation, along with the role of the Christian church. As the Hebrew prophets and the apostle Paul indicate, God will, in the future, restore His vineyard. The process began with the rebirth of Israel as a nation. God will also graft back into the tree those branches that were removed through unbelief.

For discerning believers, the signs indicate that, within a few years, a major transition will unfold. According to prophecy, a major seventh empire will form in the area of the old Roman Empire. Many scholars believe this is the European Economic Community. When this powerful unit of nations finally becomes one with a new currency and free borders, America will be in a peculiar situation. We will be forced to follow Europe into a new global order, or else lag behind. Prophecy indicates that around this time, the focal point will be on the Middle East and Israel.

With the possibility of so many prophetic Scriptures and situations coming to pass in the next few years, where does that leave America? Only with the passing of time will we fully understand the final destiny of America. I do believe we have an open window at this time, and we must continue to take every opportunity to reach the nations while the doors remain open.

We can allow God to pluck the eagle's wings when the prophetic time comes or, through our disobedience to God's Word, we can watch as the eagle dies a slow death in the wilderness of unbelief and sin. It is my prayer that we will choose to follow God, complete our assignment, and fulfill our complete destiny as God intended. With the right leadership at the right time, and with people who know how to act upon the Word of God, I believe we will do so.

APPENDIX

Is George W. Bush the 43rd President?

Some people believe that Bill Clinton was actually the 41st president and that George W. Bush is actually the 42nd president, not the 43rd. They base this upon the fact that one American president, Grover Cleveland, served as president twice, although not in consecutive terms. Cleveland's first term was from 1885 to 1889, and his second term was from 1893 to 1897. Benjamin Harrison served between Cleveland's two terms. Because of this unique situation, some say Cleveland should be counted only once.

Presidents are counted in the order in which they serve. When a president serves two consecutive terms, such as Presidents Reagan and Clinton did, he is not counted twice, but his two terms are considered to be a complete cycle. He is not the 40th president for his first term and the 41st president for his second term. He is simply identified as the 40th president.

Historians and political scientists consider George W. Bush the 43rd president; therefore, in this book I consider him to be the 43rd president and not the 42nd president.

The Presidents Beyond Number 43

I want to make it clear that, from a prophetic perspective, I do not believe George W. Bush will be America's final president. Since I teach that the church is the 43rd generation from Abraham, and the blood was sprinkled 43 times to complete the atonement, it could be inferred from this research that the 43rd president will be the last one in America. This could not be true.

According to those who accept the teaching of a pre-tribulation Rapture, America will have a leader during the seven-year tribulation. The Bible indicates that there are ten kings that will give their kingdoms over to the future Antichrist. America will have a 44th president and perhaps several others before the predicted time of the end and the final formation of those ten kings of Biblical prophecy.

My emphasis is on the number 43 to show how this number is connected to the time frame of the fullness of the Gentiles. Just as Jesus revealed signs of things that would happen before the destruction of Jerusalem and the Temple, the cycles, patterns, and prophetic numbers are signs to get our attention today. These signs reveal the fullness of America's assignment to preach the message of Christ to the world.

"And this Gospel of the kingdom shall be preached in all the world as a witness unto all nations, and then the end will come."
(Matthew 24:14)

I emphasize again that the word "end" in this passage does not allude to the end of the world, but to the end of one assignment and the beginning of another. When the assignment of the true church is completed, God will turn His attention to Israel and the false world church will be given control of the nations (Revelation 17 and 18).

It is interesting to note that, in Scripture, the number four represents the world system. There are four seasons in the year, four points on the compass, four rivers that flowed through the garden of Eden, and so forth. Using the meaning of the numbers, the 44th president could suggest the globalization of a new world order that would fit quite well with the prophetic Scriptures where all buying and selling are conducted with the use of a universal mark (Revelation 13:16-18).

Israel and Renewing the Covenant

Many older scholars believed that God would renew His covenant with Israel at the time when Christ would set up His kingdom on earth during the 1,000-year (millennial) reign. Yet, when reading the book of Revelation, the inspired author paints a clear picture of how 144,000 Jewish men will be protected during the first half of the tribulation. The two witnesses will be anointed to minister and to pronounce judgement on Gentile nations during the first forty-two months.

So, it becomes clear that God begins His spiritual dealing with His natural seed, the Jewish people, just after the Gentiles complete their mission of preaching the Gospel to the Gentile nations. Once the church is caught up to meet the Lord (1 Thessalonians 4:16-18), the spiritual assignment changes and the two witnesses will bring the message of the kingdom of God to the Hebrew people (Revelation 11:1-6).

This is what Paul was referring to when he wrote about the branches of Israel that were removed once again being grafted into the olive tree (Romans 11:23). While the full completion of this grafting into the new covenant will transpire when Christ returns to earth again (Zechariah 12:10; 13:1), the process of bringing the natural Hebrews into covenant with Christ will begin during the first forty-two months of the period of time called the tribulation. The purpose of the two witnesses is to bring the Gospel of the kingdom to the 144,000 Jewish men in Israel (Revelation 7:1-17).

Translating English Names into Hebrew

When translating an English name into the Hebrew alphabet, it is important to note that the Hebrew alphabet contains twenty-two letters, which are all consonants. Sometimes, if certain vowels appear in the middle of a word or name, they may be translated to the letter vav. When translating the names of Bush and Gore, note that the "u" in Bush and the "o" in Gore are translated as vav. When a vowel is at the end of a name, such as in Gore, the vowel is dropped and not translated.

I want to point out again that, in this book, we used the symbolism of the Hebrew letters to give meaning to the names Bush and Gore. This is not the normal way of translating someone's name, so a person should not place too much emphasis on this method. I placed this in the book as a point of interest.

Beyond 2008

The world is not coming to an end. When the Bible uses the term end of the world, the word world is a Greek word meaning *age* (Matthew 24:3). Literally, it means the end of the age. The end of the age alludes to the time when the kingdoms of this world become the kingdoms of God, and when Christ will rule on earth for 1,000 years (Revelation 20:6). This transition is part of a time called the Day of the Lord (1 Thessalonians 5:1-3).

It is impossible to calculate the exact year when the Rapture will take place or when the day of the Lord will begin. All forms of calculation are futile. Therefore, I ask the reader to exercise caution when understanding the time frame of 2001 to 2008. I believe this time frame relates to the fullness of the true Gentile church and its assignment of reaching the nations with the Gospel. It does not speak of the end of the Gentile powers (nations) that will invade Jerusalem. Remember that during the final half of the tribulation, the future antichrist will take control of Jerusalem for forty-two months (Revelation 11:2).

It is important to understand that America is not directly identified in prophecy, but appears to be identified indirectly when you compare the patterns, cycles, and Hebraic symbolism. Only time itself will reveal how accurate the time frame of 1967-1968 to 2007-2008 will be as it relates to the fullness of the church age.

I am sharing this with you so that nobody can say that Perry Stone believes things will "end" on 2008. I certainly do not. We will have another presidential election and the nations of the world will continue to form in the manner predicted by the Hebrew prophets. The number forty-three should serve as a sign to get our attention, so we will notice the many prophetic events now unfolding before our eyes!

The Final Assignment

As mentioned in the book, the true church has an assignment to reach the nations with the Gospel of Christ (Matthew 24:14). The true church consists of all believers who have a born again experience with Christ and who are actively living according to the Word of God. When the assignment of reaching nations with the Gospel is complete, there will arise an end-time counterfeit religious system, identified in Revelation 17 and 18 as a woman riding on a beast. A man who is identified as a false prophet (Revelation 16:13; 19:20; 20:10) will control this system. This false system will control the area of the Middle East and Europe. It will severely persecute anyone who does not follow its rules and regulations. It will be this system that will issue a special mark for buying and selling (Revelation 13:16).

At the present time, there is freedom in many nations to preach the Gospel. Yet, missionaries inform me that this is changing. In many nations, the traditional religions are threatened by the spread of Christianity, and they are persecuting and even murdering many Christians. The spread of radical Islam is making it extremely difficult in many areas. In India, the Hindu religion is beginning to rise up against Christianity.

We can see the time when those who believe Jesus is the only way to salvation will be persecuted, as leaders will attempt to silence their voices by passing laws and jailing the dissidents. The book of Revelation describes a large number of believers who are martyred for their faith in Christ (Revelation 6:9).

When the true church has completed her assignment, then the false church system will dominate the world scene, with the help of ten kings who will rule over ten major kingdoms in the future (Daniel 7:24; Revelation 17:12). It is interesting to see the emphasis being placed on a global government and a global economy. The next phase will be a global religious system. Let the reader be aware that this future system will deny the truths of the Scripture in order to have many world religions join as one unit. But also be encouraged that the true believers will be those who will rule and reign with Christ!

Again, it is impossible to know the exact time frame for many of these events, but we are able to discern the signs of the times and we are not in darkness in our understanding (Matthew 16:3; 1 Thessalonians 5:4).

BIBLIOGRAPHY

Bauman, Louis S., D.D. *Russian Events in the Light of Bible Prophecy.* London and Edinburgh: Fleming H. Revell Company.

Beliles, Mark A. and Stephen K. McDowell. *America's Providential History.* Charlottesville, Virginia: Providence Foundation. First Printing, December 1989. Eighth Printing, March 1996.

Brinkley, Alan and Davis Dyer, ed. *The Reader's Companion to the American Presidency.* New York, New York: Houghton Mifflin Company. 2000

Carnegie, Dale. *Lincoln the Unknown.* Garden City, New York: Dale Carnegie & Associates, Inc. 1932. Dorothy Carnegie, 1959.

Church, J. R. *Guardians of the Grail.* Oklahoma City, Oklahoma.

DeMoss Foundation, The Arthur S. *The Rebirth of America.* Arthur S. DeMoss Foundation. 1986.

Durant, John and Alice. *Pictorial History of American Presidents.* A.S. Barnes and Company, Inc. 1955.

Edersheim, Alfred, D.D., Ph.D. *The Temple: Its Ministry and Services as They Were at the Time of Jesus Christ.* Grand Rapids, Michigan: William B. Eerdmans Publishing Company. Reprinted May 1978.

Freidel, Frank. *The Presidents of the United States of America.* Washington, D.C.: White House Historical Association with the cooperation of the National Geographic Society.

Harris, Bill. *The Presidents.* Surrey, England: Archive Publishing, a division of Colour Library Books Ltd, Godalming. Portland House. 1990.

Johnson, Paul. *A History of the American People.* Harper Perennial. 1997.

Lapin, Rabbi Daniel. *America's Real War.* Sisters, Oregon: Multnomah Publishers, Inc. 1999.

Lindsay, Gordon. *American Presidents and Destiny.* Prepared for Layman Reading and Our World Correspondence School. September, 1960.

Marshall, Peter and David Manuel. *The Light and The Glory.* Fleming H. Revell Company. July, 1977.

McTernan, John. *God's Final Warning to America.* Oklahoma City, Oklahoma: Hearthstone Publishing, 1996, 1998.

Millard, Catherine. *The Rewriting of America's History.* Camp Hill, Pennsylvania: Horizon House Publishers

Moore, Judy Hull and Laurel Hicks. *The History of our United States.* A Beka Book Publication. 1981, 1990.

Prolman, Marilyn. *The Story of the Capitol.* Chicago: Children's Press

The Lives of the Presidents. New York City, New York: The New York Book Company.

Metzger, Bruce M., ed. *The Oxford Annotated Apocrypha.* New York, Oxford: University Press, Inc. *The Apocrypha of the Old Testament Revised Standard Version. Expanded Edition Containing the Third and Fourth Books of the Maccabees and Psalm 151.* 1965, 1977. *The Apocrypha.* 1957. *The Third and Fourth Books of the Maccabees and Psalm 151.* United States of America: Division of Christian Education of the National Council of the Churches of Christ. 1977.

Vine, W. E., M.A. *Vine's Expository Dictionary of New Testament Words* (unabridged edition). Peabody, Massachusetts: Hendrickson Publishers.

Whiston, William, A.M., trans. *Josephus Complete Works.* Grand Rapids, Michigan: Kregel Publications. 1960, 1978.

Willmington, Dr. H.L. *Willmington's Guide to the Bible.* Wheaton, Illinois: Tyndale House Publishers, Inc. Fourth printing, May 1983.

"God's Final Call to America! Will America Stand with Israel?" *God's News Behind the News.* Televised 2000.

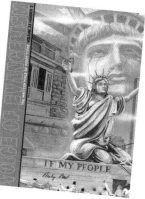